More Beautiful Purses

by Evelyn Haertig

Gallery Graphics Press

More Beautiful Purses

by Evelyn Haertig

Photography by Milton Haertig

PUBLISHED BY: GALLERY GRAPHICS PRESS
Post Office Box 5457
Carmel, California 93921

Copyright 1990 by Evelyn Haertig
Design: Allen Weathers/Publishers Art Service
Typography: Metro Typography
Printed in Japan

Library of Congress Cataloging-in Publication Data
Haertig, Evelyn
More Beautiful Purses
Includes: index, illustrations, bibliography.

ISBN 0-943294-009 Hardcover

Contents

Contributors

We are indebted to the following collectors who unselfishly shared their collections and materials for inclusion in this book and heartily thank them:

Private Collectors

Charmay Allred	Janice Gruenwald	Joan Kroll	Bernadine Pohlers
Frances Barbour	Genevieve Gillaizeau	Janet Krumm	Yvonne Puig
Angie Cash	Patricia Halligan	Mary Lauderdale	Norma Roth
Nettie Charney	Kathryn Hunter	Judith Leiber	Johanna Ryker
Mrs.Donald Flannagan	Ginger Hyland	Sheila Macdonald	Helene Sutter
Susan Fuhrer	Helene Iacobellis	Suzi Mounts	Beverley Steppler
Sally Getzelman	Molly Klupfell	Evelyn Marie Musser	
Monica Greenburg	Martie Koskoff	Rhett Owings	

Museums, Institutions, Manufacturers, Experts

The Ebenezer Alden House, Union, Maine
Bath Costume Museum, Bath, England
Bethnal Green Museum of Childhood, London, England
Boston Museum of Fine Arts, Boston, Massachusetts
Gawthorpe Foundation, Burnley, Lancs, England
Vreni Landot, Turlock, California
Doris Langley Museum, Bath, England
Louvre Museum, Paris, France
Museum of Leathercraft, Northampton, England
Manchester Museum, Manchester, England
Meeker Manufacturing Comany, Joplin, Missouri
Metropolitan Museum of Art, New York, New York
Mozart Museum, Salzburg, Austria
Museum of Fine Arts, Boston, Massachusetts
Dr. Edgar Page, Corticelli Thread Company, New York
Charles Whiting Rice, Wrentham, Massachusetts
Smithsonian Institute, Washington, D.C.
Societa Veneziana Conterie, Venice, and Murano, Italy
Stefan Mann Company, New York and Carmel, California
Susan Swan, Winterthur Museum, Delaware
Traquair House, Peebleshire, Scotland
Victoria and Albert Museum, London, England
Whiting and Davis Company, Plainville, Massachusetts
Winchester City Museum, Winchester, England

Thanks To:

Charles Rice for reading copy, and supplying information heretofore unknown; thanks beyond measure. My heartfelt gratitude to Rhett and George Owings for their tireless computer training and assistance which brought this manuscript to fruition. A special thanks to Mrs. Isabel Slomowitz for her many kindnesses. Last, but by no means least to my husband, Milt, for his seemingly endless photographic chores, patience, and confidence over many years.

4

Preface

When **Antique Combs and Purses** was finished in 1983, I had the feeling that never hearing the word purse again would be too soon! In the intervening years I have learned almost as much again about them, and felt the necessity to write this final book on the subject almost as much to thank all the truly nice, dedicated, interesting collectors, museum personnel, dealers, instructors, artists, writers and general public that I have met as a consequence of the first book, as for any other reason. So many of you have become more than mere acquaintances and have, as the song goes, "lighted up my life".

This book is for you. Hopefully it will illuminate every aspect of antique purses and bring the new meaning and joy to your collecting that increased knowledge of any subject always brings to those who are learned.

Every chapter has as thorough coverage, without tiresome repetition of material previously covered in **Antique Combs and Purses,** as it was possible to achieve. For those who have no prior knowledge of the above book some introductory material on the history and development of the purse was essential. The text and photography are completely new. As **MORE BEAUTIFUL PURSES** deals only with purses, each section has been greatly expanded and a multiplicity of examples assist in best identifying, classifying, and maintaining a collection.

In order to keep it from falling into the "coffee table" classification and from its true purpose as a definitive reference, the textual information is of prime importance; the illustrations reenforce it. There are fewer photographs, but they are larger, of better quality, and have almost exclusively been drawn from private collections. This should reassure the reader they are available. Museum pieces have been used only where they were significant and not obtainable from any other source.

Where color is essential, almost all the photographs are in full color. For some meshes and leathers, where shades do not vary greatly, or where there is no particular advantage to color, black and white photographs have been useful in reducing publishing costs.

To assure accuracy and authenticity my husband and I journeyed to Venice, Vienna, Paris, Germany, London, in fact every country directly connected with purses which time and credit card allowed.

The first book depended heavily on the great museums for guidance. This book lacks no assurance, for several years spent in repairing, appraising, selling, writing, lecturing and dealing first hand with purses of every kind and description have given me the kind of authority which no casual acquaintanceship could ever develop.

No prices have been included for the following reasons: Price guides are almost *worthless* for the prices must be constantly revised to reflect current conditions. Prices are not universal and a purse selling in one section of the country under one set of circumstances will sell for an entirely different price elsewhere, prices are therefore unreliable at best. This book is intended for serious research and was far too extensive and costly a project to fall into the category of a mere price guide. Prices are dependent upon so many variables that individual examples must be examined first hand to determine values with any degree of accuracy. Because examples "look alike" does not mean they are of the same value. Collectors are advised to rely on their own experience, for in the end they are best able to determine what they wish to pay for a given item rather than slavishly determining values on an outdated, limited and often *quite inaccurate* guides.

It is my hope this is the definitive book on purses. This does not imply there is no more to be said nor learned, but future research will have a firm base on which to build and I shall have done all that is presently possible to meet with your approval.

Carmel, California
1990

5

6

Chapter 1

History and Development of the Purse

For all practical purposes, the history of the purse began in the 11th century when the Crusaders, under Papal sanction, crossed Europe bent on wresting the Holy Lands from the Saracens, those present day peoples who are followers of the Moslem faith.

The Crusaders were a motley band composed of the truly pious, the military, knights and noblemen, children, the conscripted, and various and sundry tradesmen necessary to such an undertaking. There is dispute among scholars as to the actual number of Crusades, (1096–1270 A.D.) some say 7, others 9, but there is no dispute about the name of the first purse and its' purpose.

Though no actual specimens remain, it is known from old woodcuts that the earliest purse was a small leather sack about two inches square, drawn together with leather strips. It was worn suspended from a wide leather belt which might also hold a sword, dagger or other weapons. A purely functional piece at this time it was called an

almonier, amonieres sarrasnoises or *almoner,* as alms or charity in the form of gold coins were dispensed from them to the needy.

It continued to be worn exclusively by men until the fourteenth century when it became a fashion accessory worn by both men and women until the 18th century, at which time the addition of exterior pockets to mens' greatcoats became stylish. The pouch was made primarily of leather though eventually it was made of fabrics and handmade textiles.

Though certainly the contents varied over the centuries and with individuals, paper money and coins were not carried to any great extent; the contents tended to be what we might think of as trivia today. Commonplace items were precious and costly so such articles as keys, sewing implements, legal documents, medicines, writing equipment, combs, mirrors, religious relics, beads, pomaders, silverware and miscellaneous small things were included.

From the 14th century on, purse sizes increased, elaborate ornamentation was

Plate 1

17th century Limoges Wedding Purse. Enameled ceramic and gilt lace. (Victoria and Albert Museum, London, England.)

Figure 1

Silk embroidered linen pocket. England, 18th century. (Museum of Fine Arts, Boston, Mass.)

added, purses were prominently displayed, and for both sexes it became a status symbol in middle and upper class ensembles. This is not to imply that the lower classes did not use pouch purses, in fact tradespersons would have included coins and objects connected with their businesses rather than trivia, along with a sharp, short, knife which was worn in conjunction with the purse. This knife was both fork, spoon, scissors, toothpick, weapon, and was handy for a multitude of other uses.

Men continued to wear purses trimmed with ermine tails, tooled leathers, fabrics embroidered with coats of arms and fancy designs, studded with jewels, and closed with metal frames and chains. By the 14th and 15th centuries they were suspended from the waist on long chains and braided cording reaching to the knees and below. They were particular favorites of the French and Italian courts for in these countries needlearts had reached elegant heights; velvets, tapestries, embroideries, and loomed materials were sumptuous indeed.

The women affected purses which almost reached the floor. Some of these round reticules had little bells, ribbons, and tassels running gracefully down the sides. They were capped by embroidered sections, slashed much like their sleeves, to expose the rich fabrics beneath. These pomadors may have contained ashes of roses, oranges pierced with cloves, citron peelings, and other sweet smelling preserved fruits and/or flowers. It was a time which knew little about personal hygiene and neglected the benefits of the baths practiced by both the Greeks and Romans before them. The smells were probably as evil as the spirits presumably warded off!

Women's styles changed little over the centuries; voluminous skirts were to the floor, only a suggestion of a waist and bodice were indicated, sleeves ranged from tight fitting to enormous. The purse continued to be displayed outside the skirt.

Pockets

By the 16th century a radical change in skirt styles and the use of metal hoops permitted an innovation of sorts and *pockets* became fashionable. Pockets were worn under the skirts and were reached through slits in the dress and undergarments. They were huge sack like affairs capable of holding a vast assortment of whatever could be stuffed into them, tied, buttoned, or otherwise secured about the waist and worn over the hips. *(Figure 1.)*

Figure 1

One would think that it would be difficult to steal from such an intimate location, but it was not uncommon to read such lost and found advertisements as the following in the *Boston Weekly Newsletter* of August 9, 1753: "Stolen out of a Person's Pocket last week, in the Common, a Work'd Pocket-Book with a Pair of Stone Earrings, two Pair of Stone-Buttons which wanted mending, silver thimble marked Hanna Bill, a large plain Stay-hook in the shape of a Heart, a silver Teaspoon broke off in the middle mark'd P.M. and sundry Papers in it. . . ." Not only a curious theft but an equally odd assortment of things carried in the pocket and the obvious thing, money, is not even mentioned!

Pockets were made of a coarse linen material or crash, crewel embroidered in fanciful large patterns or in the white-on-white tamboured syle then in vogue in France. Pockets, being commonplace items of clothing, have not survived as well as more elegant articles and the few that remain are in museum costume departments.

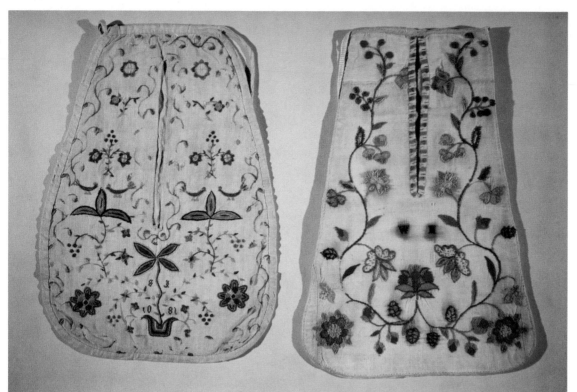

Plate 2

The driver's whip unfolds its torturing coil.
"She only balks — go, lash her to her toil."

Figure 2

9

Figure 3

Handwritten verse side of The Slave Purse

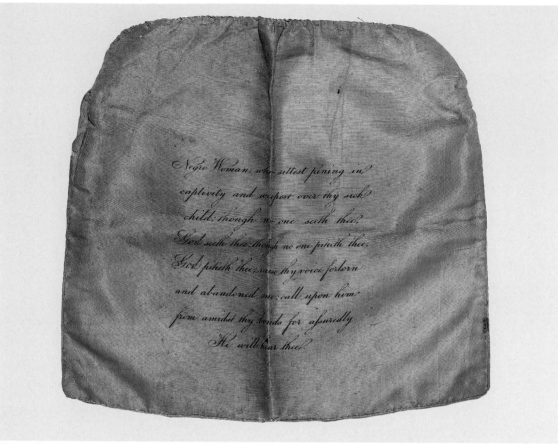

Figure 3

Doris Langley's great museum collection contained what may be termed the *slave pocket. (Figures 2 and 3.)* Moved by the plight of women slaves, some society matrons sold these pockets to fund the effort to end slavery in Britain. Whether they directly effected the end of this barbarous custom is not known.

The Pocketbook

The pocket is not to be confused with the pocketbook. The *pocketbook* was a rectangular, envelope-shaped piece usually covered in some form of embroidery such as bargello work, needlepoint, leather, which might be embroidered or stamped, or some sort of fabric. Some fine examples surface from time to time such as *Figure 303.*

This is a (5 × 8¼ inches) pocketbook of bright carnations, tulips, and strawberries, done on a dark green ground. Made in 1764 for Loammi Baldwin, a distinguished Revolutionary officer and engineer who built the canal between Concord and the Merrimack River, and who also developed the Baldwin Apple. It has had the good fortune to be held by his descendants until offered for sale by a Maine anitque dealer in 1984. It is an American pocketbook and representative of others now in American museums. There are European examples scattered among the many costume departments of European museums.

The pocketbook had relatively standard sizes varying by an inch or less in each dimension. It was approximately 4–5 inches long and 7–8 inches wide. Women's pocketbooks tend to be somewhat smaller than men's but both sexes carried them. Both men and women had their names worked into the pattern along with the date of presentation or working, which has proven a great boon in accurately dating a purse. It consisted of a long strip folded like an envelope with a flap and metal closing. The two equal divisions were folded through the middle and secured by long tapes attached to one end. The edges were bound with twill or silk. The linings were of cotton, silk, or linen. They were embroidered in simple stitches including flame, tent, and Hungarian point, best suited to canvas. *(Figure 4.)*

Seal Bag and Game Bag

Although not specifically purses in the modern sense, two early English examples are nonetheless fascinating and singularly well preserved. The first is the *seal bag* and the second is the *game bag*.

The seal bag, trimmed with the seal of the royal house, was used to transport state papers and important documents. The Guildhall in London has on exhibit one of these bags dating from the 14th century.

Small bags such as *Figure 5* elegantly tasseled and done in couched silver and gold threads were gifts, a subtle form of bribery, to the reigning monarch. When delivered,

Figure 4

Small flame stitched pocketbook (4 × 3) dated 1789. Indistinct word, KNOCK. (Wilmington, Delaware.)

Figure 4

Plate 3

Envelope pocket-book embroidered with silk and metallic threads. (Museum of Fine Arts, Boston, Mass.)

Plate 3

they contained a substantial sum in gold coins. The monarch in return gave the subject a smaller sum. It is not known if the exchanged bag was as fine, but it is known the bag presented to the monarch was considered quite valuable.

Tassels at the ends and middle of the bag were more than decorative, they weighted the bag and thus helped retain its shape. Though not all 17th century bags have such rich netted tassels, square or straight bottomed bags are invariably tasseled.

The embroideries might contain a coat of arms, a crown, the lion and unicorn, a maxim, florals or leaves, and/or comical, heavily padded human faces in a form of embroidery the British call *stump work.* The metallic threads were made of drawn gold or silver and were as elaborately and perfectly applied as the needleworker could make them.

The game bag was, as its' name implies, used to carry game home from the hunt, though cut velvets with turreted iron tops do seem a trifle plush for such purposes. They

are thought to be game bags because of their generous size, and some have an exterior rounded iron flap which could be lifted to more easily insert the game. They all have one element in common, an ornamental iron/steel frame. Some are topped by a silhouetted castle which reenforces the theory they belonged to the nobleman who dwelt there; at least it is an intriguing conjecture. Fine examples are owned by American museums: (Metropolitan Museum of Art and Boston Museum of Fine Arts).

A steel engraving from an obscure volume in the British Museum Library entitled, *Costume in England,* spoke of a *gipciere* an ancient name for a game bag. The drawing was so similar to the actual bag from the Metropolitan Museum, that it deserves to be included along with the text. It is possible a row of tassels once extended across the base of *Figures 6 and 7.*

Another fascinating bag is from The Victoria and Albert Museum. This fabric purse appears to have been worn at the side attached to a wide embroidered belt. The holes where the buckle tongues secured the belt are visible, along with the loop which held the excess material in place. The coat of arms and embellishments are exquisitely done in gold thread. Careful examination of the circle containing the shield, shows it also is a belt and buckle arranged much as the purse itself would have looked when worn. The words pertain to the divine right of kings to rule and thus the bag could have been used by tax collectors or a representative of the crown. (Circa 17th century.) Note the current absence of tassels stressing the utilitarian nature of this bag. *(Figure 9.)*

Figure 8 presents two purses with long, slender cords or tapes attached to their

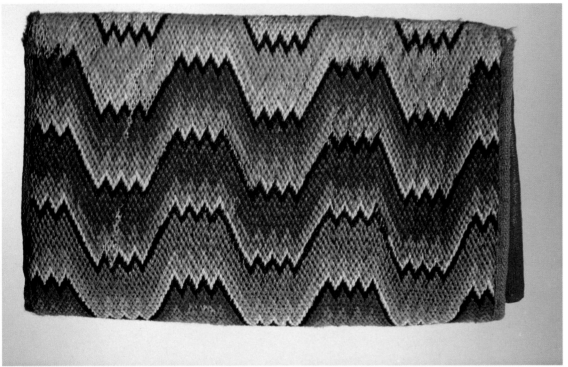

Plate 4

Plate 5

13

14

Figure 5

Figure 6

Cut velvet Game
Bag with iron
frame. Circa
15–16th century.
(Victoria and
Albert Museum,
London, England.)

Figure 6

15

Figure 7

Fine engraving of a 15th century gipciere *from actual example in the Louvre, Paris, France. Velvet embroidered in colored silk, gold threads and laces. Elaborately chased steel frame attached to the gridle through the ring at the top. Frequently they contained religious inscriptions. (British Museum Library, London, England.)*

Figure 7

corners. The tassels were secured by a series of purely decorative metal rings, both covered and plain. Worn in conjunction with this type of bag were pin cushions, thimble holders and other small sewing impliment cases. The three examples shown are also held by long cords. The looped cording made for easy wear at the wrist, or as a chatelaine, or attached to the tassels of the bag itself.

All of the examples thus far have been tapestries or embroidered. Beads are introduced in *Figure 10.* Tiny seed beads appear on the onion shaped side tassels done in a simple diamond pattern.

The shield became a favorite shape for the purse carried in the hand and later the purse with attached chain. Modified escutcheon shapes, rounded at the top and blown out at the sides continue to this day and are among the most graceful shapes.

Limoges Wedding Purse

By the 17th century, ribbons, gold lace, pierced silver caps resembling acorns, metallic threads, bright colored silks, and push latched frames appear. Surely the most interesting is the Limoges, (France), wedding purse. *(Plate 1.)* Surrounded by stiffened gilt laces, the bride, her face adorned with beauty spots, fixes her eyes upon us across the centuries.

The 2–3 inch portrait section was made of porcelain enameled with the likeness of the wedding couple. Both the groom and bride exchanged bags much as rings are now exchanged. The custom of wedding portraits is here fulfilled in ceramic. The round or oval was fitted at the top with two large metal-trimmed holes through which a substantial cord was passed on each side and drawn together. The lining and rich materials were attached to the ceramic by a series of small holes on the outer edge of the portrait.

These extravagances were for royalty only. The subjects in all their wedding finery were neither glamorized nor sentimental; royal marriages were political in nature, not romantic. Considering the difficulties of rendering a likeness in any form other than photography (not developed until two centuries later) the needleworker and painter did well indeed.

Closely related to the Limoges purse is a carved 3 inch ivory bag. *(Figure 11.)* Here the holes and connecting cord are clearly seen. The remaining tassel resembles an overgrown strawberry. One of the tassels evidently has been lost.

Several examples of fine beaded French pocketbooks and reticules from American museums which deserve further study are shown in *Antique Combs and Purses* Chapter 1.

Sterling Chatelaine

Moving in and out of favor as it did for centuries, it is difficult to decide exactly where to place the chatelaine in the scheme of things.

Many people have rather hazy notions as to exactly what a chatelaine is, aside from a decorative piece which is attached to the belt or waistband, or as in antiquity, a part of a wide girdle. This excellent chatelaine *(Figure 12,)* momentarily lacks the small purse which might be included, but it does show the accouterments which were traditional to fine sterling chatelaines.

Figure 8

Rare belted 17th
century bag with
royal coat of arms.
(Victoria and
Albert Museum,
London, England.)

Figure 8

17

Figure 9

*Two pouches and
three pin or needle
cushions with long
cords done in silk
and metallic
embroidery. Bead-
ing is noticeably
absent. Patterns are
primitives drawn
from nature.*

Figure 9

These tiny matched objects are as follows
from left to right: a retractable writing tool; a
match safe, (which kept matches dry and
from accidentally igniting); a thimble holder;
a penwipe or needle holder, and an ivory
writing tablet. All the pieces are marked Bir-
mingham, England. Each piece is attached to
a ring at the base of the chatelaine and to the

implement by a swivel hook much like those
used on watch chains.

Sixteen inches overall, it is a showy piece
and quite valuable. Such chatelaines are still
available but the sterling ones with so many
hooks are fetching prices in the thousands of
dollars, if the pieces are matched, marked,
and original. Quite aside from the value of

18

Figure 10

Figure 10

Limoges wedding purse (center), small oval bag with pom-pom ribbon, shield and dome shaped metal framed coin purses. 17th century. Metallic and silk embroideries. (Victoria and Albert Museum, London, England.)

the sterling, the beauty of the workmanship has intrinsic value.

Just such a chatelaine could have been worn at European courts hundreds of years ago.

The Beaded Reticule

Beaded reticules first appeared in 1791 (*Figures 13–17*) with the introduction of slim straight skirts. They are considered the first ladies' bags as they are currently known. Reticules dating from 1800 are infrequently offered for sale, but before this date it is most unlikely, for wealthy donors have enriched the museums with those few remaining extraordinary bags just discussed. Considering their fragility and scarcity, it is as well.

Subsequent chapters will illustrate only those items which can be acquired. Not only the finest and rarest, but those which are **representative** of a class or type of purse. It would be impossible to include every example, for the book would never be concluded and the sheer weight alone would prevent anyone from lifting, let alone ever reading it!

19

Figure 11

Carved ivory purse
shown nearly
actual size. Missing
base tassel. (Victo-
ria and Albert
Museum, London,
England.)

Figure 11

Figure 12

Sterling chatelaine
and fittings. Proba-
bly 19th century.
(Privately owned.)

Figure 12

Figure 13

British noble-women in 16th century costumes.

Figure 14

Knights Templars with almonier.

Figure 15

15th century Italian courtier with tasseled bag suspended from girdle.

Figure 16

16th century merchant's wife with a type of muff purse.

Figure 17

17th century serving women with girdles holding knives, keys, and pouches.

Noblewomen, London, 1590

Figure 13

22

Templars

Figure 14

Mid-century   Apothecary
(1st half of century)

Figure 15

London, 1590:   Servant woman   Townswoman
Merchant's wife

Figure 16

Denmark: Upford   Dithmarschen   Eiderstadt

Figure 17

Chapter 2

Needleworked Purses
Some Embroidery Definitions

One of the most durable and beautiful classes of purses is the textile purse, as its' many admirers and collectors will attest. Too often all works in this category are classified as being needlepoint.

As the various other needleworked processes are not as well known, nor as easily identified, the following clear and concise definitions should prove helpful.

Hand Tapestry

Hand woven tapestry must not be confounded with embroidery. It, in itself, constitutes a cloth, and the process of its production is essentially weaving. The design is formed as the cloth is being woven, by the use of differing colors and by the shuttle which contains any one color being carried over and under the warp threads so far only as that particular color is required by the design. The example is shown partially worked leaving the warp threads exposed at the top of the illustration with a strand of wool lying ready to be beaten up into them.

Hand woven tapestries and Aubusson work are still found and the prices are surprisingly modest considering the quality of the workmanship. *(Figure 18.)*

Turkey Work

Turkey work was made in the same way as the Turkey rug which it imitated. Tufts of wool were knotted, in rows, onto the warp threads and secured in place by a strand of the weft after each row of knots, the whole being thus wound into a cloth which had much the texture of a pile carpet. Most of the examples still in existence are worn almost completely threadbare, and, the better to match these, the piece shown has been faked to imitate a partly worn specimen, the top edge being unravelled to show its construction. *(Figure 19.)*

Crewel Embroidery

This embroidery is executed in wool on closely woven cloth. The work is done with stitches of different lengths, the direc-

25

Figure 18

Enlarged view of hand woven tapestry showing warp and weft threads, and wool ready to be beaten up into the pattern.

Figure 18

Figure 19

Figure 19

Antique turkey
work stitch no
longer used. An
existing sample was
unraveled to illus-
trate the knotting
technique.

Figure 20

Crewel embroidery.
The threaded needle
illustrates the direc-
tion of the next
stitch to be taken.

Figure 20

tions of the stitches being varied, to give added expression to the design. Fancy stitches are also frequently introduced, to heighten the effect. The cloth on which the design is embroidered is generally used as a background, but occasionally the entire surface is covered with needlework. The example given is shown with the needle in place ready to make the next stitch, as it would be when worked in the hand. *(Figure 20.)*

Most crewel worked pocketbooks are now in museums but occasionally a fine antique such as *Figure 4* does surface. Naturally an authentic 18th century pocketbook will be very expensive regardless of its' condition.

Petit Point

Gros (large) point, point (square) carre, cross stitch, and needlepoint are types of embroidery worked on open canvas. The fine work or petit point is formed by stitches taken across from one opening in the canvas to the next in a diagonal direction. The coarse work, or gros point is formed by similar stitches twice the length, thicker wool, cotton, or silk being used. The stitches thus formed are sometimes overlaid with other stitches crossing them. Hence the name cross stitch embroidery. *(Figure 21.)*

Tent Stitch

Tent stich is also known as Hungarian point, flammo work or flame stitch. Embroideries of this type are worked in wool or in silk onto canvas. The stitches are made over a given number of threads, uniformly throughout the design and they lie always in the same direction—up and down, never across, the design. The ground is completely covered; the pattern generally being small and worked as an exact repeat, although this type of work is sometimes applied to large designs. *(Figure 22.)*

Berlin Work

During the Victorian Era (loosely 1837–1901) the most popular form of embroidery was the Berlin work mentioned in the beaded section. Done in soft wools in harsh, bright colors the Germans

produced from aniline or synthetic dyes, (as opposed to vegetable dyes used previous to 1858), tapestry work could be done with or without beads. Originally the patterns were based on Biblical or mythological themes as well as copies of celebrated paintings, but by the 1870's the patterns had become so inferior the passion for Berlin work faded.

It is the canvas on which tent stitch and needlepoint was done which allowed for a differentiation between stitches. The closer and more numerous the warp and weft threads, the finer the canvas foundation. Berlin work was done on a coarse canvas or even stiff paper, and the stitches were of the gros point type. It has been estimated the canvas contained only 576 stitches to the square inch, as opposed to the fine Austrian tapestries done on silk gauze early in the 20th century, containing a staggering 1,800 to 3,122 stitches or points per square inch.

Differentiating Between Machine and Hand Made Embroideries

How does one tell the difference between machine and hand made needlepoint and other embroideries? A relatively simple method of closely examining the ground. If the squares appear not to be "filled in" so much of the color of the backing shows through, and it appears that some of the stitches are "missing", the tapestry is most likely to be machine made. Machine tapestry is sometimes done with thin, dull-colored thread and has a flat lifeless appearance.

If all else fails, modern tapestries are plainly labeled hand made or machine loomed on a small cloth tape sewn to the side lining, along with the country of origin.

The collector should be aware that many tapestry bags are now imported from China. They are definitely hand done but they are also poor imitations of the dainty, multi-shaded hues found in the intricate scenics and florals usually associated with this exquisite form of embroidery originating chiefly in Austria.

Figure 21

Enlargement of
petit point work
showing unworked
canvas and worked
pattern. Note the
mixture of stitches.

Figure 21

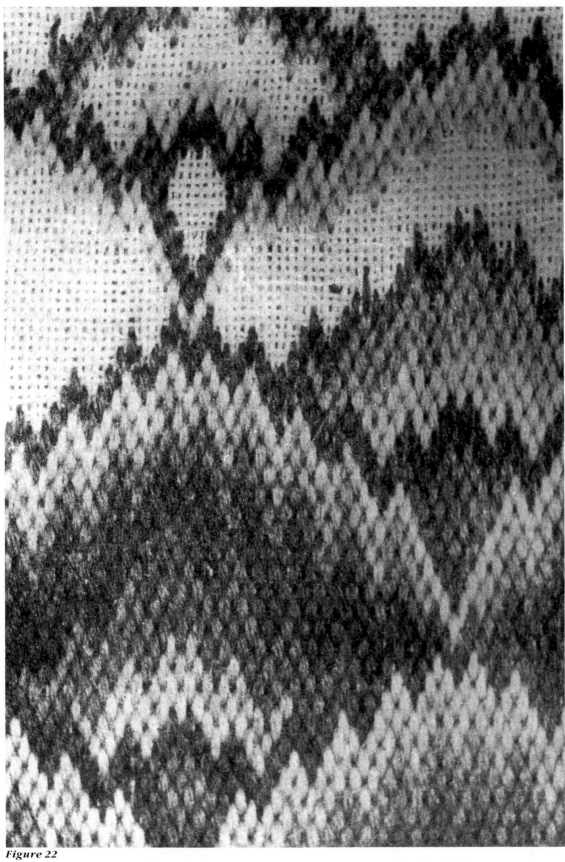

Figure 22

Tent stitch, var-
iously known as
flame or flammo
stitch and/or
Hungarian point.
Usually done in
brilliant colored
wools. Canvas and
length of stitch is
clearly shown.

31

Figure 22

Chinese needlepoints are hand made and quite well done, and the designs are pleasing, but their colors tend to be harsh, lack the subtlety and the refined elegance of Austrian hand made purses.

The quality of the work is determined by the evenness of the surface when seen from the side rather than from above. Experts in the field say the Chinese needlepoints now so prevalent, are uneven and have other deficiencies which would go unnoticed by the layman.

European hand made tapestries have a slit left in the weaving where one weft color meets the weft threads of another color. In Oriental tapestries the weft threads of one color are dovetailed with adjoining weft threads of another color. Unless one is sophisticated in construction and/or can examine the reverse side of a tapestry it is difficult to use this method of substantiating the country of origin, if the marks are missing.

In all true tapestries both sides are the same except that the loose ends of threads usually appear on the wrong side. A machine imitation is an entirely different weave and not reversible.

Handwoven Tapestries

Handwoven tapestries should not be confused with needlepoint or other types of embroidery for it in itself constitutes a cloth and the process of its production is essentially weaving not filling in a canvas. The unworked portions of the tapestry are composed of a series of threads called the *warp*. The warp threads run the full length of the cloth parallel to the selvedges. The *weft* is a series of threads woven in, thread by thread, with the shuttle. These threads run across the cloth at right angles to the warp and interlock with it. Woven materials require some sort of loom whereas embroidered materials such as needlepoints, have both warp and weft threads already formed in the canvas. The surface of hand woven tapestry is not smooth as the yarns have a nubby quality quite unlike petits and there is no differentiation between stitches for the effect is vertical. The beauty lies in the shading created by the almost constant changes in colors. The gusset will be a complimentary color or a color found in the pattern; usually a solid color.

Some fine examples of hand woven tapestry are seen at *Plates 7, 8, 9 and 10.* Some of the characteristics of handwoven materials can readily be seen. Notice they all have magnificent frames of sterling, gold, or vermeil for the amount of work involved warrants the finest materials. They may have been wall hangings made into purses at some later date, as the front and back sides are seldom ever the same. The patterns are taken from old tapestries. They are usually romantic scenic/figurals but on occasion are florals. They are invariably pouch shaped, the single tucks being arranged at the corners. The frequent color changes are subtle and give depth and richness. They are two to three times as large as petitpoints (some as large as a foot long and ten or eleven inches wide) which may account for their tendency to sag slightly as they are heavy though not unwieldy. The linings are ordinarily heavy faille, fitted with a beveled mirror, change purse and side pockets.

Hand woven tapestries are durable, classic, appropriate for almost any occasion, and a sure sign of discriminating taste. Hand woven tapestries were not mass produced and are not plentiful. They are not appreciated in the United States and like hand made petitpoints are undervalued against their flashier beaded counterparts which actually required far less skill, take very little abuse, and are seldom works of art.

History and Needlepoint Techniques

Hand embroidery can be traced to the Middle Ages (12th century). During the Crusades when knights were often gone from home for years at a time, their noble ladies waited more or less patiently for their return. Their vast stone castles and chateaux were cold and colorless, heated only by mammoth but inefficient fireplaces and meagerly furnished with an occasional chair and essential bed, the mattress of which was filled with straw! (Mattresses

Plate 7

Handwoven tapes-
try with unusual
floral divided by
ribs. Geometric
design is repeated
around the body.
Sumptuous wide
sterling frame with
griffith pattern.
Circle intended for
engraving.

Plate 7

33

Plate 8

Superb hand woven
purse with wide
sterling fret frame.
Typical cherub
design in frame.
Court figural/scenic.

34

Plate 8

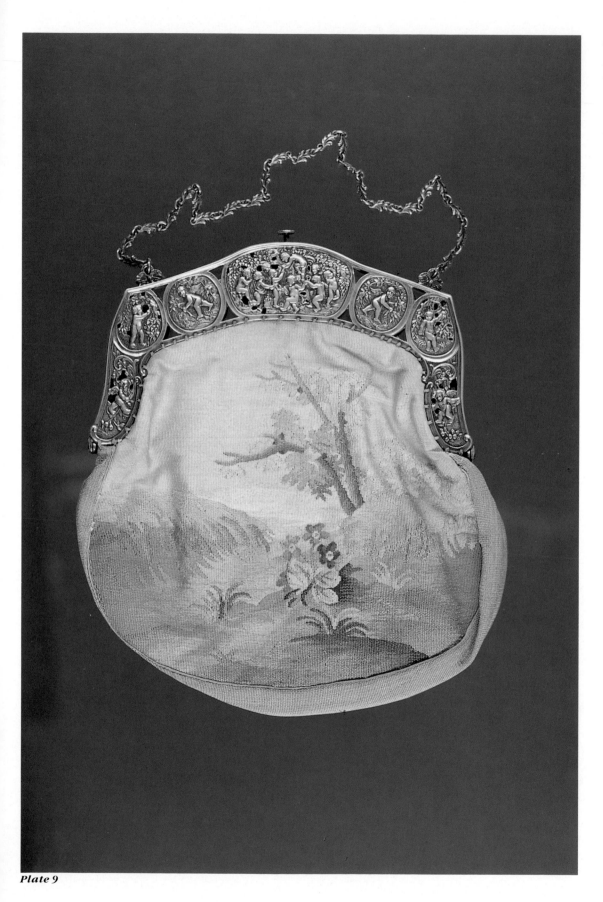

Plate 9

Reverse side of
Plate 8.

The pastoral is
representative of the
back side of all
handwoven scenics.

Plate 9

35

Plate 10

*Romantic figural/
scenic with exqui-
sitely scrolled gilt
frame. Unusual
griffin motif.*

36

Plate 10

Plate 11

Plate 12

Plate 13

may still be filled with straw to this day, even in a three star European hotel).

Needlework was one of the few pastimes considered proper for high born women and it occupied much of their time. Skillfully executed, they were both decorative and functional, relieving the bleak monotony of the cold stone. Adding warmth and color, they were the focal point of interest in the great halls. They eventually reached in ex-

cess of twenty feet in width and almost as long. With time they came to be made in studio conditions by teams of embroiderers working on each section. There is still a tapestry school in Paris which is open to the public on specified days, where this ancient art may be observed first hand.

Fortunately for the generations to follow, they also gave an historical account of notable battles, village festivals, mythological

Plate 14

Atypical bird and
floral handwoven
example employing
delicate pastels.
Unusual frame is set
with a cameo sur-
rounded by jewels.
Plunger closure with
drop tab.

Plate 14

and Biblical episodes, and events in their daily lives such as weddings, journeys, and court scenes.

Such masterpieces as the Bayeux Tapestry reveal the types of arms, the significance of powerful military and political figures, even the progress of a battle and its' eventual outcome can be gauged. They were the manuscripts of the time, for few were learned enough. nor aside from the monks in the monasteries, had any need to read.

Centuries of refinement resulted in rich costumes, comfortable housing, and a proliferation of personal possessions. Finer stitches and more elegant patterns confined to smaller and smaller areas such as the purse, chair seats and backs, table coverings, bell pulls, and a host of other objects resulted.

During the reign of Empress Maria Theresa (1717–1780) the art of needlepoint reached great heights in the Hapsburg royal court, and eventually was adopted by those outside court circles. By the mid 19th century needlepoint had become a leading Austrian export. An entire dining room set of 18 chairs and numerous side chairs all done in handmade tapestries can be seen in the Hapsburg Summer Palace. It is hard to keep ones eyes on these mundane objects when there is more gold on the walls than in Fort Knox, for the proud Hapsburgs nearly bankrupt the empire with their insatiable appetite for art and sumptuous living.

NEEDLEPOINT MATERIALS

To understand needlepoint embroidery, one must first know the nature of the canvas on which the work is done. Needlepoint done by a nonprofessional in the home is done on a stiff open canvas . With proper instruction and experience needlepoint can be done quite nicely by an amateur.

Fine Austrian needlepoint bags are done by *expert* and *professional embroiderers* on a gauze similar to that used in bandages, though even finer and of a softer silk web-bing, having virtually no relationhsip to the canvas familiar to the amateur.

Both vertical and horizontal threads are double. The open space between the warp and weft threads constitutes a small square which accommodates the embroidery material and needle. The threaded needle is inserted diagonally (as shown in the diagram *Figure 23*) to complete a full stitch called a needlepoint. When half a stitch is taken it is called a *petit point* or small point or stitch. When a stitch covering twice the area is taken it is called a *gross point* or large stitch. It is not uncommon to find all three types of stitch, gross, petit, needle on one piece of work. It adds greatly to the total affect.

The thread used in valuable petit point bags is either cotton or silk slightly thicker than a human hair, not wool, which is too coarse for such delicate stitchery.

Generally embroidery involves a variety of stitches so the concept of needlepoint as an embroidery form employing a crewel needle, extends only to the technique, as the diagonal stitch is the sole stitch used. The stitch itself is easily mastered, it is the quality of workmanship which is exacting. The constant changing of colors, the size of stitch, the intense concentration required, and the absolute necessity of following a pattern (which is merely mounted in view of the embroider) make the work so time consuming and fatiguing that few are willing to commit themselves to the months, which may stretch into years, in order to complete a single piece. Most of the petit today is done by Austrian village women in their homes, presumably during the winter months when there is less to occupy them than during warmer weather. Of course they work on bell pulls, chair coverings, wall hangings, and other types of objects d'art rather than bags exclusively.

In order to prevent the complete disappearance of this art form, the Austrian government has underwritten needlepoint work to a handful of these dedicated women whose slender output has become so valuable it is eagerly snatched up and the choicer pieces are placed along with jewels and other valuables in safe deposit boxes.

Figure 23

*Self explanatory,
way petit point
is made.*

Figure 24

*The painters at
their work.*

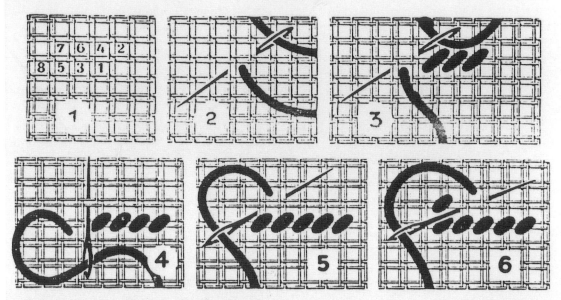

THIS IS THE WAY PETIT POINT EMBROIDERY IS MADE

1. The numbers indicate how the stitch is made — 2. - Leading the needle with the first stitch — 3. - The first row of the petit point work has begun — 4. - How the second row is started — 5. and 6. - The second stitching row before being finished

Figure 23

STEPS IN PRODUCTION

An extremely helpful small booklet was published in January, 1955, by the Viennese Embroidery and Art Studios of J. Jolles, Andreasgasse 6, Vienna, Austria, outlining the steps involved in the production of needlepoint. Similar books cover the needle arts from the viewpoint of the amateur, whereas this booklet, which was once given to those who visited the now defunct Jolles Studios, concerns itself with professional and commercial production.

The first step in creating a new design requires the pattern be drawn in charcoal. Classical art works from the Dutch masters, the French, English and other romantics, along with floral arrangements, still lifes and original designs by the individual studio artists are utilized. *(Figures 24 and 25.)*

Next a water color is made indicating the desired color scheme, then carefully examined to make certain it will be suitable. The watercolor is than transferred to millimeter graph paper and mounted on stiff cardboard; at which point it resembles a mosaic, each

Figure 24

square being a separate color. This step requires enormous skill and experience as the graph now becomes the actual pattern for the embroidery. *(Plate 15A, B and C.)* Professional embroiderers call this pattern *the point*.

Next *the point* goes to a color expert who selects the various colors of yarn to complete it. Some points require as many as 500 different shades. This person must be extremely

Figure 25

broidery pattern stands in front of the embroider's head. She counts the color, point by color point, from that pattern and embroiders it onto the guaze. There is no transfer of the pattern directly to the silk guaze itself. *(Figure 27.)*

For each printed square on the pattern two stitches are made on the silk guaze. The first stitch is started on the left side of the material and is worked upwards, the second is worked from the top downwards. The yarn is constantly changed in accordance with the pattern. The front and back of the bag are done simultaneously. The work may take six months or more to complete, depending on the size of the piece and the amount of time devoted to it.

When completed, a magnifying glass is used to see if any stitches were missed and then filled in. Tapestries may contain different grades of embroidery and when the human body is involved in the design, twice the number of stitches are used so the work is almost impossible to count with the naked eye. As many as 3,122 points to the square inch may be done with the aid of a magnifying glass.

skilled for it is the infinite number of delicate shades which makes the difference between an ordinary point and a great one. *(Figure 26.)*

Once the yarn is selected by a color expert it is put into an embroidery frame. The em-

Plate 15A

41

Plate 15B

Plate 15C

The bag is then assembled by adding an embroidered strip between the front and back sections bordered by welting which helps prevent wear on the edges; and a frame and carry chain are added. Some petit has a grosgrain insert rather than an embroidered one. This operation was traditionally done by men whereas the other steps were done

Figure 26

Figure 27

Figure 28

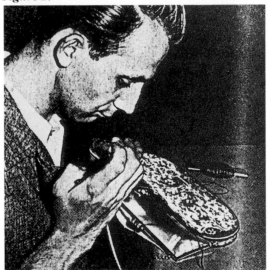

Figure 29

Figure 26

Skilled colorist in the shading room selecting the yarn for the embroidery.

Figure 27

Embroiderer working with a magnifying glass. The embroidery is stretched into the frame from the pattern in front of her.

Figure 28

Here the petit point is assembled and fitted with a frame.

Figure 29

In the final step the embroidery is joined to the frame using special devices.

by women, though the designers could have also been men. An interlining of linen is added and an exposed satin lining is attached. The two linings create virtually separate bags and give substantial protection to the delicate exterior petitpoint. *(Figures 28 and 29.)*

Modern Viennese Studios

Though the Jolles Studios were gone when we visited Vienna, we did find an interesting wholesaler at the top of two wide flights of marble stairs in a building which must have been built before Napoleon. It is a myth that all the world speaks English and even more discouraging to find this out in a city where

only the taxi drivers and hotel personnel are passingly conversant.

It was obvious we were foolish Americans but the aproned ladies decided to allow us to photograph the shelves stocked with sample petitpoints after it was determined we did indeed wish to make a purchase. The prices were so staggering we decided on some small souvenirs that were easily transported and have subsequently been doled out as gifts to our customers. The first in a long series of purchases we should have done without! The walls do enable one to see the repetition of designs and some unusual designs. Many petits now are fitted with leather straps rather than chain handles and the in-

43

Plate 16

*Detail of modern
petit point purse at a
wholesale shop in
Vienna, Austria.
Classical motif.*

evitable identical frame regardless of the design. *(Plates 16, 17 and 18.)*

Antique and Modern Petits Compared

Some recent purses tend to have simpler designs than they once had. An identical design may be used and appear quite different when the background color is changed from cream to black, for instance, and the size and/or shape altered. (See *Plates 17 and 18.*) They favor stylized florals, have fewer color changes, tend to have quite similar patterns, are larger than antique purses (probably in response to popular demand for larger purses). A few are done entirely in modish black and white patterns, the more costly ones are still traditionally elegant scenics done in countless pastels, and all are easily distinguished from antiques by one simple detail, the frames; which are all alike! *(Plate 16.)*

FRAMES

The frames are the best measure of the age of the purse, if the collector is in doubt. Years ago frames were designed for individual purses, the finer embroideries demanding the most valuable frames. Note the standing incised closure in *Plate 19.* rather than a twist, and the absence of pearls, enameling or other jewels. Older bags are most likely to have jeweled frames, the chains are longer, heavier, may be double, and may have interspersed beads, enameled insets and jewels in the twist ends. *(Plates 20, 21, 24, 25, 26, 27, 28 and 29.)*

Modern frames are made of sterling silver with an incised pattern, lightly engraved. They are not unattractive but are an indication of the decline in cherished artistry. The shop windows in Vienna, Strasburg, Innsbruck and other Austrian cities are crowded with petitpoint purses, but the price will quickly alert one to the handmade, which outwardly appear the same quality as the machine made.

Machine made containers, bags, coin purses, cases for eyeglasses and a variety of other uses sell for about one tenth or less than the handmade and unless the reverse side can be examined (an obvious impossibility) only an expert can tell the difference between them. I have no reason to believe the merchants will be less than honest with potential customers as a matter of national pride. As of this writing the finest handmade new petits are offered for sale at $3,000–$4,000 (U.S.).

Plate 16

44

Plates 17–18

Shelves of modern petit point purses awaiting purchase by retailer. Note identical frame on each.

Plate 17

Plate 18

J. Jolles Studios

Petitpoint bags made at the Jolles Studios, as well as the box in which they were sold, contained their label. Recently a purse was found incorporating the signature in the pattern itself, shown at *Plate 30*. It is evidently a part of a series from the books of the Bible entitled Esther, which appears in the enclosed area below the scene. Although nicely done, the frame is not as ornate as that on many other subjects. It is possible that religious subject matter was considered inappropriate for jeweled framing.

Other houses must have had different opinions for *Plates 21 and 22* present Biblical tableaux framed by enamels and blue rhinestones.

45

Plate 19

*Classical motif with
sterling frame;
standing closure.*

Plate 20

*Enameled frame.
Extremely fine silk
gauze underlaid
with gold threads.*

Plate 19

46

Plate 20

Plate 21

Plate 21

Biblical motif on fine gauze. Frame set with blue rhinestones.

Plate 22

Reverse side of Plate 21 depicting Christ with disciples at communion table.

Plate 22

Plate 23

Needle point with simple design. Jeweled frame with standing closure.

Plate 24

Petit point with mythical motif. Enameled frame set with seed pearls. Enameled standing closure.

Plate 25

Petit point. Elaborate classical design. Enameled frame of raised roses, marcasites, and polished agate clasp.

Plate 26

Cobalt beads strung through ornate filagree. Padded figures typical of pre-French Revolutionary romantic designs.

Plate 23

Plate 24

Plate 25

Plate 26

Plate 27

Plate 27

Jewel set frame on small petit point. Closure tilts to open.

Plate 28

Figural enclosed by pastel florals. Jade set frame.

Plate 28

49

Plate 29

Enameled floral frame set off by seed pearls. Standing closure. Fine classical motif.

50

Plate 29

Plate 30

Plate 30

Rare signed J. Jolles petit point. Signature beneath figure to the extreme right. Biblical scenic from the court of Esther.

Jolles states, "As soon as the embroidery for an evening bag is ready it is made into a handbag and a frame is designed and made by jewellers according to the value of the embroidery. The frames are also Viennese handicraft work and show the great skill and craftsmanship of the Viennese gold and silversmiths guild."

It is difficult to tell much from photographs but *Plate 55* is a machine made purse. Notice the dull colors, the eveness of the weave, the expanse of background which is not embroidered, and the coarseness and uniformity of the stitches. However, not all machine made purses are as uninteresting as this one which I keep to illustrate the difference between techniques.

Given the huge price differential why should one invest in the more costly hand-made petit? Fewer of a particular design in the handmade petit are likely to be made than the machinemade. The designs used are handsomer and greater attention is paid to the selection of the colors, as well as a wider more suble range of colors used. Any skillfully done handmade object is a work of art and as such cannot be compared with a machined product. Handmade articles usually outlast machine made, as the finest materials are used and the workmanship is executed with pride.

Identifying the Antique Petitpoint

Antique petits may be identified also by such characteristics as:

1. Subdued colors, partially due of course to uniform fading.

2. The welting may be covered by a gold thread sections which may be worn. Time, patience, crewel needle, and matching fine needlepoint yarn can restore these unsightly worn spots.

3. Antique petits are inclined to be from two to three inches smaller in length and width than modern ones.

4. The patterns are more likely to be different on the front and reverse sides on antique petits as production time involved was less of a factor.

5. Religious themes are very unlikely to be found on current commercial petits whereas they were used on antique bags.

6. Very old petits may also have sections of the pattern where the silk has worn away and the gauze is exposed. There are petit restorers and of all the types of antique purses this would be the most successfully restored, provided the silk gauze was intact. If one had the time and skill, rest assured it is easier to do this sort of work than restore beading.

7. Again, look at the *frames*, for modern petits are monotonously alike.

Needlepoints done on canvases on which the central motif has been worked by an expert and the background is completed by a novice at a later date, *(Plate 23)* are much simpler, the stitches are true *needlepoint*

Plate 31

rather than tapestry, and the patterns greatly simplified, bearing practically no resemblance to the fabulous Austrian tapestries. This is not to belittle them for many of these domestic purses have the singular appeal not found in commercial needlework. Excellent examples of fine woolen needlework are seen at *Plates 32, 33 and 34.*

Contrast these relatively simple works with two of the most extraordinary needleworked purses one could hope to find. *(Plates 35, 36 and 38.)*

Maintaining the Petitpoint

Caring for petitpoints is not nearly as difficult as for beaded purses but naturally the question of cleaning antique petits constantly arises. I would not recommend washing them as can be done with beaded purses, as they lose their shape. The dyes are virtually colorproof. Fading occurs over an extended period of time giving the antique petit an even more pleasing mellowness than newer ones.

There is available a commercial cleaner which needlepoint shops can supply, but I

Plate 32

Needle point. Scenic oval center with florals. Plated frame.

Plate 32

53

Plate 33

Needlepoint. European scenic with leather back. All metal frame.

Plate 34

Coarse needle point. Simple scenic design. Plain frame. Inexpensive to moderate value.

Plate 33

Plate 34

54

cannot personally vouch for either its effectiveness nor safety.

Wear occurs on the petit exactly as it does on any purse in the area just below the opening of the frame, along the gussets, and below the top of the frame. These are the areas where the purse comes in contact with other objects, is rubbed or snagged. This seldom occurs to the face or back areas.

It is a sad fact that the silk gauze is fragile and some of the most exquisite patterns have been given little regard by their indifferent owners. Who would think of scuffing or mistreating a painting or sculpture? This idyllic scene, *Plate 38* slightly reminiscent of Whistler's grim and aged mother is a case in point. The subject is restful, the colors soft and becoming, the bouquets add depth to the sun dappled piazza. Even the tiled floor is carefully delineated showing the great detail which is not done today at any price. The reverse side shows no wear and the colors are muted to perfection.

The handmade petitpoint is timeless, always correct no matter where it is carried, makes a cultural statement that few accessories can, will last a lifetime if given reasonable care, increases in value, and will enhance any costume. What more could one ask of a purse?

Petitpoint Descriptions

LION AND UNICORN DESIGN

One of the oldest patterns used on tapestries of all kinds, drawn from 12th and 13th century wall hangings, is one of the most interesting and a fair guarantee of age in a petit purse; The Lion and The Unicorn.

The pattern may vary from one rendition to another but there are certain elements which are fairly constant such as the ever present unicorn, that fabulous beast which was similar to the horse in most respects save for the one huge horn protruding from the center of its forehead and the lion rampant. The animals are nearly always attributed that most pleasing of human characteristics, the grin or smile. This comical aspect is a sure fine winner. *(Plate 37.)* Moreover they are capable of holding flags and standards, acting as domestic pets fond of sitting on a queenly lap or dancing about on two legs for the amusement of onlookers.

This particular salmon grounded, 6 × 9 inch petit, is magnificently set with genuine lapis lazuli and pearls. The stitch count may run to 3,000 in this purse. Close examination discloses the favorite of the exotic animals beloved of royalty; the monkey. A rabbit, a dove, a pug dog, and a crane or stork, a small fox, and a lamb fly about or are hidden in the grasses.

The humans are nobles, Biblical figures, warriors or their attendants whose representations are purposeful and significant. Here a queen is seen in the doorway of her field tent inspecting the jewels/crown tendered by her lady-in-waiting. The three words above the tent door read *Mon Seul Plaisir* (My Only Pleasure). One wonders if the queen is a greedy and haughty woman or a pawn in the matrimonial game which wed both men and women with only the continuation of the monarchy a paramount factor. Is she left with only her jewels for comfort?

The fact that flowers, animals, fruit and other unlikely things are floating about in space somehow seems quite fitting and the whole is crowded with strange and wonderful details. Everyone is having a fine time in this Medieval world.

This favorite pattern is also shown at *Plates 35 and 36* which was donated by its' owner to the Los Angeles County Museum after appraisal. The frame and background colors are clearly different but the pattern is identical to *Plate 37.*

See also Figure 2, Page 252, *Antique Combs and Purses*, in which the background stitch is needlepoint and the animals and seated figure are tapestry quality petit.

BIBLICAL SCENE

This Biblical allegorical is 6 by 7 inches with a different story on each side. One side depicts Christ preaching to four women wearing rich Medieval attire but Christ is wearing traditional robes and carrying a staff. The mixture of cultures separated by fifteen hundred years was quite common. The principal figures were traditionally dressed for immediate recognition as few

Plate 35

Royal figure and her lady-in-waiting. Lion and Unicorn with standards. Jeweled frame and drop. Circa 19th century. Ancient pattern which was used by both French and English courts.

Plate 36

Reverse side of Plate 35.

Plate 35

Plate 36

Plate 37

Another version of Plates 35–36. Dusty rose background. Frame set with genuine lapis lazuli and pearls. Base is slightly varied. Note the vast difference in the total effect.

Plate 38

Petit point with 3,000 + stitches per square inch. Unfortunately severely damaged and lacking frame.

58

Plate 38

people could read or write and the allegories were a method of teaching the faithful. The subordinate figures were clothed in contemporary garments with no regard for the disparity in time.

The background is a mixture of Gothic arches, an elaborate banner running across the top. The opposite side shows Christ with two male figures, probably disciples, loaves of bread and bits of food, along with a large jug of water or wine. The table cover is extraordinary for it is done in pale white and lavender silk giving it the illusion of being transparent. The columns and arches are marvels of perfection. Probably no fewer than 100 different shades are discernable.

The blue enamel frame is jewel set. An enameled plunger-fastening with a similarly set tab indicates the front panel. The lining is of watered faille finished with gold braid. There are no markings but they are really not necessary as it is without a doubt Austrian. It is significant from the standpoint of ecclesiastical art and an outstanding example of a dedicated needlewoman. *(Plates 21 and 22.)*

GOLD THREAD

This fine (5¼ by 5 inches) petit of chenille florals and leaves is a most unique purse. The background is purposely left blank to reveal the gold thread beneath the fine silk gauze. This one is different because the leaves and buds still show faint traces of having been done in chenille outlined in gold thread. French knots secure the outer gauze.
The corners of the frame are ormalu, the center a brilliant crimson enamel with a matching plunger fastening. *(Plate 20.)*

CLASSICAL MOTIFS

This antique petitpoint, *(Plate 28),* has all the elements of a classical motif; garden scene, statuary, female figures pursuing butterflies and a delicate floral framing all. It has imitation jade sets on both front and reverse sides of the frame and the pattern is the same on either side. The chain holders face left or right, a very clever method of

making each side functional. The lining is cream colored satin. The colors are subtle blues, lilac, fuchsia, touches of gold, and olive green.

Quite different is the modern oval purse with classical motif whose frame is so plain. *(Plate 40.)* It speaks volumes about an attempt to keep costs within bounds even at the expense of appeal.

An untraditional size and shape in addition to an original, lively, peasant motif done in joyous colors distinguish this petitpoint. *(Plate 42.)* A bit of advertising was included in the form of a card bearing the makers' initials *L.K.W.* and the message, "This is a hand made petit bag. The embroidery has 1800 stitches per square inch." A generous 10 × 9 inches make it a serviceable purse as well as a decorative one. The raised clasp, fretted frame and snake chain handle are indicative of recent vintage; it is probably thirty or more years old.

No more perfect petit can be found than this costly dusty rose bag which features a gold washed sterling frame set with three groups of marcasites and a marcasite set tab. The splashy varigated bouquet almost covers the body. The footed vase is classic; the colors striking. Each flower has upwards of ten different shades. It has the customary beige satin lining; coin purse and mirror still intact. Its elegance indicates it was probably made in the first quarter of this century. It is an extraordinary example of a purse which has been maintained in pristine condition for nearly a century. *(Plate 39.)*

A fine, small (7 × 6) petit was *(Plate 25)* made early in this century. It has an enameled frame of raised roses, and marcasites with a polished agate clasp. It has an unusual brass wire-braided carry chain with sliding rings never seen on any other purse. The design is traditional and balanced, with a tremendous range of shades. The cupid figurals in each base corner are as inconspicuous as the birds at the top. The pattern is identical on the reverse side. The excellent lining is a mustard color fitted with an oval mirror and two pockets.

Plate 45 is an interesting tiny purse because it has some fine petit on an extremely fine linen body and a beaded fringe. Beading

Plate 39

*Superior quality
petit point dusty
rose floral. Sterling
frame marcasite set.
Nice shading on
assorted florals.*

of any sort on tapestries is seldom, *if ever* seen, and this piece must have been fringed because the owner liked fringing. The narrow sterling frame is attached with a cording as most purses of this type were. The flat basket of naturalistic flowers is definitely drawn from an 18th century pattern, presumably a section of a much larger design. The overall dimensions are 4 × 3½ inches.

The romantic subject matter is only part of the uniqueness of *Plate 26* for the frame is typically French though the needlework was in all probability done in Austria. A band of jewelry size cobalt-blue glass beads is threaded on a wire through the fine pierced frame. The figures are lightly padded and the skin and features are done in the smallest

conceivable stitches. The costume is not classical Greek or Roman, but very characteristic of the 18th century ideal prior to the French Revolution.

Recently a fine petit was offered for sale the frame of which was missing some inlay work. Inside were several incomplete pieces of various grades of gauze. Only the central portion was completed on all but one, so we have a rare opportunity to see first hand how the work was done and how very fine the gauze is. Each piece was priced and stamped Made in Austria. Whether they were for export or were purchased in Austria is not known. The frame would indicate the purse had been made at least sixty to seventy years ago. *(Plates 44A and B.)*

Plate 39

Plate 40

Plate 41

Plate 42

Plate 43

Plate 40

Modern petit point showing undistinguished frame and unusual shape still using an 18th century theme.

Plate 41

Refined scenic showing skillful use of perspective.

Plate 42

Modern peasant scenic with standing frame and snake chain handle.

Plate 43

Narrow elongated needle point done in woolens. Gussets done in dark blue grosgrain. Sterling frame with daisy chain.

61

Plates 44A–44B

Fine gauze with center portion completed. Background unfilled. Their purpose is not clear as only one was found and the work is far too difficult for an amateur to complete. Note Made in Austria tags.

Plate 45

Unusually fine petit point on cream ground featuring a flat basket of flowers after an 18th century pattern. Beaded fringe never before seen on a petit point, was added at the owner's preference.

Plate 46

Fine floral tamboured evening bag. Center oval of satin stitch embroidery surrounded by seed pearls. Pearls in frame and a pearl is used in the plunger. French.

Plate 44A

Plate 44B

Plate 45

Plate 46

62

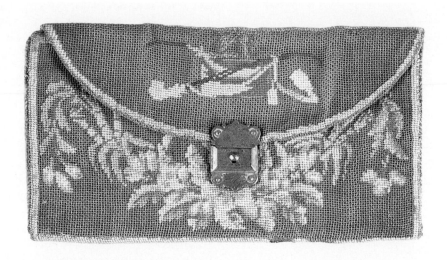

Plate 47

Plate 47

Needlepoint pocket-book with tin lock. Thought to be 18th century vintage. Purpose undetermined.

Plate 48

Leather backed needlepoint beside an open fan for purposes of size comparison.

Plate 49

Grospoint Art Deco bag with large composition stones in frame.

Plate 48

Plate 49

63

Unconventional Petitpoints

Plate 47 is a puzzle to both the owner and the dealer from whom it was obtained. This is an example of a fine oblong petit in which the major part of the canvas lacks embroidery. The design is difficult to discern but it appears to be a pair of crossed, long stemmed clay pipes such as were commonly used in the 18th century, a flag or emblem, and a crest above. The reverse side bears the initials A. M. The tin or steel lock is much the same as those discussed by Susan Swan, (Henry Francis de Pont Winterthur Museum), in her *Needlework, an Historical Survey.*

Although it may be a tobacco pouch it is more likely a gentleman's pocketbook for important papers, bank notes, and the like. There remains not a hint of tobacco scent, if indeed it was a tobacco pouch. Overall dimensions are $7 \times 3\frac{1}{2}$ inches. It is in remarkably good condition despite the fact it was made in the last half of the 18th century, for it has been part of a well preserved collection.

Plate 49, another unconventional petit has a panel of fine colorful florals attached to a carmel colored suede forming the gussets, sides and back. There is no damage to either material and the suede lining is in good condition, so it can reasonably be assumed the purse was made in this fashion. Actually it is a sensible combination for the suede is a rugged material which can withstand abuse more readily than the delicate tapestry. The frame is of the type commonly used in the early 1920's. Size $5\frac{1}{2} \times 6$ inches.

A remarkable purse is seen at *Plate 6.* The frame is set with two enormous pieces of high quality turquoise and four smaller ones. The fresh water Scotch pearls are lustrous and large. Neither the turquoise nor pearls have been cut or shaped. The front section is done in elegant petitpoint. Note the rendering of the facial skin tones, the shimmer on the taffeta gown, the delicately molded hands and the minute details of the wig, cap and laces.

The back is a gaudy random floral gros point. The contrast between front and back is so marked it is hard to believe they were intended for one another. This is a purse of unparalleled beauty.

All prior examples have been of petitpoint, *Plate 32* is entirely of the coarser needlepoint embroidery, as is *Plate 34.* The latter has an undistinguished frame indicative of a German origin and is not sought after by American collectors even though its' scenic pattern is more desirable than the former floral. Both have identical patterns on either side and display a harmonious blending of colors.

The embroidery in *Plate 48* is very coarse, the design has a Near Eastern flavor, the rectangular shape is boxy, but the frame is outstanding. The needlework which is almost as heavy as that done on rugs, is used on one side only, the reverse side being of sateen matching the large, mock-jade stones. It is the kind of purse which was popular with an avant-garde section of society near the turn of the century.

Other Embroidery Techniques

TAMBOUR WORK

The great American portrait painter, Gilbert Stuart, painted two charming young girls in 1787, a Miss Vick and her cousin, Miss Foster. A little known portrait, it is most interesting to this study because Miss Vick is shown doing tambour work, while her cousin holds her pattern to the side. Her well rendered left hand holds the hook and under the huge hoop, her right hand is guiding the thread. Over two hundred years ago children of the leisure class were skilled in the use of the tambour hook. Reading patterns from sight was an accomplishment indeed. Today machines do the tambouring, especially of sequins, bangles and the attachment of many forms of beads to fabrics. *(Plate 54.)* It is nearly impossible to chose a favorite among the thousands of purses seen each year but if forced, *Plate 59* would have to be high on the list of esteemed bags. Both it and *Plate 56* (as well as *Plates 57 and 58*) are examples of tambour work but there is a vast difference in age, delicacy, quality of workmanship, artistry and general appeal.

The huge cabbage roses are done on watered taffeta silk and framed by a most distinctive sterling frame with blown out decoration. The carry chain is of double,

Plate 50

Plate 50

Whimsical English
needlepoint. Several
different sizes of
points are used in
the beast and
flowers.

Plate 51

Tilted basket of roses
on black ground.
Needlepoint quality.

Plate 51

Plates 52–53

Scenic abounding in activity. A study of the detail strongly reminiscent of St. Stephen's Square in Vienna, Austria. Both front and back shown. Fabulous petit point.

Plate 52

Plate 53

Plate 54

Plate 54

embossed heavy sterling links, the lining of pale pink silk. It was hand done probably in China or the Near East at least 100 years ago; the tambour work has that refined and slightly faded quality of great antiques.

The second example is a lovely purse but of recent vintage, about half the age of the first. The body is a silky black satin, the tambour work small, sparce and insignificant. The frame is enameled over sterling but narrow and tending toward gaudiness. Both purses are done by hand but the former ex-

ample has more tambour work and an outstanding pattern.

Tamboured purses where only the thread shows and there is no attached beading have wonderful frames. Great care is taken to coordinate colors shown in the pattern with jewels or/and enameling. Silks and satins were selected most frequently and the pouch shape was most popular. The motif in *Plate 58* is decidedly Near Eastern. The mounted falconeer rides among his prey within the confines of a Moorish cartouche. Not your

Plate 55

Machine made needlepoint. Note the dull color scheme and pedestrian pattern.

Plate 56

Satin evening purse with enameled frame and tab. Tambour work is sparce and unimaginative. French.

Plate 57

Antique tambour. Base completely filled with fine, subtle pattern. Turquoise set frame.

Plate 58

Antique tambour featuring Moorish theme. Nice jeweled frame and drop.

Plate 55

Plate 56

Plate 57

Plate 58

Plate 59

Magnificent antique tambour. Note the soft shades, lush pattern, fine sterling frame and chain. French, but the tambour may have long ago been done in China.

Plate 59

everyday design for a woman's purse, but clearly reminding us of the origins of the art of tambouring.

Occasionally one finds a French purse solidly beaded with minute brass beads resembling round edged cut steels, filling in all the space between the tambour work. Such an example is seen in *Plate 60*. The major peony blossoms are large and fully open, nicely surrounded by realistic fuchsias below the jeweled frame. These purses are always rather small in size and the tambour and bead work are that high quality seen prior to the First World War and seldom seen since.

HAND EMBROIDERY

No more representative example of mid-Victorian (1820–1850) stitchery could be found than this velvet gold thread bag. *(Figure 30.)* The simple, utterly classic pattern with metallic cord side tassels was so appealing it could not be passed over, and it's hard indeed to move my jaded spirit. I can turn away from lesser purses as a matter of course.

It is the same embroidery technique favored over four centuries ago. The threads of what must be acorns and carnations are raised somewhat but are not heavily padded. The original alabaster pure silk lining is in unbelievably good condition. It measures

69

Plate 60

Envelope style tambour with box frame. Note as with older tambours, the amount of tambour work is sharply contrasted to the ordinary and stingy use on current machine made tambour. French.

Plate 61

Body is entirely hand done in satin stitch. Prohibitively expensive if done today. Fine jeweled frame. French.

Plate 60

70

Plate 61

Plate 62

Plates 62–63

Modern petit points showing the difficulty of determining age as the quality is as fine as ever, economizing reflected in the monotonous framing. Bottom plate shows the completed petit ready for finishing steps.

Plate 63

Figure 30

Silver and gold embroidery on black velvet. Metal braid side tassels. Circa mid 19th century. British.

Figure 30

seven by six inches. The elegant frame and chain are 24K gold over sterling silver. It many be American, but more likely is English in origin.

A different type of embroidered purse *(Plate 61)* was made in France of stitches covering the entire body surface. A time consuming process, this delicate work, done in a blend of silk and cotton, would be prohibitively expensive to produce on a commercial basis today.

As in hand woven tapestries, the front features a court scene symbolic of the artificial pastoral life favored by the French aristocracy prior to the French Revolution. The reverse side is an oval floral medallion lacking the complexity of the figural. The frame is exquisite. Large, amethyst colored raised cabachons are set off by three Renaissance rose groups of garnets and pearls. This type of frame is very choice. Representative of the elegance of French textiles made in the mid nineteenth century this 9½ × 8 inch bag is a jewel itself.

French purses made full use of Marie Antoinette's court, for she appears again and again, as in this silk embroidered evening bag. Here the likeness is done entirely in satin stitch embroidery. The oval is surrounded by a ring of small pearls matching the larger pearls set in the gold colored frame. The pale pink and green floral embroidery is all hand done and the faux-pearls are of good quality. The size is 5 × 7 inches. Circa 1920. This style is seen in both silk and satin. The richness of the embroidery makes it a most popular bag with collectors. *(Plate 46.)*

Chinese Embroideries

K'SSU WORK

Though petit-point may contain 3,000 + stitches per square inch, there is one type of embroidery which was so delicate embroiderers went blind doing it and the Chinese government passed legislation forbidding its use. It is not the forbidden stitch

Plate 64

Plate 65

Plate 64

Lovely Japanese figural petit. Note the use of latern, robe and hair ornaments to iden- tity an exotic country. Stylized peacock feathers on black ground.

Plate 65

Abstract embroidery with modern feeling; quite different from all the other patterns.

generally thought of (a type of tight knot peculiar to ancient Chinese embroideries) in this regard, but a stitch so microscopic that it can barely be seen with the aid of a ten power magnifier. Variously spelled *k'ssu* or *kussu* work, there are few references to it in literature and examples are not abundant. *(Plates 66 and 67.)*

This superb and costly example is mounted and framed on suede with an ob- long piece of carved muttonfat jade in a brass bezel underlaid by a strip of suede to protect the embroidery.The scene is of mounted and foot combatants reminiscent of charging Monguls. If it seems an unlikely, even inap- propriate subject matter for a lady's purse, it was never intended to be used in this fashion. An expert dealer in Oriental antiques assures it was originally an ornamental embroidery. K'ssu tapestries were done from the 18th century through the first quarter of the present century. This one uses pure gold thread as part of the background. Colors are confined to grey, rust, black, and a delicate

rose. The eyes and brows are painted as was traditional in some embroideries. The pure silk lining is badly frayed.

The ancient Chinese were fond of yellow and few other cultures made quite as effec- tive use of it as they did. In fact, yellow is a difficult color to use alone. Here, *(Plate 69)* the traditional chrysanthemum bloom and leaf motif is boldly done in shaded gold, yel- low, brown and bronze. The design is curva- ceous, stunning, and showy. It comes as near as any to being an "Oriental Purse" for this type of embroidery was intended for export to Western cultures. Oriental women did not use purses as we do.

In a similar vein, Chinese embroideries with Peking glass bracelet handles and beads were popular on huge sack-like bags about eighty years ago in America. Standard were the side tassels attached with a cord and couched gold and silver thread within the Oriental motifs. The embroidery was unusu- ally fine, as are antique Chinese embroi- deries in general. *(Plates 68 and 71.)*

Plate 66

Rare Chinese K'ssu
work. Mutton fat tab
with leather protec-
tor. Literally count-
less silk stitches were
underlaid with gold
threads.

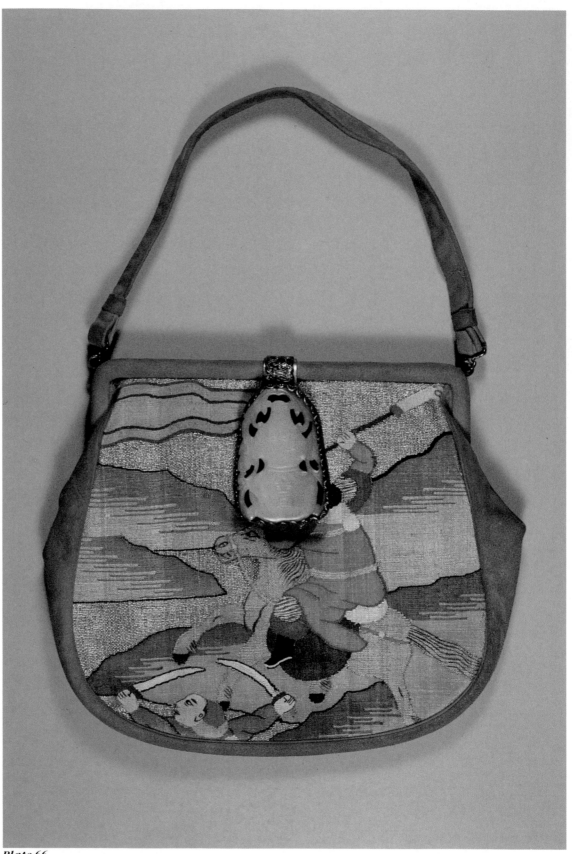

Plate 66

Plate 67

Reverse side of K'ssu revealing the difference in the pattern.

75

Plate 67

Plate 69

Plate 68

Plate 70

Plates 68–70

Variations on Chinese embroideries popular at the turn of the century. Plates 68 and 70 are huge, sack-like, open sided with gold thread touches and satin stitch embroidery. Each has side tassels except for the elegant gold peony design at Plate 69 intended for export.

Plate 71

Plate 71 is much smaller than the previous examples.

77

Plate 71

Plate 72

Fashion doll from
Bethnal Green
Museum of Child-
hood, London, Eng-
land. Circa 1830.
Composition head
and kid body. Silk
reticule matches
gown.

Plate 72

Fabric Purses

Those purses which cannot be neatly classified as petits, tambours, crewels, embroideries, or other woven materials are here loosely termed for convenience sake, as *fabrics* . They constitute a relatively narrow grouping encompassing that richest of all purses, the plain silk or velvet purse framed in sterling or gold repousse.

Sterling Topped Fabrics

This most sophisticated purse was made in suede, antelope skin, suede cloth, satin, velvet, peu-de-soie, taffeta, cordé and other silks in a solid color, almost invariably black. On occasion they are found in red, various shades of blue, violet, dark green, cocoa brown, salmon and/or deep purple.

They were pouch shaped, generously proportioned, occasionally beaded, (but in such a simple fashion that the beading is irrelevant). The elaborately pierced wide frame predominated both fabric and random bead-ing. Cordé or fine pleated material was not beaded. Since they differ from one another only in slight details such as beading, pleating, pattern weave and rarely, oh, so rarely, fringing, only six outstanding examples are presented in which the frames are unusual as well as the bodies.

I am repeatedly asked which purse among the thousands is my favorite and aside from the one on the cover, for some inexplicable reason it would have to be *Figure 31*. Since it has no such effect on others, perhaps my taste is faulty, or there is no accounting for individual taste after all.

In its defense it is the only one of its ilk with a fringe; a natural outgrowth of the symmetrical cut steel pattern. The sterling frame is only moderately wide and embellished simply with a raised square punch, but the tab is set with fine, old, stones which have a glow not found in present day marcasites. No mere afterthought, this tab has a prominent place in the design. The cut steels are French and unusually small, brilliant cut,

Figure 31

Black velvet bag
with small French
cut steel beads.
Drop tab set with
marcasites. Circa
1900–1914.

Figure 31

much like those examples in the beaded section. The beading is outstanding but since it
is confined to a small area of the purse, it may
belong here rather than under the chapter on
beads. It is 9 inches wide and 8 inches long;
rather standard dimensions for this type of
purse.

More traditional and perhaps more spectacular are *Figures 32, 33, 34, 35, 36 and 37.*
They all measure approximately eight or
nine inches in each dimension. The linings
are colorful silk; one is a brocatelle in yellow
and black, another is a teal brocatelle edged
in black silk. *Figure 38* is hand made, navy-
blue, watered silk faille, and has the ear-
marks of a non commercial body, but is every
bit as elegant as the others.

Similarity of Sterling Design

One design appears on
many of these frames
but because of the
shape, color, and differ-
ent purse bodies, the
sameness is curiously overlooked. Drawn
from Greek and Roman antiquity, it consists
of a center panel of cherubs playing ring-
around-the-rosy, while two others have
scaled a tree or large vine and are busily
handing the fruit to those on the ground
beneath. The side panels contain more
cherubs and vines and for variation a mythological creature or floral. Since the sterling
marks are not the same, it is unlikely they all
had the same manufacturer, but this is an
area best left to sterling researchers.

Figures 32–35

Group of four sterling mounted bags. Chief glory of this category of purse is the superb frames featuring florals, cherubs, birds, mythological figures, swags and fret work. Usually the chain links are sterling, but on occasion material matching the body was used.

Figure 32

Figure 33

Figure 34

Figure 35

Figure 36

Tissue silk body with raised velvet dots, an extremely popular fashion accent early in the century on veiling and fabrics.

Figure 37

Finely pleated silk material on the body was called cordé. Permanently pleated, it required no stitching.

Figure 38

Ornate figural frame atop a watered silk body. Probably created in the home as the shape is most unusual. May have had a tassel.

Figure 36

82

Figure 37

Figure 38

More restrained designs included the swag, floral baskets, cherubs and baskets, and single cherubs holding engraved name-plates.

The shape of the sterling frame permits the sides to extend four inches into the material deliberately creating an elongated pear shaped body. This shape of frame may also have a heavy interior bar to which a coin purse or lining is attached. This construction is costly and was used on only the finest purses. These purses had to be assembled in a factory because the linings were inserted into the frames and secured with special equipment and a cording or belting. *(Figure 148.)*

A truly different and early (1860–70) velvet is shown at *Plate 80* for the base of this purse is a heavy cardboard which has been preformed and covered with silver and gold thread and set with dull silver beads. There is extensive damage but it does show the lengths to which manufacturers went to produce a unique bag.

Both ring chain and fabric handles were used, though it must be conceded that the more valuable examples use the sterling (and on rare occasions gold or gold plated frames) and matching chain.

Early examples were of the chatelaine type *(Figure 43)* even though they were large and it would appear, inappropriate for wear at the waist. Not all were large, as *Figure 44* is shown nearly actual size; five inches long including hook and four inches wide. It is European silver (800) with a gold wash. The fret work depicts a wild boar hunt deep in the forest. Typical of the twist top, the cap extends down the face of the body for one and a half inches. Quite atypical is the chain arrangement for this is the only three chain chatelaine I know of, though presumably there are others. The third chain is attached to the hook, thus preventing its accidental loss. It is hallmarked in several places. The forest green velvet shows some wear appropriate to its age which is early 19th century.

Shirred silk finished with a blown out filagree frame *(Plate 77)* was much favored for evening use. Small sized, delicate and very feminine, they appeal to all serious collectors.

Sack shaped velvets terminated with a silk cord, either dangling from or affixed to the base of the purse, were also popular early in this century. *Plates 73, 74 and 78* are examples which respectively feature a carved and colorful celluloid.

Irish Crochets

About 1900, when dresses were made of a fine lawn, pleated, tucked, embroidered, and shirred, a crochet purses called Irish Crochet became extremely popular.

It could be done by anyone who could crochet, required no frame, lining, or beads and could be made in a minimum of time. As they were monotonously the same, only three are presented at *Figures 40, 42 and Plate 75.* They were always made in white, cream, beige, or some off shade of white. The patterns were remarkably alike, so much so, once having seen an example, it will not be confused with any other. They were always reticules as well and might be decorated with large oval or round crochet-covered, light weight balls or drops.

Comparable to the modern tote bag, they were the perfect accessory for the summery white dresses worn by any lady under ninety. Like the miser's purse they were made in such quantities that they can be readily found at a pittance, and in fine condition at that. Because the linen or cotton crochet thread was very thick, they were not beaded; beads would have been totally ineffective.

Some ingenious shapes and patterns evolved using ribbons, chenille pompoms, laces, cords and all manner of embellishments. The Museum of Decorative Costume in Paris showed a delicate French version in their recent display of 1920 fashions. *(Figure 41.)*

Plate 73 is crochet but a different type, with a celluloid frame and chain. Another modification is the chenille bag seen at *Plate 76.* The body is embroidered on a lush cream colored plush with a simple drawstring cording.

83

Plate 73

Large netted purse with stylized swan, celluloid frame and chain. Rhinestone set eyes.

Plate 74

Soft suedecloth body and strap. Ivorytone celluloid frame with mock Oriental figure on stippled background.

Plate 75

Large Irish crochet with side and base crochet ball trim.

Plate 76

Very large plush velvet body embroidered with silks. Flowers and pom-poms of chenille plush.

Plate 73

Plate 74

Plate 75

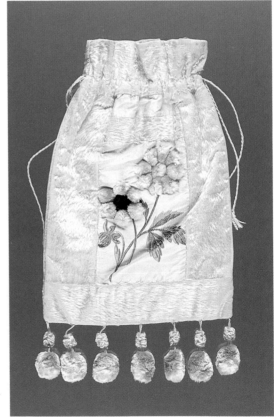

Plate 76

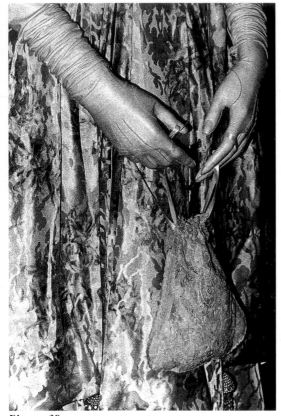

Figures 39–42

Figure 39 is a lace reticule from the Musee of Decorative Arts, Paris, France. Probably hand made lace. Figures 40 and 42 are representative of Irish crochets. Note pattern similarities. Figure 41 is a whimsical canary yellow, crochet, funnel shaped reticule with chenille pom-poms.

Figure 39

Figure 40

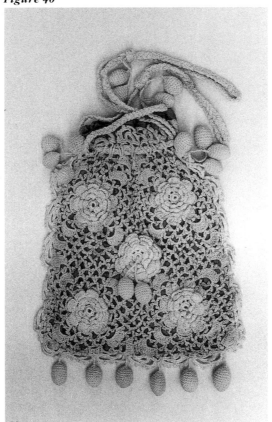

Figure 41

Figure 42

Figure 43

Black suede cloth bag framed with sterling crenulated edges. Chain of flat pierced links. Shallow hook topped by an engraved cupid. Central oval often engraved with owner's initials.

Figure 44

Small, early 19th century (possibly earlier) three chain chatelaine. The elongated oval piece clamped over the waistband or belt, though the presence of the third chain would have made this awkward. Primitive hunt scene done in sterling with gold wash. Rare example.

Figures 45

Reticule. Jet beading on body and loop fringe.

Figure 43

Figure 44

Figure 45

86

Figure 46

Figure 47

Figure 46

Paris fashion model May, 1911, displaying velvet reticule with tassels. Note the use of polka dots and dotted veiling on the hat. It was considered quite alluring to cover the face with this veiling.

Figure 47

Velvet pouch shaped bag with silk tassel. Sterling frame with a butterfly used as an ornament, not as a drop.

"Made-To-Match Fabrics"

Fabrics made into purses to match a particular outfit are far from a 20th century idea, for reticules were "made to match" in the 18th century.

Bethnel Green Museum of Childhood in London, England, contains some of the most delightful exhibits in the world. From it comes this English fashion doll circa 1830. *(Plate 72)* Its head is composition and the body is kid leather. Note the reticule is two toned and of material which matches her gown. For many years the dolls themselves were costly and playthings for only children of the wealthy.

Advanced doll collectors know the practice of presenting the latest fashions from abroad (usually France) to the continents through dolls which were dressed in the most minute detail. This allowed a fashionable and wealthy or royal patron to order a specific gown to her measurements and fabric requirements. It was an ingenious idea in an age when ocean travel was the sole means

Plate 77

Dainty evening pouch in forest green satin. Ladies' choice rhinestone set frame.

Plate 78

Velvet sack-like bag with colored celluloid frame and matching fabric handle. Colored celluloid is currently choice.

Plate 79

Beaded cover hides a large beveled mirror on this otherwise common bag.

Plate 80

Very rare paper molded purse overlaid with silver and gold threads. Gilt replacement frame and chain. Circa late 19th century.

Plate 77

Plate 78

Plate 79

Plate 80

Plate 81

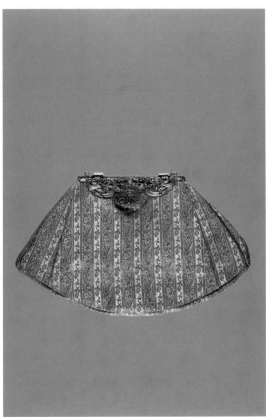

Plate 82

of transport and even that took months.

Pattern books including fold out patterns made of tissue thin paper, with almost incomprehensible directions, given in French, appeared in the mid 1870s.

As early as 1723, the Dictionnaire du Commerce stated, "...those beautiful dolls richly dressed and with beautiful head dresses are sent to foreign courts to exhibit the latest French fashions"

Mrs. Smith, (*Antique Collector's Dolls*) points out that bisque headed dolls on kid, wooden or cloth bodies (which were popular from the 1860's on), were not the only types of dolls used. All these dolls were small, about eighteen inches or less, and were dressed to show the current fashions, however. Having the latest fashions was important to European royalty and American upper classes as well. Even Lanvin dressed dolls made by Sevres. After a period of time such dolls were used for children's play as well. Such dolls were not a classification of doll, merely those dressed in the latest fashions and accessories. *(Plate 72.)*

Modern fabric purses worn for special occasions such as weddings or a particular ball are likely to be small and made of exotic materials. The sterling frame was marked Tiffany and Company above hand made Turkish cloth. An amazing number of people overlooked this fine purse when it was offered for sale, preferring something bolder.

A short chain completes *Plate 82* made of imported French brocade and set with a nicely carved cornelian tab. It could be carried as a clutch if desired.

The Carpetbag

The carpetbag came into being both in this country and abroad with the advent of the steam locomotive. By the mid 1800's trains made it possible to venture across great distances which would have once been unthinkable, especially for women and children.

They were called carpet bags for their strong resemblance to colorful Wilton rugs. They were only slightly more feminine than the oak foot lockers, steamer trunks, and canvas satchels used at this time. Light in weight, they were all approximately the

89

Plate 83

Genuine American
carpet bag fitted
with dated lock and
key. Circa 1884.
Some damage to the
brilliantly colored
wool. Handle of two
ply black leather.
Lined with figured
cotton material and
watercolored
portrait.

Plate 84

Three carpetbags
from the Metropoli-
tan Museum, New
York. The two at the
bottom are of car-
peting material
whereas the one at
the top is gross point
needlepoint. It is
smaller than the
others and has much
wear at the right
side; the rest is in
good condition. Note
subtle differences in
each bag such as
leather gussets, whip
handle, and over-
bound edges.

Plate 83

same dimensions; fifteen inches by eighteen inches.

Many if not all, were fitted with a lock and key, as they contained a lady's valuables as well as immediate necessities for the journey. *Plate 83* has a chain and key holding the reenforced steel edges together, somewhat like tongue and groove flooring.

The wool was harsh, dyed with strong aniline German dyes which had only recently been perfected. The coarse wool and wool and cotton blends insured a few have survived, for a better grade of wool, would have been ruined long ago. Some are more restrained but reds, yellows, oranges and warm colors were preferred. The colors are amazingly bright even today.

This one was purchased in New England some years ago and it is cherished over a host of purses far handsomer. The thick red, beige, black, bronze and cream colored wool shows some wear, possibly from moths, exposing the canvas beneath.

The soft sides of the interior are covered with a small print wall paper and a hand colored print of a lady in a hoop skirt and bonnet lives eternally within its cover. A

small skeleton key fits the patented keyhole dated February 26, 1884. The delicately scrolled brass nameplate is blank.

Three from the Metropolitan Museum of Art show various handles and slight variations in shape; there is a strong similarity in patterns and colors. *(Plate 150.)* Note the handles and frames are different on each bag. One is also covered with carpeting material, another is of rolled leather, while the third is of red and white silk cording. The thin leather is drying out and turning into a powdery substance.

People made one to two trips in their lifetime, savoring each detail for decades. The carpetbag as a travel instrument received little use and if moths and neglect have not consumed them, they are among the most precious of bags and *very* difficult to find.

Cut Velvets These purses have been a mystery for some time. No one seems able to determine whether they are clever imitations or genuine. Not too common, they appear in pleasing color combinations of

Plate 84

Figure 48-1

Figure 48-1

*Dimensions 16"
wide by 11" long.
Done on heavy
canvas. Coarse wool,
loop left loose on
exterior giving a
high pile surface.
Leather base and
strap handles. Bit of
interior edge shows
the now faded exte-
rior wool was rose,
gold, brown, beige
and light green. The
interior is covered
with coarse glazed
linen. The center is
divided into two
sections by a metal
rod. Trade name
"Manuel L. Post.
Saddle, Mattress and
Trunk Manufac-
turers. Corner of
Broadway and North
Murray Street, New
York" is stamped on
the linen. Undated;
typical carpet bag
circa 1860–1870.*

cotton velvet, and various patterns, even slightly different shapes, but the frame is always the same and all the more noticeable because of the baseness of the metal. It is heavy, dull, very poorly engraved with silhouettes and various crudely rendered figures and objects nearly impossible to decipher.

The center post is fitted with a ring through which some heavy chain is passed. The reverse side has three large script letters, M.W.G., always the same. There may be

no attempt to claim these cut piles as antiques or if they are new, their design causes them to be confused with antiques. It is the absolutely dreadful metal casting which casts doubt on their authenticity.

They are made of a nice quality of cotton velvet, the background or weft threads in one shade and the warp threads in a contrasting color. The linings are always secured by large metal brads and three cotton flowerettes near the brads. It is the repetition of details which makes for suspicion. *(Plates 85 and 86.)*

Plates 85–86

*Cut velvets different in size, color, pattern, and ring fittings yet made by the same company and always signed **MWG** on the back side of the frame.*

Figure 48

A group of English picknickers, circa 1907. Note the ladies are clad in summer white and carry very small, black, framed bags.

Plate 85

Plate 86

Figure 48

Chapter 4

The Enduring Leathers

*I*t is doubtful that any purse ever made could tolerate as much punishment and remain as enduring a favorite as the tooled leathers which first made made their appearance in America at the turn of this century.

With the exception of metal mesh purses all other types were made by individuals; either beaded, woven, or embroidered, in the home or hand assembled in a factory/studio type of situation. The leather purse was the first purse to be entirely commercially made, commencing between 1880–1900. However, they involved so much handwork it is difficult to view them as a machine made product.

About this time purses were called handbags to distinguish those which were hand held from those which were worn, such as the chatelaine. The chatelaine has had a long costume history. Chatelaines made of leather were worn outside the home; velvet, satin or plush being reserved for social events. *(Figure 128.)*

Dyed green shagreen was a favorite material, as it was considered a romantic shade in Victorian times. Morocco leather was also esteemed as were seal, walrus, ostrich and other exotic leathers. Leather has remained an ideal material because it is lightweight, supple, and durable. Genuine leather has in recent years met stiff competition from vinyls, and various synthetics. However, there is no comparison between the wearing qualities and good looks of leather and its substitutes.

Leather purses have traditionally been oblong shaped, square, or rectangular. Circular leathers, diamond or other unusual shapes would surely be exceptions in early leathers. When compared to reticules and most meshes, the leathers were relatively spacious. The interiors were divided into two or three compartments to accommodate a mirror, coin purse, comb, compact, handkerchief and other small items. *(Figures 129 and 130.)*

There were many companies producing leather purses and related items; among

Plate 87

Custom made Roycrofter Purse. Hand laced sides; lariat strap, shape not found in mass produced bags. Modifications of this design were used, but not the soft-as-butter leather. Signed and dated 1903.

them were such names as Meeker, McKinnon, Cameo, Reedcraft, Bestmade, Bosca, Cordova, Kaser, and Roycroft. Each of these companies used the trade name above and some added a symbol as well. Their shops were located chiefly in the eastern states of Ohio, Missouri, New York, New Jersey, and Illinois.

Elbert Hubbard and the Roycroft Movement

One of the most interesting producers of leather bags was in no sense a manufacturer, quite the contrary. He was Elbert Hubbard, writer, lecturer, entrepreneur, and founder of the Roycroft Shops located in East Aurora, New York. *(Figure 53.)*

In 1988 the mention of the name Elbert Hubbard would elicit either a resounding "Elbert who?" or a blank stare from all but a handful of artisans. But between 1895 and 1938, when the movement which he founded quietly faded into near oblivion, his was one of the most famous names in the United States.

His admirers did not hesitate to compare him favorably with the great men of his day, but such admiration seems absurd in the light of history.

He was a flamboyant, interesting man whose lifestyle and philosophy had such a tremendous influence upon society in general that he deserves consideration as a patron of the arts and a practicing advocate of "rugged individualism."

Resurgence of the movement he founded is due in large part to a renewed interest in hand crafts and communal life style experiments. Still, Hubbard was soon disenchanted with socialism and would have looked askance upon the social permissiveness practiced today.

The only surviving son of a country doctor, Hubbard was born June 15, 1856, in Bloomington, Illinois. He received a grade school education comparable to that of most children, though his father's profession offered the family an element of refinement and academic appreciation far in advance of his day. His sister, Mary Hubbard Heath, in her biography, wrote of his youthful yearning

to become a farmer, much to the disappointment of his father. But when another sister, Hanna Frances, married John D. Larkin, an enterprising soap manufacturer and an offer was made to employ the strapping, handsome, sixteen year old as a salesman, he enthusiastically took up the challenge. He soon became a junior partner and when he was twenty-five years of age he married Bertha Crawford. In 1884, the family moved to East Aurora, a rural community sixteen miles from Buffalo.

Hubbard was a successful business man and skillful advertiser, especially in mail order sales, which proved a boon to rural purchasers. Out of his passion for reading, he developed a keen interest in writing aside from these commercial broadsides. In order to enhance his limited formal education he enrolled as a special student at Harvard University where he appears to have been less than erudite and curiously indifferent to his studies. He withdrew after a year and sold his interests in the Larkin Company in 1893, to become a lecturer, writer and publisher.

The first issue of *The Philistine,* a pocket size magazine, was in June, 1895. This was followed by fine press books, advertising tracts, pamphlets, and illuminated mottoes. As an outgrowth of these literary endeavors he established a colony of printers, leather-workers, illuminators, artists in metal-work, bookbinding, pottery, sculpture, painting, culinary arts, gardening, furniture, architecture, music and virtually every other artistic expression. *(Figure 49.)*

Hubbard was impressed with the work of the English social reformer, William Morris, and in 1899, after visiting the European colony he was able to establish his own complex where youthful artists could study and produce handwork which could be profitably marketed. Virginia Hamilton states in her pamphlet, "The best artisans were attracted to East Aurora and the Roycrofters received expert instruction in printing, bookbinding, metalcraft, and as a sideline from bookbinding which in those days was done in leather, the production of *modeled leather* articles. About 250 employees worked happily in this corporation, which paid wages and was not the communal experiment as some erroneous accounts indicate."

The BOOK of he Roycrofters

Being.
A Catalog
of
COPPER
LEATHER
and
BOOKS
1919

Figure 49

Catalog originally
issued in 1919 and
reprinted around
1926. It included
fine photographs of
copper and leather
items available
through the
Roycrofters.

Figures 50–51

The Copper Shop
Furniture and
Leather Shop build-
ing is still standing
as is the Chapel and
Main Building.

Figure 49

IN this building our Modeled-Leather Craftsmen, Bibliopegists, and Cabinetmakers do dexterous deeds. They are practical craftsmen and their work is the product of head, hand and heart coordinated. And the things they make are lasting, beautiful and worth while. Many, many thousand homes have been made more beautiful by these creations and many more thousand individuals are happy and proud to possess them.

Figure 50

Figure 51

Figure 52

Figure 53

Figure 52

Roycrofters' Chapel and Main Building which presently houses the municipal offices for the town of East Aurora, New York.

Figure 53

Elbert Hubbard, the vital spirit behind the arts and crafts Roycroft Movement. He and his wife were passengers on the S.S. Lusitania which was torpedoed in 1915.

Coeducation gave the movement a Bohemian flavor, and they *were* radical, but these artists were vegetarians, neither drank nor smoked, and enjoyed such activities as baseball, dramatics, musicals and bowling; hardly the racy activities expected of libertines!

The essential difference between the Roycrofters and similar groups which sprang up in America about this time, was the magnetic personality of its founder and his strong paternalistic stance. The artisans were his employees and though fostering and assuring a continuation of hand made items and skills, the loosely knit group was strictly a capitalistic venture.

Both men and women were engaged in producing these items on a virtual custom made basis. Naturally the volume was limited. It was sold through speciality shops throughout the nation in a featured Roycroft section. The prices were amazingly competitive and the quality was never compromised. The Roycrofters never allowed their high standards to waver or decline. They were

victims of the depression, a technological revolution which radically altered styles, and the impending World War II.

All of this was made possible by the publication of one of the most famous essays ever written, *The Message to Garcia* (which should be required reading for all secondary students). Luckily, the public was sympathetic to the work ethic he espoused and here advocated. It has been printed over 80,000,000 times. Its popularity made Hubbard a highly paid lecturer and he became a columnist for Hearst Publications.

Hubbard and his second wife, Alice, were lost at sea when the S. S. Lusitania was sunk at the outset of World War I. His community projects were continued by his heir, Elbert Hubbard II. Rather than reduce the quality of their crafts, the Roycrofters, seriously effected by the depression, disbanded in 1938.

Their products are rare and valuable, leather handbags in particular, because they were subjected to considerable wear and

Figure 54

The town of East Aurora presently has its offices in one of the Roycrofters buildings and the campus has been maintained as undisturbed as possible. A gift shop, museum, inn, (now defunct) and some craft shops are housed on what was the site of the leather and furniture shops. *(Figures 50, 51 and 52.)*

Trademarks

As an interesting sidelight, master leather worker, German born Frederick Kranz, was engaged to instruct apprentices in the leather workshop. Under his leadership the workshop was eminently successful and many highly skilled workmen, including George Scheide Mantel emerged.

Kranz subsequently established his own leather studios in Buffalo, New York, which he called the **Cordova Shops.** He signed his works with a *K* within a diamond shaped punch on the outer side of the purse back, as opposed to the common company practice of lightly stamping the purse lining.

As many of these craftsmen trained together it is not surprising their output shows a marked similarity in shape, designs, and materials. The artists working originally with the Roycrofters opened their own studios once they had sufficient skills to become entrepreneurs.

The Cordova advertisements are from an old salesman's sample book and the note is indicative of the way one factory monitored the activities of another. Whether *us* was intended to be *our,* or stood for United States, is a puzzle. *(Figure 62.)*

I believe the two purses at these figures are signed Kranz purses for they are most unusual. The date on the frames is 1918 and they are assuredly signatures. Quite similar in pattern, each features a rose and leaves on dark steerhide, with hand lacing and copper Jemco frames. *(Figures 63, 64 and 65.)*

H. E. Kaser Modeled Leather Corporation located in Buffalo, New York, at 1870–72 Genesee Street, was a contemporary and competitor of the Roycrofters, whose superb hand crafted leather goods were second to none.

Figure 54

were ultimately discarded. There are those who collect only Roycroft items and they now command exceedingly high prices. *(Figures 55, 56, 57, 58 and 59.)*

Mrs. Hamilton feels, "The Roycrofters were dedicated to the glorification of fine craftsmanship. They wielded the tools of their various crafts with the same zeal Hubbard put behind his pen. And so, as they earned a living, they also left a legacy of collectibles and a legend that has become an indelible part of the history of arts and crafts in America."

Figure 54

Roycrofter Symbol as it appears on the card of Hubbard's granddaughter, Linda Hubbard Brady.

99

*Roycroft handbags
as illustrated in
the Book of the
Roycrofters, 1919.
Bag number 2120
sold for $35.00,
whereas number
2116 sold for
$10.00 retail.*

HAND-BAG—2119
Bold grain cowhide. Fitted with
coin purse and mirror. Silk lined.
Size 7 x 7 inches.

These illustrations show the shape
and designs, but no printed pictures
can do justice to the rich coloring—
two-tone gray-blue or two-tone
brown

HAND-BAG—2118
Bold grain cowhide. Fitted with coin
purse and mirror. Silk lined. Size 7½
x 6½ inches. Hand laced edges.

HAND-BAG—2120
Calf, leather-lined. Fitted with card case, coin
purse and mirror. Size 7 x 8¼ inches.

Figure 55

HAND-BAG—2126-A
Spanish steer hide. Fitted with coin
purse and mirror. Velvet ooze lining.
Gun-metal frame. Size 6 x 7 inches.

HAND-BAG—2125
Spanish steer hide, laced edges, gun-metal
frame, soft, ribbon-effect handle, velvet
ooze lining. Fitted with coin purse and
mirror, in pockets. Round bottom.
Size 7¼ x 8½ inches.

HAND-BAG—2126-B
Spanish steer hide. Velvet ooze lining.
Fitted with coin purse and mirror.
Gun-metal frame. Size 6 x 7 inches.

Figure 56

Roycroft Hand-Bags and other hand-modeled leather come in two colors: two-tone gray-blue, two-tone brown. In filling orders we will use our own judgment, unless you specify which color you prefer.

HAND-BAG—2116-2117
ENVELOPE-SHAPE
No. 2116 is 4 x 6 in. fitted with
2 x 3 in. purse.
No. 2117 is 5½ x 6½ in. fitted
with coin purse and mirror.
Moire silk lining.

HAND-BAG—2105-B
Spanish steer hide. Soft handle, round bottom, ooze morocco lining. Fitted with coin-purse and mirror. Size 7½ x 7¼ in.

HAND-BAG—2109
Spanish steer hide. Ooze leather lining. Fitted with combination coin and bill purse, mirror, memo-slate and pencil. Size 5¼ x 5¾ in.

Figures 57–58

Roycroft and H.E. Kaser Shop handbags showing the whole-sale prices handwritten at the end of each description. It is estimated current prices are in excess of ten times those asked in 1900; a bag which sold for $30.00 would currently be worth approximately $300.00. This is still a bargain consider-ing the quality and rarity of the bag.

Figure 57

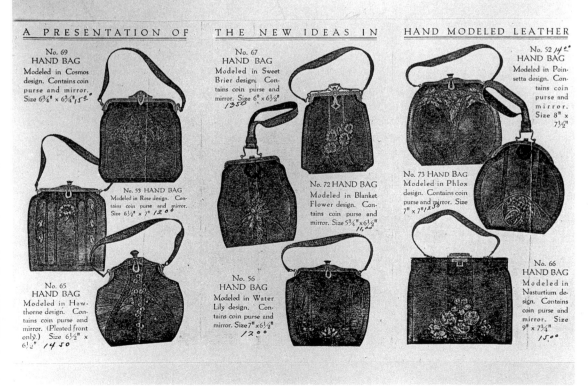

A PRESENTATION OF   THE NEW IDEAS IN   HAND MODELED LEATHER

No. 69
HAND BAG
Modeled in Cosmos
design. Contains coin
purse and mirror.
Size 6¾" x 6¾" 15.²

No. 67
HAND BAG
Modeled in Sweet
Brier design. Con-
tains coin purse and
mirror. Size 6" x 6½"
13.50

No. 52 14.²
HAND BAG
Modeled in Poin-
setta design. Con-
tains coin
purse and
mirror. Size 8" x
7½"

No. 53 HAND BAG
Modeled in Rose design. Con-
tains coin purse and mirror.
Size 6½" x 7" 12.00

No. 72 HAND BAG
Modeled in Blanket
Flower design. Con-
tains coin purse and
mirror. Size 5¾" x 6½"
11.00

No. 73 HAND BAG
Modeled in Phlox
design. Contains coin
purse and mirror. Size
7" x 7" 12.50

No. 65
HAND BAG
Modeled in Haw-
thorne design. Con-
tains coin purse and
mirror. (Pleated front
only.) Size 6½" x
6½" 14.50

No. 56
HAND BAG
Modeled in Water
Lily design. Con-
tains coin purse and
mirror. Size 7" x 6½"
12.00

No. 66
HAND BAG
Modeled in
Nasturtium de-
sign. Contains
coin purse and
mirror. Size
9" x 7¾"
15.00

Figure 58

Figure 59

*Envelope and coin
purses from the
Roycroft Studios,
1919.*

PURSE—504
Large pocket for change.
Closed pocket for folded bills,
cards, tickets, etc. Laced edges.
Leather lined. Size 4¼ x 2¾

PURSE—513. ENVELOPE-SHAPE
Moire silk lining. Fitted with coin purse,
mirror, memo-slate and pencil
Size 3¾ x 8 in.

BUSINESS-WOMAN'S POCKET-BOOK
507. Leather lined. Strap on back
Pockets for bills, change and cards
Mirror, memo-slate and pencil
Size 3¼ x 5½ in.

SADDLE-PURSE—501-A
Large pocket for coins, smaller
one for tickets. Size 3 x 3½ in.

PURSE—535. ENVELOPE-SHAPE
Suede leather lining. Strap handle on back.
Three compartments. Fitted with mirror, memo-
slate and pencil. Size 3¾ x 7 in.

SADDLE-PURSE—505-A
Laced edge. Large coin pocket.
Ticket pocket. Size 3 x 3 in½.

MEMO-BOOK—701
Pad of 90 sheets, renewable.
Size 2½x3½. 702. Size 3x4¾ in.

PURSE—536. ENVELOPE-SHAPE
Same as 535 except the design and a different
bottom construction

MEMO-BOOK—704
Pad of 90 sheets, renewable.
Fitted with pencil and card pocket

Figure 59

Whether all of their line was signed is uncertain, but the elegant example at *Figure 66* is deeply impressed with the words **ORIGINAL KASER, GENUINE HAND TOOLED** and signed with a **K** after the fashion of Fredrick Kranz. Did Kaser use the master craftsman's signature with permission? Did Kranz work for Kaser or was Kranz deceased and the **K** released from copyright? Was Kaser another pupil of Kranz? It is an intriguing mystery.

It is currently most unusual to discover a signed bag and I was delighted with the 6 × 7 inch example above. The hammered brass frame dated July, 1918, is topped by an embossed button plunger and the front shows a stylized daffodil in high relief. The strap handle was worn and had to be relaced, other than that, both the ooze leather interior and smooth exterior were in excellent condition.

Roycroft craftsmen (and craftsladies) did not usually place their own initials or personal marks on the pieces they turned out, rather, they affixed a special Roycroft trademark. *(Figure 49.)* Hubbard explained that it

evolved from the basic mark first used by Cassiodorus, a monk who lived in the Middle Ages. "He was," as Hubbard liked to relate, "one of the first bookbinders and on every book he illumined and bound, he placed his mark which was the cross and circle representing unity and infinity."

Adopting and adapting this mark, Hubbard divided the circle into three parts signifying, he explained, Faith, Hope, and Love. In the lower portion of the divided circle he added the letter *R* to stand for Roycrofters. He pointed out that Roycroft was coined from *roi craft* or *royal craftsmen* and as such could be interpreted as the Kings Craft.

The significance of the signature is tantamount to that of any artist whose signed work confirms the authenticity of the piece, though the work is not necessarily superior to similar unsigned items.

Roycrofter purses were not as unusual as one might expect them to be. It is possible their designs were copied by other manufacturers. This practice has been used since the beginning of time by making slight modifications in designs to avoid outright pirating.

USEFUL CRAFTSMANSHIP

No. 302 4 8°
BILL FOLD
Modeled in Pinecone, Grape
and Acorn

306 22⁵
No. 306
BILL FOLD
Modeled in
Pinecone and
Thorn Apple

No. 305
BILL FOLD
Modeled in Ivy,
Grape, Acorn
and Pinecone

305 · 3⁰⁰

DAME FASHION
HAS DECREED

NOTHING is quite as appropriate with a finely tailored
ladie's suit as an—EXQUISITELY
"TAILORED" SMART
HAND BAG.

H. E. Kaser's creations in hand
modeled hand bags are considered
ultra smart and are really "tailored."

SAMPLES ON REQUEST

H. E. Kaser Modeled Leather Corp.
1870-72 GENESEE STREET
BUFFALO, N. Y.

TRADE K MARK

All articles GUARANTEED

H.E.Kaser
Modeled
Leather
Corp.

Figure 60

The designs were simple often utilizing rather traditional florals such as: cosmos, sweet brier, blanket flower, poinsetta, phlox, nasturtium, water lily, hawthorne, and rose. They are very difficult to differentiate from one another.

They were fitted with pencil, mirror, memo-slate and coin purse. *(Figures 71 and 72.)* The linings were of green suede or moire silk. Green suede was widely used by all leather purse manufacturers as it was considered less apt to soil and wear than smoothly tanned leathers.

Some models are found still containing the coin purse and mirror. *(Figures 71 and 72.)* The mirrors were treated with quicksilver and a backing of porcelain. The silver is usually badly age cracked, but collectors find them strangely appealing even though they are no longer usable. They often are backed with the same leather used on the purse exterior, but they are no better preserved than the porcelain backed types.

Roycroft Designs In the autumn of 1986, we passed a pleasant af-ternoon with the late Vir-ginia Vidler, (who was closely associated with the preservation of the Roycroft Movement) shortly before her

untimely death, discussing the leather craftsmen and purses in particular.

Three genuine examples from the Roy-croft Museum were available to be photo-graphed along with a few done by George Shiede Mantel. They are shown at *Figures 73, 74 and 75.*

We noted *Figures 73 and 74* are so simple of design that they are exceptionally beauti-ful. A realistic grasshopper dominates the focal point, arching the slender blade in a semi circle conforming to the modified tri-angular shape of the purse. One half expects the weight of the grasshopper to break the grass and cause it to fall on the daisy be-neath. The single bloom and scattered buds are so restrained that the personality of the unknown artist shines through.

The first two are of particular interest be-cause of their similarity to *Plate 87* known to be a Kranz purse.

Both of these purses are ten inches long and six inches wide at the widest parts. The copper plates at the top have a eye through which the lariat is threaded. The softest, smoothest leather imaginable, almost like butter is used. *Plate 87* is rather traditional Art Nouveau, the front and back unalike in small detail. Unfortunately the gussets were not generous enough and over the years have torn away from the lacing. The outer sides

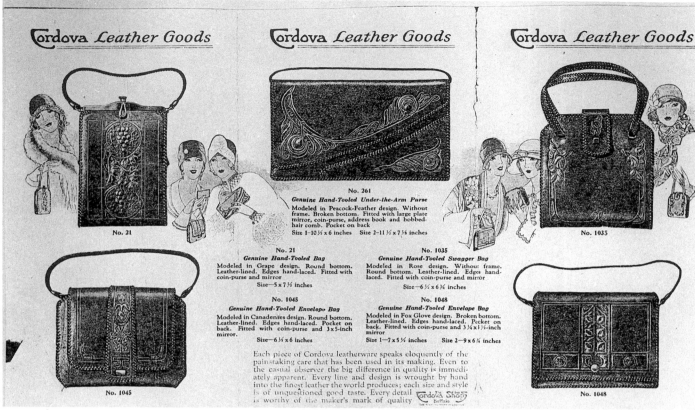

Figure 61

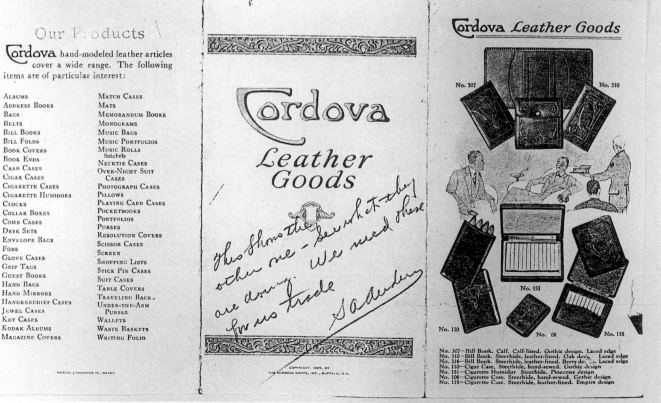

Figure 62

Figures 61–62

*Interesting advertise-
ments (date 1925)
from Cordova.
Charming hand
rendered drawings
and penciled note
from a person
named Saunders.
"See what they are
doing," he suggests.
Either poor grammar
or lack of capitali-
zation is indicated
in the advice to the
salesman.*

Figures 63–66

*Three signed purses
by Fredrick Kranz
featuring the rose
motif and a ham-
mered-brass framed
floral from Bosca
Reed.*

Figure 63

Figure 64

Figure 65

Figure 66

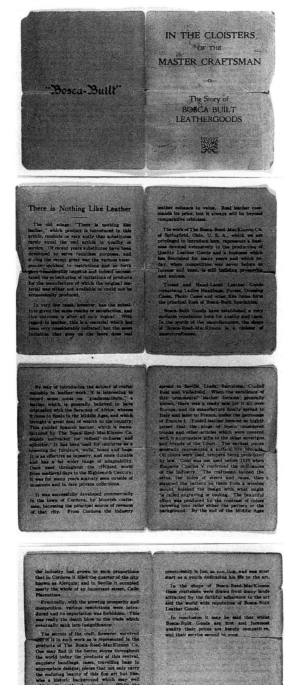

Figure 67

Figure 68

Figure 69

Figure 70

are attached to a gusset, so with loving care, it can be restored. The interior was lightly burnished, so lightly it is now nearly impossible to read the words, Cordova Shops, Buffalo, N.Y. 1913.

The second example, *(Figure 74,)* is equally distinctive. Note the symmetrical design so nicely integrated with the straps and flap. Again it is the simplicity of the constrained pattern which adds to the feeling of length and exclusivity. This purse is dark maroon, Moroccan leather.

The third example *(Figure 75)* is not as individualized as the others adhering as it does to the central design of blossoms, leaves, vines, and side decor. The frame is a

Figures 71–72

*Art Nouveau design
on fitted purse. It is
unusual to find all
the fittings intact.*

Figure 71

Figure 72

standard plunger or stud type made of copper. The handle is a laced leather strip of the sort commonly used on leather bags. It has the advantage of being larger than the others. These flat leathers were not as expandable as modern bags which are more conveniently pouch shaped.

These bags are all hand tooled, laced and finished. Unless one is an expert, it is very difficult to differentiate between the hand tooled and die impressed, especially from a photograph. The depth of the design is important but more indicative of hand tooling, is the originality of the design.

There are on display in the East Aurora Museum, some purses by George Shiede Mantel, a gifted pupil of Fredrick Kranz. Sheide Mantel became head of the leather shop himself from 1915–1918 directing a staff of approximately ten people. His leather artistry was exhibited in major museums during his lifetime and he enjoyed a considerable reputation.

A design by Sheide Mantel along with a card which accompanied the object is shown at *Figures 76 and 77.* It is not known if the design was for a purse, but it is quite possible.

TYPICAL ROYCROFT PURSES

From *The Book of The Roycrofters,* sizes, linings, fittings, colors, leathers and designs are shown. The ooze leather refers to sheepskin or calfskin tanned by using a decoctuion of oak, bark, sumac, and mud to create an ooze which is forced through the skins to produce a soft, finely granulated finish sometimes called a velvet finish. It was invariably dyed green.

The salesman's prices are handwritten into the margins. If a handbag was offered for $15.00 just prior to World War I, does $200.00 seem an inflated price for one in mint condition seventy-five years later? Hardly.
(See Figures 55, 56, 57 and 58.)

*Other
Hand
Made
Examples*

About this time an extremely soft suede leather purse was being beaded (some were laced) possibly sold in kit form, as they are all very similar in shape, beading and design. *(Figure 79.)* They were

Figure 73

Figure 74

neither attractive, nor durable and apparently were made in huge quantities. The leather was usually a dull brown and the beads black, chunky glass or cut steels.

From England's Victoria and Albert comes this hand tooled Egyptian motif bag. It shows the world-wide effect the discovery of King Tut's tomb had on fashion as well as other art forms. *(Figure 80.)* It is undoubtedly a custom made piece and rather modern in style. Particularly interesting is the wide strap handle which is a continuation of the body itself.

Figure 81 is done in pale green print on light grey suede. It is not a very functional purse but the design is striking and much along the lines of others made during this momentous time of discovery. The hieroglyphics are handsomely done as are all these flat representations of ancient Egypt.

Figure 75

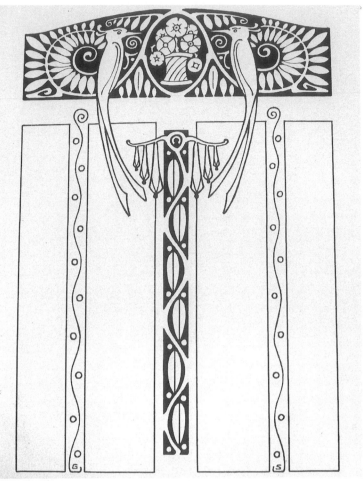

Figure 76

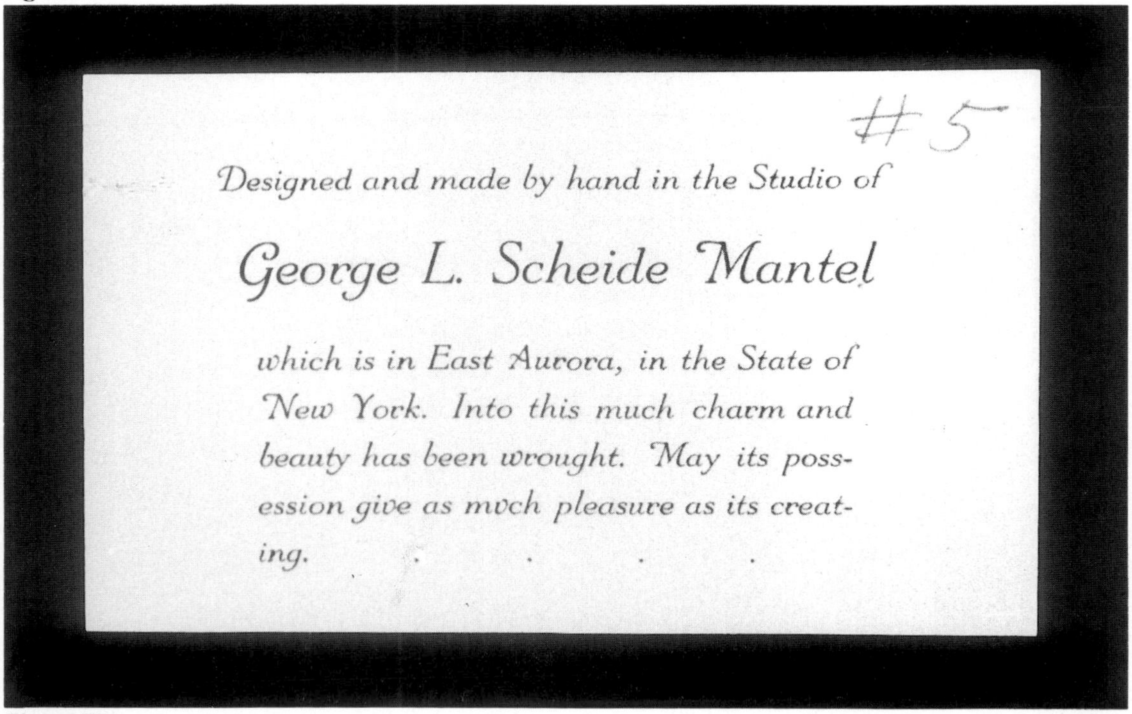

#5

Designed and made by hand in the Studio of

George L. Scheide Mantel

which is in East Aurora, in the State of New York. Into this much charm and beauty has been wrought. May its possession give as mvch pleasure as its creating. . . . .

Figure 77

***Figure** 73*

Custom made Roycroft purse done in simple grasshopper design on smooth leather.

***Figure** 74*

Custom Roycroft purse with unique strap mechanism.

***Figure** 75*

Original Roycroft design with plunger fastener. Copper frame.

***Figure** 76*

Original design possibly for use on a purse or book cover.

***Figure** 77*

Card accompanying an art ojbect in the Roycrofter Building.

Figure 78

*News article and
George Scheide
Mantel at work,
dated 1936.*

BUFFALO COURIER-EXPRESS, MONDAY, JANUARY 6, 1936

CALLS LEATHER COMING MOTIF

Craftsman predicts its use in interior decoration

East Aurora, Jan. 5—Leather wall hangings, plaques and other examples of leather adaptations for interior decoration are being prepared by George L. Scheide Mantel, East Aurora leather designer and craftsman for the annual exhibition of Buffalo and Western New York artists to be held in the Albright Art Gallery in March.

"A plain piece of leather has a beauty that nothing else has," Mr. Scheide Mantel said, exhibiting examples of his craft in the small white studio in his home at 363 Oakwood Avenue. "Leather has a texture you don't get in a woven fabric, and the clever use of light accentuates its hidden beauty."

Inca, Maya Inspiration

Several wall hangings Mr. Scheide Mantel has made were inspired by Incan and Mayan art, of which he is an admirer. One of these is a long panel of tooled leather which he did for the public works of art project a year or so ago with an exhibition at the Albright Art Gallery.

His panel representing an Incan high priest with a kneeling figure on either side was a total of 345 hours in the making, over a period of weeks. Commenting on a colored reproduction of one of these figures, Capt. Mitchell O. Hedges, British authority on art of South America, complimented the artist on capturing the atmosphere and feeling of the Incan in his work.

The primitive African motif was Mr. Scheide Mantel's inspiration in creating two life-size leather masks. The first one he made is the figure to the left in the accompanying picture. As the African woman seemed to be lonesome at her plight of perpetually "jawing away at no one," the artist took pity on her and created the warrior facing her who is doomed to listen and say nothing.

The eyes, lips, hair and headdresses of the African pair were touched with bright hues of water color, and the faces highly waxed before the photograph was taken. Since then, Mr. Scheide Mantel decided that the masks would be more effective in all-leather, without paint.

Inset Colored Pieces

He inset small pieces of colored Morocco leathers wherever color was called for in the masks. The faces are in the original steerhide, highly waxed. He also mounted each mask on a board of white birch about sixteen inches by eighteen and had a whitewood molding placed as a border.

A hideous full-face view of an Inca god is the subject of a leather mask, mounted on a brown stained birch board with brown molding. Many observers shudder at this one and ask Mr. Scheide Mantel why he made such an ugly thing, but he only smiles and replies that he guesses he was successful in making him.

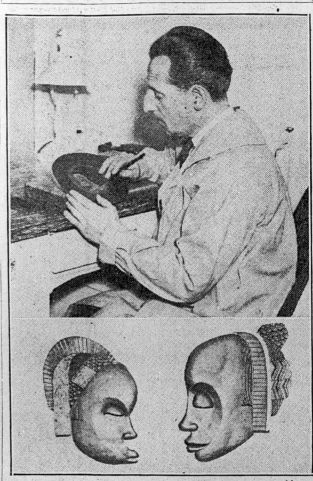

His Inspiration, Inca, Maya

East Aurora—George L. Scheide Mantel, artist in leather, working on a plaque. Lower, primitive African masks.

Figure 78

Figure 79

Figure 79

Laced purse with beaded fringe and outside pocket. At one time a popular kit project with home beaders.

See following page:

Figure 80

Leather purse with Pharaoh's profile from the Victoria and Albert Museum, London, England. Circa 1920. Unusual strap construction.

Figure 81

Drawstring rough finished purse with very fine Egyptian motif done in pale green. Religious rite is being performed by the Sun God, Amenhotep. Historically accurate costumes and symbols.

Figure 82

Fine purse made in Egypt showing view of the Nile River. Circa 1920. Interior of salmon colored smooth leather. Note lacing is different than that done on Western bags.

Figure 83

Printed leather reticule. French. 18th century costumes contemporary with date of manufacture. Boston Museum of Fine Arts.

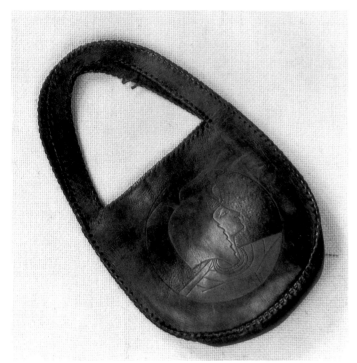

Figure 80

Figure 81

Figure 82

Figures 80–83

See page 111.

Figure 83

112

Figure 84

Figure 85

Tourists have tended to purchase items with some reminder of a visit to a foreign land for centuries, so this hand painted purse advertises the Nile River, the distant pyramids, date palms, and a typical desert scene. The ancients were abandoned in favor of a more modern approach. *(Figure 82.)*

Made in the late 1920's or early 1930's it is a magnificent signed work done in soft leather, possibly camel. The many compartmented interior is dyed a coral color. Notice the lacing done in wide strips is different from domestic lacing.

Printed leather reticules were done as early as 1840. The Boston Museum of Fine Arts owns this fragile example which so resembles a paper bag or sack. *(Figure 83.)* The

Figure 84

MEEKER AD

Figure 85

In 1908, Meeker employees were largely ladies, a rather unusual fact in itself.

113

Figure 86

formal, romantic subject matter of this French reticule is in sharp contrast to the simple Egyptian motif. It is worth noting each has a border or background which emphasizes and complements the central design.

Commercial Leather Manufacturers

MEEKER COMPANY

During the heyday of the leather bag, one of the largest and most renowned manufacturers was the Meeker Company of Joplin, Missouri. They discontinued the tooled or modeled leather purse in 1959. The present owners are William E Fowks, Jr. and his brother, Michael Fowks, nephews of the founder, Mr. Cory Meeker.

Mr. William Fowks Jr. generously donated a wealth of material which in fact enabled the inclusion of this chapter and we thank him most profoundly. Up to this point in time the leather purse has been something of a mystery, few people outside the environs of the Meeker Company remembering much about these famous purses other than the fact that a relative had once owned one. An endorsement to the quality of workmanship which went into their creation is their longevity.

Mr. Cory Meeker established the Meeker Company in 1908, in a small two story brick building with about two dozen employees, most of them women. A tiny photograph, *(Figure 85,)* shows them standing in the doorway beneath the company sign. Whether they were first engaged in leather production is not clear, but in 1923, the sign on the one story newer brick building read, "Calendars, Leather Goods, Signs and Specialties MEEKER ADVERTISING." It would appear at this time that paper products of various kinds were the firm's principle manufacture and leather was merely one of the sidelines.

Figure 87

Letter

THE MEEKER COMPANY
INCORPORATED
JOPLIN
MISSOURI

April 9th, 1932

Style-right--
quality-right---

--and price-right!

Handbags which really sell at full mark-up -- that's what you're looking for, isn't it?

Well, here they are! Eighteen representative numbers of our spring and summer offering -- in just the colors and the shapes your customers will be demanding. They spell TURNOVER in capital letters -- for they team-up perfectly with the season's tailored ensembles, and are correctly in tune with predominant style trends.

These bags were designed by one of the country's foremost stylists (now working for us exclusively), and smartness is built right in! Don't you think they deserve a place-- a prominent place -- in your handbag department?

Take advantage of this advance presentation -- the opportunity given you to get these stunning bags NOW, while they're newest in a style way. There is adequate stock for speedy delivery.

We are so certain you'll like these bags that we'll be glad to send you a trial order. Specify any quantity you like. Then, you be the sole judge. If they don't meet every up to the minute requirement, return them at once.

Very truly yours,
THE MEEKER COMPANY, INC.,

President

CM:EN

(The order-envelope needs no postage).

HANDBAGS
VANITIES
BILL FOLDS
KEY CASES
CIGARETTE CASES
GIFT SETS
BRIDGE SETS
DESK SETS
TOILET CASES
BOOK COVERS
BOOK ENDS
WRITING SETS

SEVENTH AND
SCHOOL STREETS
TELEPHONE 1271

Figure 87

115

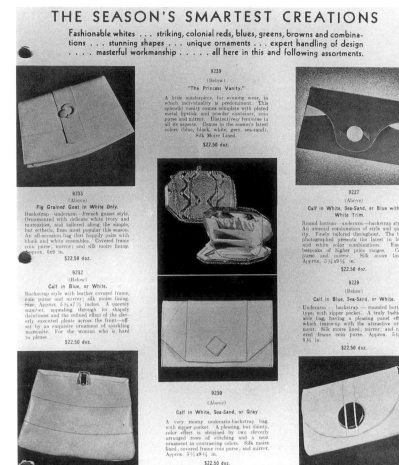

THE SEASON'S SMARTEST CREATIONS

Fashionable whites . . . striking, colonial reds, blues, greens, browns and combinations . . . stunning shapes . . . unique ornaments . . . expert handling of design . . . . masterful workmanship . . . . . all here in this and following assortments.

9239
(Below)
"The Princess Vanity."

A little masterpiece, for evening wear, in which individuality is predominant. This splendid vanity comes complete with plated metal lipstick and powder container, coin purse and mirror. Distinctively feminine in all its aspects. Comes in the season's latest colors (blue, black, white, grey, sea-sand). Silk Moire Lined.
$22.50 doz.

9233
(Above)
Pig Grained Goat in White Only.

Backstrap—underarm—French gusset style. Ornamented with delicate white ivory and marcasites, and tailored along the simple, but esthetic, lines most popular this season. An all-occasion bag that happily pairs with black and white ensembles. Covered frame coin purse; mirror; and silk moire lining. Approx. 6x9 in.
$22.50 doz.

9232
(Below)
Calf in Blue, or White.

Backstrap style with leather covered frame, coin purse and mirror; silk moire lining. Size, Approx. 5½x7½ inches. A queenly number, appealing through its shapely daintiness and the refined effect of the cleverly executed pleats across the front—offset by an exquisite ornament of sparkling marcasite. For the woman who is hard to please.
$22.50 doz.

9227
(Above)
Calf in White, Sea-Sand, or Blue with White Trim.

Round bottom—underarm—backstrap style. An unusual combination of style and quality. Finely tailored throughout. The bag photographed presents the latest in blue and white color combinations. Easily bespeaks of higher price ranges. Coin purse and mirror. Silk moire lined. Approx. 5¾x9¼ in.
$22.50 doz.

9229
(Below)
Calf in Blue, Sea-Sand, or White.

Underarm — backstrap — rounded bottom type, with zipper pocket. A truly fashionable bag, having a pleasing panel effect which teams-up with the attractive ornament. Silk moire lined; mirror; and covered frame coin purse. Approx. 5¾x 8¾ in.
$22.50 doz.

9230
(Above)
Calf in White, Sea-Sand, or Gray

A very roomy underarm-backstrap bag, with zipper pocket. A pleasing, but dainty, color effect is obtained by two cleverly arranged rows of stitching and a neat ornament in contrasting colors. Silk moire lined; covered frame coin purse; and mirror. Approx. 5½x8¾ in.
$22.50 doz.

SIX CAPTIVATING LEATHER NUMBERS
IN LEAGUE WITH QUALITY » » IN TUNE WITH THE YEAR'S LATEST VOGUES

Figure 88

Figure 88

AD

Figures 89–96

On the next four pages:

The following Meeker factory photographs were taken about 1930. They emphasize the handwork then required in manufacturing leather purses made between 1900–1940.

Before World War II, companies located in small towns tended to be somewhat paternalistic as a high percentage of the local population constituted their workforce. Group photographs taken at company picnics, assembled in front of the expanded facilities and at parties, indicated the company's growth and also revealed a slight increase in the number of male employees, although women continued to outnumber them about three to one. Light industry benefitted from their employ as their salaries were lower than men's. They were undoubtedly more dexterous at the various tasks involved in purse production.

It seems ironic that a company bulletin masthead reads Vol, I Number I and the date is October, 1929. The thrust of the message informed merchants that Meeker, like Whit-

ing and Davis, had undertaken an advertising campaign in virtually the same magazines as Whiting; *Vogue, Liberty, Harper's Bazaar,* and *Photoplay* were selected. They also had prepared literature for merchant distribution to selected customers.

How successful this campaign was is not known, but the courage of any company which continued to keep afloat when caught in the grip of the terrible depression *has* to be admired.

In July, 1929, ten very pretty showgirls posed with Meeker purses, the latest in cloche hats, and what appears to have been chic that year, the sheath, complete with accordion pleats. Each girl has a different style and size of purse and each carries the purse in a different manner. *(Figure 86.)*

By 1932 the the company was housed in a modern three story building where they are still located. At this time four hundred skilled men and women were employed during peak seasons.They had become incorporated and a company letter listed the following line: handbags, vanities, bill folds, key cases, cigarette cases, gift sets, bridge sets, desk sets, toilet cases, book covers, book ends, and writing sets. Clearly they had moved into the leather business and away from paper goods. *(Figure 87.)*

Nearly seventy years ago these plant photographs were taken of the various departments at the Meeker factory. I assume the following order of assembly was followed. (There may be more or fewer steps, as there was no accompanying explanatory text and the order may be incorrect).

The hides were first selected, the pattern determining the size and shape traced and cut, the decorative die impressed, the desired dyes applied, the glazing applied, the various parts assembled, the lining glued into place, the sides and flap laced, the framing, strap, and hardware added and finally the fittings inserted i.e. mirror, coin purse, possibly a comb, and addressbook. The completed purse was stuffed with tissue paper and boxed for shipment to the retailer. The retailer was a department store, speciality shop, or luggage shop rather than a jeweler. *(Figures 89, 90, 91, 92, 93, 94, 95 and 96.)*

Figure 89

Figure 90

Figure 91

Figure 92

Figure 93

Figure 94

Figure 95

120 *Figure 96*

Why the Leather Purses Survived

One of their most endearing qualities is the nostalgia connected with leathers. They seem to remain in the memory of an astonishing number of elderly ladies, much like Whiting and Davis purses. A plausible theory is that the leather purse was the workhorse of purses and it was used on a daily basis. "When I was a little girl I remember my mother (or my grandmother) had a purse just like that," they muse. "She carried it for years everywhere she went." No purse arouses thoughts of happier days for them as they dreamily reminisce; almost always concluding, "I wonder what happened to it?"

They frequently surface, especially in the Midwest. Admittedly, they are not always found in mint or even good condition, but this should not deter the collector from adding at least a few to any well rounded collection.

They have the added advantage of being relatively easily restored at a modest price by any master leather worker. Beaded purses require extraordinary skill and expertise in a field which is already obsolete, (and which really should not be repaired by a novice). There are many highly adroit and innovative leather workers throughout the country working in modern mediums, who are both competent and willing to restore antique leathers. The cost of repairs depends to a large extent on the area and of course on the amount and degree of damage to the leather.

They were made in the United States but some advertisements placed heavy emphasis on the fact that the steerhide leather was of English origin. Other manufacturers such as the Roycrofters claimed their leather was Spanish steerhide. One such ad ran as follows: "These bags are made in this country of the finest quality imported steerhide. English steerhide is noted for its long wearing properties. The tooling and the coloring are done by modern methods after an ancient formula developed in Medieval Spain." How superior English leather was may have more to do with the price quoted than the leather itself, for purses made of domestic leather were offered for much lower prices.

For many years almost all European goods, services, educational institutions, and the arts, were considered superior to their American counterparts. It was a snobbish attitude which Americans rather willingly tolerated, if not outright encouraged. Ours was considered almost an upstart civilization and those who could afford to buy imported goods, educate their children abroad, indulge in foreign travel and fashions, (particularly French), did so. It was an appeal to those who wanted the best and could afford to buy quality items.

BOSCA, REED, BESTMADE AND OTHERS

Guarantees have always been important but they were highly stressed a half century ago. Women bought fewer purses and expected, nay demanded, they last. And last they did, as any lady of that era can attest.

Leather purses came with a card such as is seen at *Figures 67–70;* extolling the virtues of each manufacturer. Bosca Built even included a story of the ancient manufacture of leather goods, how they came to be known as cordova, and their Spanish-Moorish origins.

There were also, Bestmade, Reed, and other names as the various manufacturers united forces and disbanded as their businesses prospered or languished over the years. *Cordova,* you recall, was the name given by Fredrick Kranz to his leather studios in Buffalo, New York.

The highly reputable Bosca Company of Springfield, Ohio, is still in business and manufactures a line similar to Meeker. One of their senior executives recalls when the company was associated with Mr. MacKinnon.

One of the cards mentions Cameo Studios and The Springfield Leather Company also located in Springfield, Ohio. It is a probable location for Reed Company as well, as they were once associated with Bosca.

See description on page 116. See figures on previous four pages:

Figure 89

A step in preparing the leather, possibly dyeing.

Figure 90

Figure 90 is marked "a general view of the factory."

Figure 91

Cutting and coloring room. Note the templates arranged on the table showing shapes and sizes then in the line.

Figure 92

These employees appear to be gluing the tooled leather in preparation for attaching frames.

Figure 93

Lacing was hand done by nimbler female fingers. The men are foremen.

Figure 94

Closeup of lacing operation. Note the vise and completed bags.

Figure 95

Producing the thin lacing strips probably from scrap leather.

Figure 96

Assembling and finishing departments.

121

Jemco and Other Frames

Thanks to the company which supplied the "hardware" known as Jemco, frames were patent dated. These abbreviated dates such as: Pat. 10.14.'04 would stand for October 14, 1904. They are invariably found on the front side of the frame, close to the closing mechanism. If the frame has an embossed pattern on both interior and exterior, it is not easy to locate this date as it merges into the pattern, but it was seldom ever omitted and is worth the search.

The narrowness of the frame usually restricted the patterns to simple narrow lines, scrolls, and leaves. Engravings were used at random and do not actually assist in dating a purse, as early purse frames may be embossed and more recent ones completely plain. The name Jemco is found on one side portion of the frame.

Copper was used as the base metal and then nickel plated; to my knowledge silver plating was not used, though sterling silver was. Frequently the frame was covered with the same leather used on the body, especially on the more expensive models.

Exotic leathers such as crocodile and alligator were handsomely encased in wide, thick, celluloid frames (such as seen at *Plate 89.*) made to resemble tortoise. Some were finished with a lariat handle which did not wear as well as the body. The welting or cording on the gussets was the first to deteriorate as it was made of cotton twill. Then the stitching on the gussets eventually separated them from the belting, necessitating costly repair.

The 1928 Sears and Roebuck's Catalog has some nice illustrations complete with details of this frame which they call Shell Frame. Of course it was celluloid but even today people are really unconvinced when told this. There was no attempt to deceive the consumer, as the word simulated was clearly printed in parentheses. Note the bag was calf not reptile, yet the price was the most expensive on the page. *(Figures 131 and 132.)*

Some of these large reptile examples were made as early as 1900 and they invariably had clip-over celluloid frames which are so attractive collectors purchase an almost worthless purse to get them.

Another style fast approaching antique status in some respects, resembles the the physician's bag. The side mounts are not rings but tubular holders which hold the strap securely in place while the closing mechanism consists of a slot and matching piece of metal. The frame allows the sides to expand much like a satchel or piece of baggage. *(Figure 104.)*

Keys and locks were used on some leathers much like those supplied with carpet bags, the steel frames held in place by small brads attached to a matching interior plate. They were fitted with a metal chain handle rather than a leather one.

Photographs of purses in hand, other than of professional models are rare, and I could not resist including an absolutely hilarious one. A woman and two children are seen about to depart on a journey. The older woman is burdened with three bags, one of which looks surprisingly like a currently popular garment bag. One child looks in danger of being swallowed by her hat, and the other shielded by an umbrella, has a small purse held in her elbow. Here is a virtual plethora of bags! *(Figure 108.)*

Leather Chatelaines With Metal Hooks

Chatelaines were popular from 1880, through approximately 1910. They were made of leather (one shown in alligator) as well as other materials and some were fitted with sterling hooks, frames and chains. As with the turnloc to come, they were dated and patented. They ranged in size from two inches in width to over six inches in length. An ad from a department store in Sacramento, California, dated 1895, even included a child's size chatelaine along with some interesting coin purses with "a clasp in the cover to hold tickets or stamps." They are remarkably similar to *Figures 109 and 110.* (note the prominent patent date).

Figure 112 has leather straps joining the rings as seen in the ad and is not much larger than a coin purse. *Figure 113* is suede with a heart in the sterling hook. *Figure 111* is large, topped by an equally large hook. Not all of the chatelaines had a hook, for the coin purses shown are either finger purses or were too inexpensive to warrant a hook. Note the most expensive purse on the page is two dollars.

Those shown in the 1902 Sears Roebuck catalog are even less expensive; but note the cost of the steel cut chatelaine, for five dollars was a high price in those days! *(Figure 128.)*

Chatelaines are a novelty today and sell briskly whenever they are offered for sale in reasonably good condition. By 1915, there were no chatelaines offered in catalogs; convenient and charming, they had been displaced by the beaded bag and commercial leathers.

The Turnloc

An innovation which greatly appealed to the manufacturers of purses at this time was called the *turnloc* and though this mechanism has not been featured on purses for years, it was interesting to find a listing under this spelling in the New York City phone book in 1986. This simple closing consists of a ball and socket which opens or locks by the turn of an ornamental ring or decorative piece of metal attached to the frame by a jump ring.

Very often the manufacturer, fearing damage to the purse or the inability of a potential customer to comprehend exactly how to open the purse when examining it in the department store, boldly engraved the instructions OPEN and CLOSE thereon. Since everyone knew how to operate the lock and those who did not initially, were plainly informed, there was little mystery for an artful purse snatcher. The turnloc was made of the same material as the frame, hammered/plain and embossed copper or brass. *(Figures 101 and 102.)*

Early Styles

Although they differed in many respects, early leather handbags usually had the following elements in common: hand laced sections, some sort of tooled front section (applied by hand or die), no zipper, for the zipper did not appear before 1930, and they were generally of steer hide.

There were a number of styles available including: the envelope shape with an exterior pocket, an under the arm style clutch with a flat strap across the top, a pouch shape with a top mounted ring and a thin strap, a short strap suitable for carrying in the palm of the hand or over the wrist, and an elongated shape with a strap across the back through which the hand was thrust and carried somewhat awkwardly. *(Figures 126, 127, 142 and 147.)*

For a very brief period, extremely long, thin shoulder straps were popular during the Second World War. Women had entered the armed forces and needed to have their hands free yet have necessary objects readily accessible. The worldwide rise in the crime rate has revived the shoulder strap, atop bags so large they resemble small trunks. Ostensibly one hand retains a firm grip on the bag while the other is free to bash potential purse snatchers. We are here concerned with antique purses so need not dwell on unhappy current aspects of the purse.

Women also have a decided preference for a purse which is longer than it is wide. The clutch shape with a close fitting strap across the top is is less manageable than the former.

Closures at this time were either snaps, or metal ball and sockets, latches, or sliding devices. The absence of a zipper is one way of determining age. Snaps were ornamental and could be covered with leather or the metal left exposed. With wear they have often torn away from the leather. This is a minor annoyance, for Tandy Leather Shops, a national chain which specializes in hobby leathers, can recommend leatherworkers who both relace and make repairs such as this.

In the early 1930's envelope shaped purses were popular because the styles had changed so radically. Hats fit tightly and low on the head, waists had fallen about the hips, dresses were simple sheaths straight lined or pleated and purses were made to tuck under the arm or were held by a strap across the back. *(Figures 106, 107, 139, 142 and 147.)*

123

Figure 97

Ad

Figure 98

An assortment of Meeker items from a wholesale catalog. Circa 1925–1935.

Figures 99–102

On page 127:

A group of tooled leathers showing the diversity of patterns used. All were made from 1915–1918, though the sizes and leather finishes vary greatly. Note the word OPEN on the tab.

No. 6106 _____ **$30.00***

Brown hand colored steerhide. Hand laced and leather lined flap. Nylon lining and stitching. Two zipper utility pockets. Cigarette pocket under flap. Adjustable shoulder strap. Size 13 x 7½.

No. 6089 _____ **$30.00***

Black or Brown hand colored steerhide. Hand laced and leather lined flap. Nylon lining and stitching. Two zipper pockets. Outside pocket under flap. Adjustable shoulder strap. Size 12½ x 8.

No. 6125 _____ **$35.00***

Brown hand colored steerhide. Hand laced and leather lined flap. Six compartments, two with zipper enclosures. Cigarette pocket under flap. Adjustable shoulder strap. Size 13 x 9½.

fifteen   * *Suggested retail price. Add 10% Federal Excise Tax.*

Figure 97

124

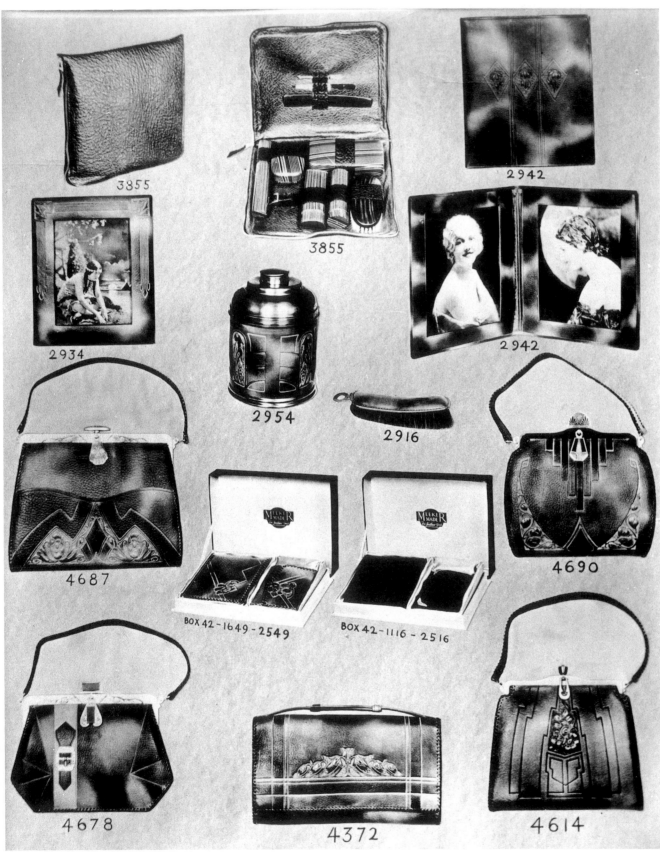

3855

3855

2942

2934

2942

2954

2916

4687

BOX 42-1649-2549

BOX 42-1116-2516

4690

4678

4372

4614

Figure 98

Figure 99

Figure 100

Figure 101

Figure 102

Figure 103   Figure 104

Figure 103

Fine example of hand tooled bag with Art Nouveau design.

Figure 104

Very old, thin leather purse adapted from the "doctor's bag" fitted with lock and key. Metal carry chain, flap front and divided interior. Seven inches wide, eight inches long. Circa 1870.

Figure 105

Ad from 1895, showing the popularity and variety of chatelaines.

Figure 105

Figure 111

Figure 112

A handsome suede tanned purse is seen at
Plate 93. It is unusual to find a leather enamel
framed and set with jewels. This one also has
a double tab which when lifted releases a slot
in the frames. One half is enameled with
Persian figures playing musical instruments,
and the opposite is an Oriental design. They
are yellowed with age but lend an air of
elegance to the purse which circa could
safely be gauged 1925. Not a domestic purse,
it could well have been made in the Near
East.

Cordova Designs Each of the five Cordova
designs shown *Figure 61* is
interesting in its' own right
but especially attractive is
the grape pattern. (No. 21) Grape clusters are
by nature nicely arranged, cascading as they
do into a wide v shape, surmounted and surrounded by their distinctive leaves. They
were a favorite theme of Art Nouveau
workers and it is not surprising to find them

130

Figure 113

Figure 114

Figure 119

Figure 121

The chief inclusions currently in this classification are the ostrich, alligator, crocodile, lizard, and snake. At one time seal and walrus skin were used but much of what was termed seal and walrus was actually pig skin, goat skin, or other hides. There were no truth in labeling laws then regulating any industry and "buyer beware" was more than a catch phrase.

As most of the exotic skins are now on the endangered species list few manufacturers are permitted to import them unless they can prove their hides and skins bear the stamp of IRV (International Reptile Leather Association). This organization strictly enforces the taking of wild crocodile and other species, maintains farms from which they obtain their stock, encourages research, animal breeding, and environmental conservation. They realize the extermination of a species upsets the balance of nature and would ultimately lead to a complete loss of their livelihood as well.

One of the leaders in IRV is a company named Stefan Mann with shops in Carmel, California, and at Trump Tower, 725 Fifth Avenue, New York. They distribute a booklet entitled, *The Fascination of Exclusivity,* to enable their customers to better understand the evolution of their creations and how to select and care for them.

Admittedly their exquisite items are costly but they pride themselves on the quality rather than the quantity of their offerings.

They suggest the prospective purchaser look to the following when making a selection: The grain pattern should be even, and rounded, with delicate pores. Know the trade name. Have a continuous tone with no unpleasant stains. Has the model been styled with fine joining of the skins or hides? Are the seams joined with small stitches and a piping used? Is exotic leather also used for the gussets and joining pieces ? Does the article have a fabric pouch and was it kept in this at the retailer? Is the sheen on a crocodile continuous with no dull patches or scratches? Does the article have an IRV seal?

These exotic bags are hand made products and each step in their manufacture is strictly controlled following age old procedures.

featured as well in the design books of every manufacturer of tooled bags. Far less common than florals, abstracts, and geometrics, they lent themselves to elongated and rounded bottom shapes. A similar example shown at *Figure 116* is not as handsome, possibly because it has seen much wear. It is approximately ten years older than the Cordova model.

The peacock feather design was also popular. What is called a broken bottom is a soft flap extending to the base of the handbag.

Birds and animals are most unusual in commercial designs though when used they were cleverly incorporated into the design and are among the choicest. *(Figure 117 and Plate 92.)*

The Exotics: Reptiles/ Animals/ Birds

It would hardly be fitting to conclude a chapter on leather without some mention of the costliest handbags, though they cannot be priced within the range of most collectors and virtually none are more than ninety years old.

Figure 114

Fine leather bag modeled after the physicians' bag with braided handles. Circa 1920, from Musee des Decoratif Arts, Paris, France.

131

Figur

Four M
circa 1
featuri
patterr
floral,
abstrac

Figures 123–125

Three very fine
examples of tooled
leathers. Figure 125
is outstanding with
hand made copper
fastener and fine
balanced design.

Figure 124

Figure 123

Figure 125

132   134

Figures 126–127

*Two oblong shaped
purses with handles
which could be
retracted converting
the purse to a clutch.
Simplicity of Figure
127 is marked.*

Figure 126

Figure 127

Figure 128

1902 Sears and Roebuck still featured the chatelaine purse.

932 SEARS, ROEBUCK & CO., Cheapest Supply House on Earth, Chicago. CATALOGUE No. III. 1902

Genuine Alligator Purse.

No. 18R2591 Genuine Alligator Purse, leather facing, with block bottom, gusseted, has three regular, one tuck and coin pocket in nickel spring catch frame, also one handkerchief pocket on back. Size, 3 x 4½ inches. Excellent style and great value. Price, each.....49c
If by mail, postage extra, 4 cents.

Paragon Handkerchief Books.

A very convenient book for carrying a handkerchief without risk of losing or soiling same. It has all the features of a regularly made book, and its special construction admits of carrying a handkerchief without increasing its bulk. All made with gusseted block bottom and made with slotted frame, preventing tearing down of pockets. Comes in three qualities.

No. 18R2593 Paragon Handkerchief Book. Leather, imitation seal, imitation seal and leather facings, two regular, one fancy card, one tuck, handkerchief and coin pocket in oval, wide mouth frame. Size, 3¼x4½ inches. Price, each..................46c

No. 18R2595 Paragon Handkerchief Pocketbook. Made of good quality seal grain leather, with calf and seal grain leather facings, one fancy card, one tuck, handkerchief and coin pocket, fine nickel frame. Size, 3¼x4¼ inches. Price, each..........72c
If by mail, postage extra, 4 cents.

No. 18R2599 Genuine Seal Paragon Handkerchief Book. Seal and calf facing. This is made similar to above Paragon books, made of finest seal leather, and best workmanship. Size, 3¼x4½ inches. Price, each..............................93c
If by mail, postage extra, 4 cents.

Ladies' Fine Seal Leather Block Bottom Pocketbook.

No. 18R2614 With chamois lined coin pocket, snap frame, faced throughout with seal leather and block bottom. Size, 3x4¾ inches. Usual $1.00 pocketbook.
Price, each...........78c
If by mail, postage extra, 5 cents.

Genuine Seal Ladies' Pocketbook.

No. 18R2615 Our highest grade book, with all the good points a good pocketbook should have. Genuine seal and calf facing, round bottom, three regular, one fancy card, one tuck and one coin pocket, in fine nickel spring catch frame. Size, 3½x4½ inches.
Price, each.........$1.62
If by mail, postage extra, 4 cents.

Ladies' Black Seal Purse, only 20 Cents.

No. 18R2617 Ladies' Black Seal Combination Purse. With fancy metal corners; regular card pocket and one leather faced pocket with flap and tuck; coin pocket with snap frame. Size, 3x4½ inches. Splendid value.
Price, each..........20c
If by mail, postage extra, each, 4 cents.

No. 18R2619 Cape goat leather, an extremely handsome pocket book, in black, brown or tan, cape goat and leather facings; three regular, one fancy card, one tuck and coin pocket, in nickel spring catch frame, mounted with open work embossed gilt rim. Size, 3¼x4¼ inches. Colors, black, brown and tan. Price, each............46c
If by mail, postage extra, each 4 cents.

No. 18R2620 Initials. Sterling silver, plain type, 1¼ inches high, have the fastenings and are easily put on. For purses, etc. Each..............................21c
If by mail, postage extra, 2 cents.

Ladies' Fine Walrus Pocketbook.

No. 18R2621 This Stylish Pocketbook has three regular, one fancy card, one tuck and coin pocket, in nickel spring catch frame. Mounted with genuine sterling silver corners. Colors, gray or black. Size, 2¾x4¾ inches. Price, each..................56c
If by mail, postage extra, each, 4 cents.

Ladies' Genuine Seal Leather Pocketbook.

No. 18R2623 With highly polished genuine calf facings. This high grade purse has three regular, one fancy card, one tuck and coin pocket, in best nickel spring catch frame. Stitched and gusseted, mounted with very handsome sterling silver corners. This is a very high grade pocketbook and sold for double the price we ask for it. Black only. Size, 3⅛x4⅜ inches.
Each. (If by mail, postage extra, each, 4c)..$1.17

Genuine Texas Steer High Grade Fancy Pocketbook.

No. 18R2627 Black and colors. Genuine steer and calf facings, block bottom, gusseted, three regular, one fancy card, one tuck and coin pocket in nickel spring catch frame, mounted with l'art Nouveaux oxidized sterling silver trimming. Size, 3¼x4½ inches. Colors, stone gray, brown or black. Each.....$1.88
If by mail, postage extra, 6 cents.

Our 96-Cent Ladies' Pocketbook.

No. 18R2631 Mexican Hand Carved Leather Ladies' Pocketbook. Assorted designs, leather facing, three regular, one tuck and coin pocket, in nickel spring catch frame. The Mexican hand carved books have an immense sale; a very nobby book. Size, 3x4½ inches.
Each...(If by mail, postage extra, 5 cents)...96c

Genuine Alligator Ladies' Pocketbook.

No. 18R2633 Genuine Hornback Alligator Ladies' Pocketbook. Fine calf facing block bottom, gusseted, three regular, one tuck and coin pocket in fine nickel spring catch frame. Size, 3x4½ inches. This fine horned alligator book is very popular, pretty and stylish, and sold by us at a very low price.
Each..(If by mail, postage extra, 6 cents)..$3.19

Ladies' Cut Steel Beaded Bags.

They have become more and more stylish. Every lady wants one.

No. 18R2637 Beaded Bag. Genuine hand made, cut steel beaded bag, with steel bead fringe, chamois back and handsome silver plated frame, chain and hook, chamois lined and inside pocket. Very stylish; all the go. Size, 4x4½ inches. Price, each....$3.29
If by mail, postage extra, 10 cents.

No. 18R2639 Hand Made Beaded Cut Steel Bag. Same style as above but larger. Size, 5x4½ in.
Price, each.................$4.95
If by mail, postage extra, 12 cents.

Ladies' Fine Beaded Chatelaine Purse.

No. 18R2643 Made of steel beads and looped fringe all around, chamois lined, chain and belt hook. A very handsome bag at a very low price. Size, 4½x6¼ inches. Price, each...............$1.50
If by mail, postage extra, 10 cents.

Ladies' Steel Bead Chatelaine Purse.

No. 18R2645 Mounted handsomely with fine nickel frame, chain and belt hook attachment, beaded loop fringe all around, chamois lined. This purse is usually retailed at $1.50. Size, 4x4¾ inches. Price, each..............................$1.00
If by mail, postage extra, 8 cents.

Novelty Metal Chatelaine Bags.

No. 18R2647 Made of fancy links of white metal, silver finish, with chain belt hook. A very stylish purse. Size, 2½x3¼ inches.
Price, each......................49c
If by mail, postage extra, 5 cents.

Ladies' Fancy Metal Chatelaine Purse in Nickel or Silvered.

No. 18R2649 The design is a reproduction of the high priced all silver purse. Chain and belt hook to match. This is a very dainty and elegant purse. Size, 3x5 inches. Price, each..........75c
If by mail, postage extra, 6 cents.

Ladies' Genuine Alligator Chatelaine Purse.

No. 18R2651 With fancy metal frame, ball catch, chain and attachment for belt. Size, 4½x4¾ inches. Price, each.........$1.25
If by mail, postage extra, 10 cents.

Chatelaine Bags.

No. 18R2653 Seal Grain Leather Bag. One leather lined pocket, gilt riveted ball catch frame, gilt chain with attachment for belt. Size, 3x3½ inches. A very convenient and pretty bag.
Price, each.....................23c
If by mail, postage extra, 6 cents.

Ladies' Chatelaine Bag.

No. 18R2655 Ladies' Seal Grain Leather Chatelaine Bag. With nickel riveted frame, the front of frame covered with leather, patent nickeled catch fastener, leather straps and belt hook. Size, 6x6½ inches.
Price, each............46c

No. 18R2657 Ladies' Chatelaine Bag, similar shape to above, made of finest real seal, leather lined, best frame. A substantial wearing as well as elegant bag. Black only.
Price, each....................................$1.00
If by mail, postage extra, each, 8 cents.

Black Leather Chatelaine Bag.

No. 18R2691 Black Leather Chatelaine Bag. Imitation walrus, riveted frame with leather front, spring catch, one regular and one outside handkerchief pocket; wide bottom and sides. Size, 5¾x6¼ inches. This is an exceptic-ally fine, stylish book and exceptional value.
Price, each..............95c
If by mail, postage extra, 8 cents.

Special Value for 43 Cents.

No. 18R2698 Ladies' Shopping Bag. Of seal grain leatherette, bound with gimp cord all around; two small outside pockets, one with nickeled catch, sateen top with drawing strings, 2 leather handles. Size, 6¾x10 inches.
Price, each..43c
Shipping weight, 14 ounces.

Seal Grain Leather Shopping Bag.

No. 18R2702 Ladies' Shopping Bag. Made of seal grain leather, bound all around with silk gimp cord, one large and two small outside pockets, with oxidized catch, good quality sateen top with draw strings, two leather handles. Size, 10¼ inches deep by 14¼ inches wid
Price, each.......[illegible]
Shipping weight, 20 oz.

Figure 128

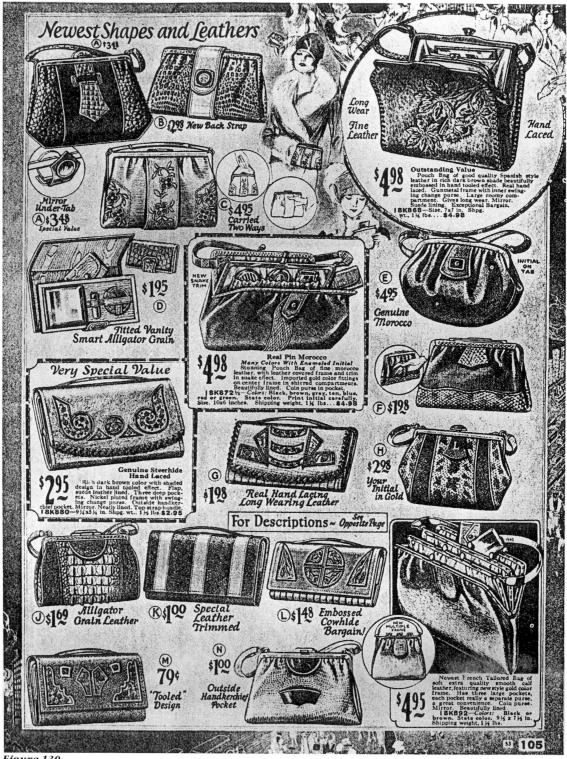

Figure 130

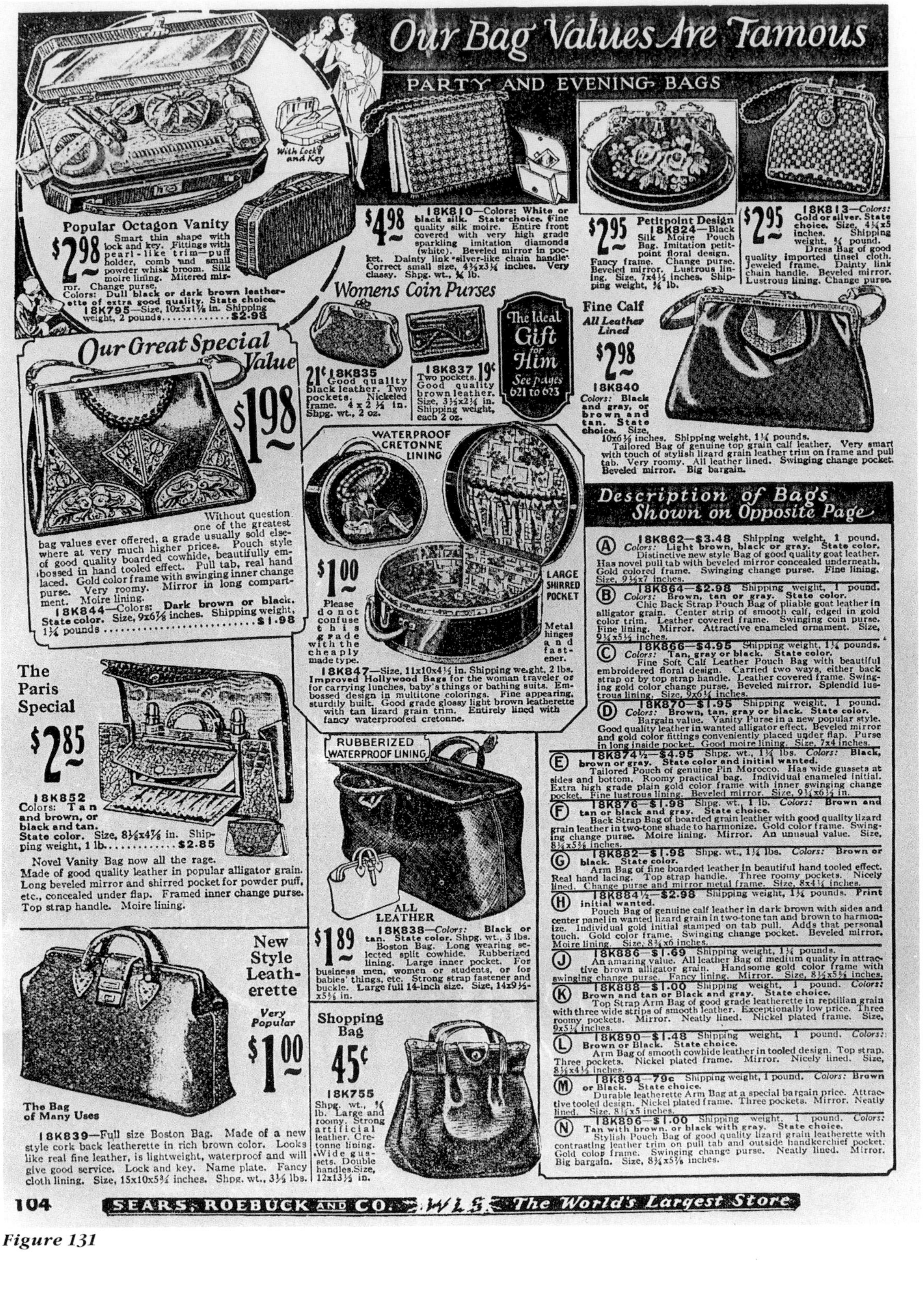

Our Bag Values Are Famous

PARTY AND EVENING BAGS

Popular Octagon Vanity

$2.98

With Lock and Key

Smart thin shape with lock and key. Fittings with pearl-like trim—puff holder, comb and small powder whisk broom. Silk moire lining. Mitered mirror. Change purse.
Colors: Dull black or dark brown leatherette of extra good quality. State choice.
18K795—Size, 10x5x1⅞ in. Shipping weight, 2 pounds............$2.98

$4.98

18K810—Colors: White or black silk. State choice. Fine quality silk moire. Entire front covered with very high grade sparkling imitation diamonds (white). Beveled mirror in pocket. Dainty link silver-like chain handle. Correct small size, 4⅜x3¼ inches. Very classy. Shpg. wt., ¼ lb.

$2.95

Petitpoint Design
18K824—Black Silk Moire Pouch Bag. Imitation petitpoint floral design. Fancy frame. Change purse. Beveled mirror. Lustrous lining. Size, 7x4½ inches. Shipping weight, ¾ lb.

$2.95

18K813—Colors: Gold or silver. State choice. Size, 4¼x5 inches. Shipping weight, ¾ pound.
Dress Bag of good quality imported tinsel cloth. Jeweled frame. Dainty link chain handle. Beveled mirror. Lustrous lining. Change purse.

Womens Coin Purses

21¢ 18K835 Good quality black leather. Two pockets. Nickeled frame. 4x2½ in. Shpg. wt., 2 oz.

18K837 19¢ Two pockets. Good quality brown leather. Size, 3½x2¼ in. Shipping weight, each 2 oz.

The Ideal Gift for Him
See pages 621 to 623

Fine Calf
All Leather Lined

$2.98

18K840
Colors: Black and gray, or brown and tan. State choice. Size, 10x6⅛ inches. Shipping weight, 1¼ pounds.
Tailored Bag of genuine top grain calf leather. Very smart with touch of stylish lizard grain leather trim on frame and pull tab. Very roomy. All leather lined. Swinging change pocket. Beveled mirror. Big bargain.

Our Great Special Value

$1.98

Without question one of the greatest bag values ever offered, a grade usually sold elsewhere at very much higher prices. Pouch style of good quality boarded cowhide, beautifully embossed in hand tooled effect. Pull tab, real hand laced. Gold color frame with swinging inner change purse. Very roomy. Mirror in long compartment. Moire lining.
18K844—Colors: Dark brown or black. State color. Size, 9x6⅞ inches. Shipping weight, 1¼ pounds............$1.98

WATERPROOF CRETONNE LINING

$1.00

Please do not confuse this grade with the cheaply made type.

LARGE SHIRRED POCKET

Metal hinges and fastener.

18K847—Size, 11x10x4½ in. Shipping weight, 2 lbs. Improved Hollywood Bags for the woman traveler or for carrying lunches, baby's things or bathing suits. Embossed design in multitone colorings. Fine appearing, sturdily built. Good grade glossy light brown leatherette with tan lizard grain trim. Entirely lined with fancy waterproofed cretonne.

The Paris Special

$2.85

18K852
Colors: Tan and brown, or black and tan. State color. Size, 8⅛x4⅞ in. Shipping weight, 1 lb............$2.85
Novel Vanity Bag now all the rage. Made of good quality leather in popular alligator grain. Long beveled mirror and shirred pocket for powder puff, etc., concealed under flap. Framed inner change purse. Top strap handle. Moire lining.

RUBBERIZED WATERPROOF LINING

ALL LEATHER

$1.89

18K838—Colors: Black or tan. State color. Shpg. wt., 3 lbs. Boston Bag. Long wearing selected split cowhide. Rubberized lining. Large inner pocket. For business men, women or students, or for babies' things, etc. Strong strap fastener and buckle. Large full 14-inch size. Size, 14x9½x5⅝ in.

New Style Leatherette
Very Popular

$1.00

The Bag of Many Uses

18K839—Full size Boston Bag. Made of a new style cork back leatherette in rich brown color. Looks like real fine leather, is lightweight, waterproof and will give good service. Lock and key. Name plate. Fancy cloth lining. Size, 15x10x5¾ inches. Shpg. wt., 3½ lbs.

Shopping Bag

45¢

18K755
Shpg. wt., ¾ lb. Large and roomy. Strong artificial leather. Cretonne lining. Wide gussets. Double handles. Size, 12x13½ in.

Description of Bags Shown on Opposite Page

(A) 18K862—$3.48 Shipping weight, 1 pound. Colors: Light brown, black or gray. State color.
Distinctive new style Bag of good quality goat leather. Has novel pull tab with beveled mirror concealed underneath. Gold colored frame. Swinging change purse. Fine lining. Size, 9½x7 inches.

(B) 18K864—$2.98 Shipping weight, 1 pound. Colors: Brown, tan or gray. State color.
Chic Back Strap Pouch Bag of pliable goat leather in alligator grain. Center strip of smooth calf, edged in gold color trim. Leather covered frame. Swinging coin purse. Fine lining. Mirror. Attractive enameled ornament. Size, 9¼x5½ inches.

(C) 18K866—$4.95 Shipping weight, 1¼ pounds. Colors: Tan, gray or black. State color.
Fine Soft Calf Leather Pouch Bag with beautiful embroidered floral design. Carried two ways, either back strap or by top strap handle. Leather covered frame. Swinging gold color change purse. Beveled mirror. Splendid lustrous lining. Size, 9x6¼ inches.

(D) 18K870—$1.95 Shipping weight, 1 pound. Colors: Brown, tan, gray or black. State color.
Bargain value. Vanity Purse in a new popular style. Good quality leather in wanted alligator effect. Beveled mirror and gold color fittings conveniently placed under flap. Purse in long inside pocket. Good moire lining. Size, 7x4 inches.

(E) 18K874½—$4.95 Shpg. wt., 1¼ lbs. Colors: Black, brown or gray. State color and initial wanted.
Tailored Pouch of genuine Pin Morocco. Has wide gussets at sides and bottom. Roomy practical bag. Individual enameled initial. Extra high grade plain gold color frame with inner swinging change pocket. Fine lustrous lining. Beveled mirror. Size, 9¼x6½ in.

(F) 18K876—$1.98 Shpg. wt., 1 lb. Colors: Brown and tan or black and gray. State choice.
Back Strap Bag of boarded grain leather with good quality lizard grain leather in two-tone shade to harmonize. Gold color frame. Swinging change purse. Moire lining. Mirror. An unusual value. Size, 8¼x5⅝ inches.

(G) 18K882—$1.98 Shpg. wt., 1¼ lbs. Colors: Brown or black. State color.
Arm Bag of fine boarded leather in beautiful hand tooled effect. Real hand lacing. Top strap handle. Three roomy pockets. Nicely lined. Change purse and mirror metal frame. Size, 8x4¼ inches.

(H) 18K884½—$2.98 Shipping weight, 1¼ pounds. Print initial wanted.
Pouch Bag of genuine calf leather in dark brown with sides and center panel in wanted lizard grain in two-tone tan and brown to harmonize. Individual gold initial stamped on tab pull. Adds that personal touch. Gold color frame. Swinging change pocket. Beveled mirror. Moire lining. Size, 8¾x6 inches.

(J) 18K886—$1.69 Shipping weight, 1¼ pounds.
An amazing value. All leather Bag of medium quality in attractive brown alligator grain. Handsome gold color frame with swinging change purse. Fancy lining. Mirror. Size, 8½x5⅝ inches.

(K) 18K888—$1.00 Shipping weight, 1 pound. Colors: Brown and tan or Black and gray. State choice.
Top Strap Arm Bag of good grade leatherette in reptilian grain with three wide strips of smooth leather. Exceptionally low price. Three roomy pockets. Mirror. Neatly lined. Nickel plated frame. Size, 9x5¼ inches.

(L) 18K890—$1.48 Shipping weight, 1 pound. Colors: Brown or Black. State choice.
Arm Bag of smooth cowhide leather in tooled design. Top strap. Three pockets. Nickel plated frame. Mirror. Nicely lined. Size, 8½x4½ inches.

(M) 18K894—79c Shipping weight, 1 pound. Colors: Brown or Black. State choice.
Durable leatherette Arm Bag at a special bargain price. Attractive tooled design. Nickel plated frame. Three pockets. Mirror. Neatly lined. Size, 8½x5 inches.

(N) 18K896—$1.00 Shipping weight, 1 pound. Colors: Tan with brown, or black with gray. State choice.
Stylish Pouch Bag of good quality lizard grain leatherette with contrasting leather trim on pull tab and outside handkerchief pocket. Gold color frame. Swinging change purse. Neatly lined. Mirror. Big bargain. Size, 8¾x5⅞ inches.

104 SEARS, ROEBUCK AND CO. WLS The World's Largest Store

Figure 131

Plate 88

Three exotics from
the modern New
York designer, Judith
Leiber. Top bag is
ostrich, the middle
lizard and the
bottom alligator.
Current dyeing tech-
niques achieve
colors never before
realized, such as the
blue-green seen here.
Note the identical
malachite set frames.

Plate 88

Plate 89

Plates 89–90

Alligator purse. Circa 1930, with a particularly handsome celluloid frame and overclasp. The style featured the creature's paws and head. Hides were once treated with less sophistication. Detail of scales differentiate alligator hide from crocodile.

Plate 90

143

Plate 91

*Typical example of a
commercial hand-
bag with engraved
brass frame and
drop. Circa 1915.*

Plate 92

*Unusual bag with
raised ornamental
frame, and animal
in the design.*

Plate 93

*Suede leather bag
with Near Eastern
motif in frame and
drop sections. Note
jewels. Possibly an
Asian import.*

Plate 91

Plate 92

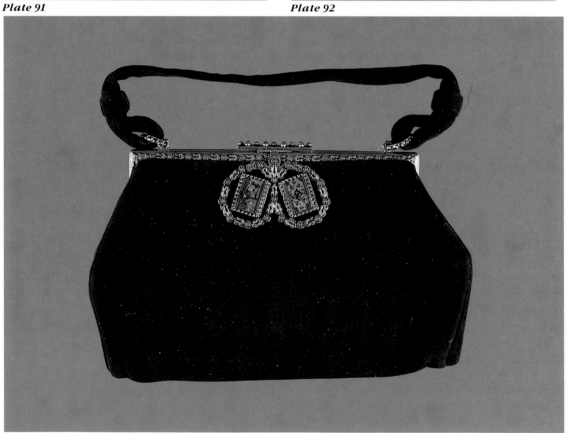

Plate 93

144

Figure 134

Soft and pliable snake skins are popular for their unusual markings. They are very expensive and are used on top quality bags only.

Ostrich leather has a regular matt grain pattern and is used for classic designs such as *Figure 135*. As it is resistant to dirt and water it is almost indestructible and can take the hard wear some crocodile cannot. It is available in many colors and styles though this example is a handsome, pure white with a jeweled set clasp.

The modern designer, Judith Lieber, has arranged a stunning grouping of three bags with identical shapes, frames, clasps and colors. Colors such as these never would have been attempted in antique purses. The group includes crocodile, lizard and ostrich skins. How dissimilar the are when closely examined and how effective is the merchandising. *(Plate 88.)*

The inoffensive, slow moving armadillo once taken for purses is shown at *Figure 133*.

It is possible the use of these creatures for handbags continues but most, if not all, will have been made about forty to fifty years ago. The practice of including the paws, head and/or other body parts is both out of style and favor.

Hand tooled steer hide purses both domestic and imported from Mexico and South American countries were popular at about the same time *(Figure 140)* but they were stiff, heavy leathers with uncreative motifs and have little appeal today. Individualized designs which tended to be quite masculine in feeling, such as the duck pattern, were less cumbersome and were nicely modeled on finer, smoother leather by leather hobbyists.

Though we are most apt to call all reptile purses alligator, it is only recently that these hides are now being taken, as the reptile has been protected for many years. There is a somewhat technical biological difference between alligators and crocodiles, aside from size, and considerable difference in the skins. A section of alligator scales as they were once used is shown at *Plate 90*.

They have made such a comeback they have become a nuisance in the United States. Retrieving golf balls from water hazards in Florida for instance, may be more hazardous than one bargains for. They are now even known to roam about backyards in Louisiana. Hunting has resumed on a limited basis under governmental supervision and control in these states.

About the turn of the century till the early 1930's, handbags such as *Figure 136* really were alligator. A 1940's style and a recent style are shown at *Figures 137 and 138*. Most of these early purses have not been particularly well cared for, are very small, and generally look shabby. These handbags are in no way comparable with the magnificent ones available at Stefan Mann stores.

In the race to protect the planet from the inroads of man who seems bent on destroying everything in his path to satisfy his unbounded greed, let us assist organizations such as IRV and humane societies so there *will be* exotics in our future.

Figure 134

Modern lizard purse conventional of size and shape.

145

Figure 135

Pure white genuine
ostrich purse with
jade sets in clasp.
Somewhat irregu-
larly spaced raised
dots are characteris-
tic of ostrich.

146

Figure 135

Figure 136

Fig

Fig

Figure 136

*Alligator purse.
Circa 1920, showing
a preferred style.
Note the skins are
matched so the
scales run down the
middle, small size,
and the fine brass
strap fitting used on
high quality purses.*

147

Figure 141

Figure 142

Figure 143

Figure 144

Figures 143–144

The shape is beginning to look quite modern though the sides and straps are still hand laced. Both tooling and lacing went out of style after World War II.

Chapter 5

The Beaded Purse

T he jewel among purses from almost any standpoint is the beaded purse. Infinite in variety, amazing in its painstaking execution, an artistic delight to behold, a handicraft which has slipped into the realm of a lost art, it holds a particularly nostalgic niche in the world of antiques.

The beaded purse is a paradox for it is certainly the most fragile of bags, yet it is more plentiful than any other single type. When the leather purse became shabby from excessive wear it was discarded. The metal purse lost fashion favor and when the mesh was damaged, it frequently was not repaired but was given to a charity or disposed of in some manner. The beaded purse seldom ever met this fate because often it was hand made in the home and the beadworker was not a faceless nonentity but a family member, (albeit one so long departed as to be beyond recall or familiarity) and therefore cherished as an inheritance.

When the contents of an estate are cataloged a beaded purse or two tucked neatly into the recesses of a drawer or stored in an attic or basement trunk is still a relatively commonplace discovery. Since they are no longer made anywhere (excluding those currently manufactured in the Orient and Italy and of such design and materials they do not even qualify for consideration), it is only a matter of time before these antique examples will have become incorporated into the large collections where all rarities inevitably disappear.

It is disheartening that so many collectors are obsessed with the *value* of their purses above all other considerations and the *bon marche* aspect of collecting takes precedence over the real worth of the object. As this is unfortunately true, it may be well to consider at the outset exactly what constitutes genuine worth in a beaded bag.

The principal characteristics of beaded purses to consider, not necessarily in the order given, are: the size of the beads, the condition, the intricacy of the pattern, the overall size of the purse, the presence or absence of a lining, the quality and unique-

Plate 94

Magnificent celluloid oak leaf frame. Overclasp in the shape of an acorn and leaf. Painted molded acorns on front side. Overall size including fringe, 12 by 8 inches. Floating center panel of crystal fringe. Beaded net.

155

ness of the frame, the skill of the beadworker in executing the work, the color scheme employed, the condition of the silk, the rarity of the pattern, the complexity of the fringing, the method of construction and the personal appeal of the purse.

Methods Since construction methods were the same regardless of date, it might be wise to deal with them at the outset.

The most often used method was knitting, followed by crocheting, beading on various kinds of canvas, beading on loose fabrics such as flour sacking, lace net, beading on soft leathers, beading on fabrics, even beading on commercially made ring meshes.

The art of crocheting originated in France and spread abroad in the 18th century. The crochet hook and threads were smaller than knitting needles and the stitch itself was tighter and very well suited to making purses. It became fashionable to carry a crochet or knitted bag to nearly every social event which in turn contained the requisite materials for constructing a reticule.

A minimum of inexpensive tools were required to make any type of purse. Crochet and knitting needles were no novelty to any well run household, for a woman who was not reasonably skilled in these arts at the turn of the century would have been thought a poor housekeeper indeed. Knitted garments and laces abounded. Canvas and flour sacking cost mere pennies or were by-products of a staple foodstuff. Remnant fabrics were always on hand in the home, for clothing was largely home made or sewn by a local dressmaker. Few purse patterns called for more than a yard of material which could be gotten from this rich source of scraps.

Silk twist spools retailed for pennies, transfer and graph paper patterns cost ten to twenty cents each. In America, net was used less frequently than the aforementioned materials, possibly because it was more expensive and far less durable. Except for the cut steel chatelaine, handsome beading on leather was done largely by American Indians. Depending on their quality and quantity, beads constituted the chief expense.

Size The most common complaint women voice about beaded purses, or antique purses in general for that matter, is their small capacity.

A number of possible explanations may be offered. People *were* smaller a century ago both in stature and weight. They carried less with them for their needs were simple. The purse was not the utility object which it is today. The **purpose** of the beaded purse was to show the skill of the beader and enhance the overall beauty of the ensemble. Today the purse is an essential to all classes of women and has less to do with esthetics than formerly.

There was, moreover, an optimum size beyond which it was not practical to extend, as the purse would have become unwieldy and the chance for beading errors greatly increased. The pattern was divided and strung in three sections. One hundred vertical rows and one hundred twenty horizontal rows was considered about the maximum for a knitted or crocheted purse. Simple or plain patterns were not a problem, but a complicated pattern could drive an otherwise sane person mad.

The largest and most complicated purse I have ever seen was made in France, uncharacteristically of fine Venetian beads. It is shown at *Plate 250.* It measures 12 inches wide and 16 inches long. It belonged to a costume designer for the then infant film industry. When her estate was auctioned I was able to purchase several extraordinary purses at an equally extraordinary price! What collector could resist, such a magnificent purse regardless of price?

Condition When being considered for purchase the condition of the beaded purse is even more important than the condition of other types of bags. If a beaded bag has numerous holes, is missing beads, has a ragged fringe or no fringe where one should be, has badly stained silk (soiled beads are easily cleaned), shows damage, particularly at the sides just below the frame, the purchase should be carefully deliberated.

If the purse is priced so as to reflect the defects and is a rare example it may well merit purchase. If one has the skill to do the necessary repair or intends to frame the bag whatever its state, condition is of lesser importance. A case in point would be a dated purse, a signed purse, a purse of extraordinary size, a magnificent frame, or superb beading.

Skill Of The Beadworker

The homemaker seldom if ever ventured into oversized, elaborate purses, though they did work with 5/0 beads, (presently numbered 20–22, the smallest known)·and some of their patterns were very pleasing. They tended to use solid colored and crystal backgrounds with comparatively simple designs. The quality of their work varied as with any hand skill. The earliest purses were possibly the most skillfully done, the manageable size was beneficial and the patterns quite standardized. An examination of the interior of an unlined early 19th century purse will reveal an almost machine like beading precision. Others are clumsily and/or crudely made, particularly those made of very large beads on various weights of canvas; knitted and crocheted specimens are generally more adroitly done.

The skill of professional beadworkers, both Europeans and those who emigrated to the United States and worked in a highly specialized area of the garment industry, could not be surpassed. Their patterns were unbelievably complicated scenics, huge florals, and figurals reflecting idealistic nostalgic or romantic settings far beyond the capabilities of the average homemaker. Many had been reared in ancient bead making environments where beading techniques and talents had been perfected for centuries.

How to gauge the skill of the beadworker? The tension on the silk should be even and smooth,the beads should lie flat and properly spaced (unless crowded for effect)there should be no obvious errors in color selection or in the pattern; if a figural, the features should be as distinct and undistorted as the size of the beads allows; the correct size of bead must be used; the body should show no signs of warp, and the sides should have been properly aligned when woven together.

There should be no silk showing at the end of the bead for this indicates the tension is too loose. If the silk is too tightly knit or crocheted, there is bunching or taughtness and the surface will warp out of shape causing the sides to be misaligned.

A ladies' magazine in 1912, estimated a purse with the simplest of crochet patterns would require 50 hours of work. As women worked only a couple of hours a day when the light was best and between meal preparation and household chores, a simple purse would take nearly a month and a difficult pattern easily a year.

158
Plate 95

Frames

Fewer than a dozen purses still survive intact from the 16th century. They are either the small leather purses which were presented to a monarch containing gifts of gold coins, (a subtle form of taxation), or bags used for the storage of game during a hunt. Neither of these examples can be considered purses in the modern sense.

Hunting bags were completed with iron frames in the shape of ornamental castle turrets as seen in *Figure 6*. The weight of the circular flap served to hold the contents in place.

The reticule type of purse was favored for roughly the next two centuries. Frames were only rarely used until the first quarter of the 19th century. A reticule could be completely finished by cords or other closures in the home, whereas certain types of frames required professional factory installation.

No other single aspect of purses arouses such suspicion and/or the curiosity of a potential purse collector than the matter of frames. I can guarantee the first question will be, "What is the frame made of?" It is curious that the frame causes more concern than the body and many uninformed people think a frame not made of sterling, silver plate or gold is inferior, if not downright worthless!

Plate 95

Three variations of French enameled frames. Earliest one (top) set with traditional glass jewels and enameling. Sophisticated middle one narrower, set with marcasites. Lower one simple and better suited to Art Deco bags.

Frames may be made of the following materials:

bone
brass
celluloid
dutch silver
enamel
gold
gunmetal
ivory
nickel
paper
plate
repousse
rhodium plate (see meshes)
self covered
silver
tin
vermeil
wood
the list is endless

Closures are:
ball and socket
ball twist
barrel slide
box
clasp or hasp
flap insert
gate top
over hinge, in celluloid
plunger

Indeed, the frame may make a purse irresistible or cause it to be rejected. The frame may also add hundreds of dollars to the cost if it is a precious metal, is jewel or stone set, enameled, dated, is engraved with the name of some celebrated owner or a great jewelry house such as Cartier, Tiffany, Fabergé, or Spink.

To illustrate the importance of a signed frame, I was once asked to appraise a stunning Cartier gold and platinum ring mesh purse fitted with an 18K gold frame. The frame appeared to be set with a single row of sapphires on one side of the clasp and a row of rubies on the other. It seemed vaguely familiar and I inquired if it had been offered before. The unabashed dealer then informed me with a laugh that the gems were *genuine*

then and now they were clever imitations. This is clearly an infringement on the great jewelery firm whose name was stamped on the frame. Such purses can easily command a price in the thousands of dollars so it is wise when contemplating such a purchase to determine both the precious metals content and have a competent, certified gemologist present a written guarantee as to the quality of the gems, rather than accept the word of a dealer who unwittingly or knowingly misrepresents such a purse. (In the absence of a certified gemologist, the Gemological Institute in Santa Monica, California, can provide unrefutable information at a nominal fee). Since these ring meshes are no longer routinely manufactured their age is not subject to suspect.

Austrian, French and Italian purse frames were downright elegant for they recognized the importance of the frame to the overall appearance and value of the bag.

French purses are likely to employ enamels, marcasites, small faceted pieces of cut steel, lapiz, seed pearls, rhinestones and elaborately pierced and extremely wide embossed sterling frames Examples of each are seen in *Plates 101 and 110* and others.

Enameled work was *not* done on brass but was usually done on sterling or copper. This side observation is important, as enameling requires a great deal of expertise, and time. It is an expensive process so it would not ordinarily be lavished on an inferior frame nor would such a frame be found on a mediocre beaded body.

The finest enameled frames such as *Figure 95* were made in France. The enameled portion is overlaid with scrolled metal bridgework or inlaid with marcasites or other types of glass jewels. Several colors may be used to create a design if no metal work is involved. A strip of enameled work may be used for emphasis between large stones. Seldom ever are these frames more than ¼th to ⁵⁄₁₆th of an inch wide. Small enameled flowers and buds had jeweled centers. The whole frame was so harmoniously refined as to establish France as the leader in enameled and jeweled frames.

Figure 148

Figure 148

Sterling embossed frame with daisy chain. Material shown is inner section. Lined body was sewn to frame through dilled holes. Bar adds strength to frame.

Figure 148

Plate 96

Figure 149

162 *Figure 150*

Plate 97

Figure 151

Plate 96

*Exceptional cellu-
loid painted frame.
Similar motif to
oversized beaded
body.*

Plate 97

*Outstanding cellu-
loid frame with shell
cameo center.
Unusual design
with side tassels.*

Figure 149

*Circular plated
frame with mirror
attached to purse
called* The Dew-
drop. *Circa 1923.*

Figure 150

*Novel monkey fur
bag. Celluloid frame
with appropriately
painted monkey.
Fabric strap.*

Figure 151

*This lovely lady
from Oakland, Cali-
fornia, was photo-
graphed in 1887. The
clarity of the picture,
charm of the subject,
costume and of
course the promi-
nent chatelaine have
always intrigued me.
It is proof positive of
how the steel beaded
chatelaine was
worn. Though a
casual purchase, she
has smiled down
from my study wall
for many years.*

Plate 98

Jeweled Austrian frame circa 1920. Synthetic sets. Nice color balance.

Plate 99

Sterling set with imitation Persian turquoise. French. Wire strung beads.

Plate 100

Double section brass set with cabachoned amethyst. Brass chatelaine style, jewels. Note twist top attached to small purse body forming suspended cap. Style infrequently seen.

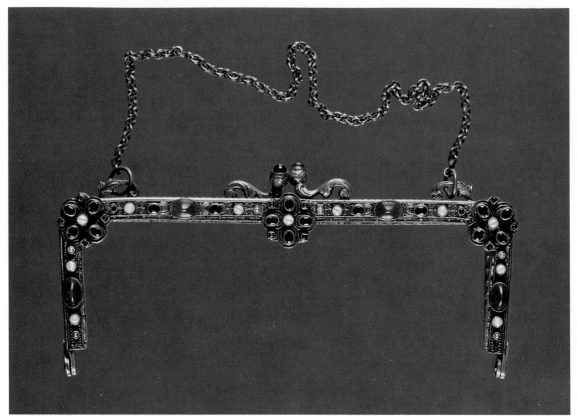

Plate 98

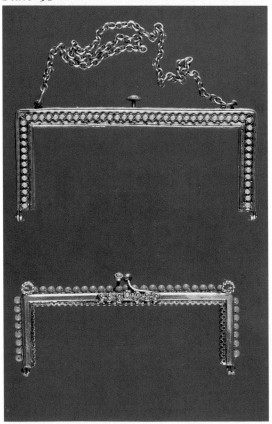

Plate 99

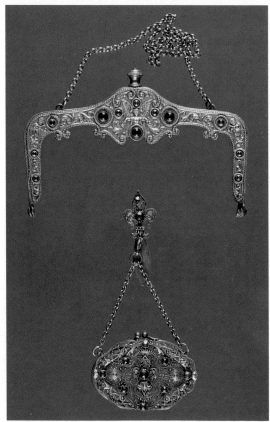

Plate 100

164

Italian and Austrian purse frames tend to use oversized (both precious and costume) stones in base metals and 800 silver. Early in the century frames made in Italy were fitted (usually in double or triple rows) with tiny, colorful, glass pieces forming flowers and abstract mosaics, resembling the picture frames and other objects which followed. This was fitting, for the Venetian glass blowers constantly searched for new ways to market their craft. Surprisingly few are to be found today, possibly the mosaics were dislodged too easily and the frames and purses were discarded. *(Plate 102.)*

Masters of rhinestone manufacture, (a faceted glass material usually gilt foiled on the back to add sparkle and depth) Austrian frame makers combined in their finest frames enameling, colored rhinestones, and pearls or other beads strung on wire and attached to the frame at the corners. *(Plate 110.)*

Very old rhinestones used in frames can be identified as smaller, more brilliant, better cut, and better set than modern ones which tend to lack luster, depth and color. Occasionally a colorful Peking glass bead or two is found, (separated by enameled caps) added to the chain, such as shown in *Plate 107* whose fine Austrian rhinestone set frame is remarkable. The body of this purse is a somewhat shapeless rich, chocolate brown velvet.

French cut steel purses traditionally had relatively narrow brass, gold or silver plated frames embossed with tiny leaves, flowers, seashells, cattails, animals, diamonds, arrows, fleur-de-lis, raised dots; some innocuous design, for they were almost unfailingly $\frac{5}{16}$th of an inch wide; the closure, a plunger $\frac{3}{8}$ths of a inch in diameter. Widths ranged from three inches to nine inches. They were to add dignity to the purse without detracting from or competing with the beaded pattern. *(Plates 229, 236 and 249.)*

The most dramatic frames were used on the plainest of bodies, the unadorned black velvet bag. This fame at its widest part can reach two inches of massive, punched, sterling silver. Such width allows for realistic cupids to play among rosebuds, garlands, and doves; Della Robbias in miniature. *(Figures 152 and 154.)*

Gold, sterling, and even platinum were used in framing, though of the three, sterling was the most commonly used. Some sterling and gold frames were unadorned, narrow, or had simple chasing, but more often sterling was pierced or fretted in designs which became classics. There were floral baskets, frolicking cupids, swags, bows and ribbons, female heads synonymous with the Art Nouveau movement, whose long tresses flowed into flower garlands, enameled leaves and flowers set with tiny pearls and sparkling marcasites, carefully placed rows of faceted Austrian rhinestones and other cabachoned, colored glass stones. *(Plate 101.)*

Others equally striking, present the Muses, each involved in her particular art; huge overflowing baskets of fruit and flowers; curving rows of rosebuds in high relief; and swags of flower chains in gleaming silver. An outstanding collector preferred the 24K gold plated over sterling frames shown at *Plate 300.* A couple even had chatelaine hooks, well marked and richly ablaze.

These sterling silver and gilt examples are traditionally not set with any ornament as they do not require further embellishment. German silver (nickel silver) frames, on the other hand, often are set with large, colorful, rhinestones or French paste.

Unlike most frames they are straight sided, have a double soldered oval link or heavy flat embossed daisy-like 12 inch chain, are arched in high curved tiers through the center and drilled with as many as fifty holes along the rim nearest the body. The sides may extend for two inches down the body but it is the width and arch which permit the frame an extension of nine inches, whereas the average purse extends about half that distance when fully opened. This is an advantage when the bag is expected to hold numerous or cumbersome items. *(Figure 154.)*

Jet black beads (colored beads were not used). were sewn in simple circles or sparingly strewn over the body at random, for the beading on a purse so framed was decidedly of secondary importance. An exception would be the colorful paisley or challis (an extremely fine wool or wool and cotton blended multicolored material), purse which was often decorated with cut steel beads following the outlines and/or interspersed at random throughout the pattern. Particularly attractive is the wide sterling frame seen on the paisley at *Plates 305 and 306.*

Rich and elegant, these bodies were not difficult to make, but the frames were and still are *very* expensive. A single ornate, wide, sterling silver frame in fine condition can currently fetch several hundred dollars.

Ordinarily, frames had straight sides and tops, others were half circles, others had curved ends, a few came to a Gothic center point, and horseshoe styles were also used. Decorative chain holders included such a range of motifs as: flower baskets, sea shells, swans, curved acanthus leaves, stylized petals, and oversized plain rings. Both twist and plunger closures could be fitted with stones. Some were real lapis, sapphires, moonstones, chalcedony or amethyst. *(Figure 148.)*

Frames made of two thin embossed brass sections were sometimes attached to the inner hinged portion from the exterior by threading through drilled holes. Possibly this prevented damage to the outer frame by relieving it of pressures. In any event this type of frame was apparently not very popular. *(Plate 100.)*

A favorite with modern women is the fret, pointed-top frame at *Plates 159 and 160,* which was usually used in conjunction with a diamond-shaped, long fringed solid color or carnival glass bead purse. Another favorite is the "blown out" type which is invariably used in conjunction with bodies of crowded beading done in bold patterns featuring vibrant, strong colors. The blown out portion has a stamped entwined pattern which was sometimes coated with a lacquer. A typical example of this type of frame is seen at *Plate 158.* These frames are always used on dainty evening purses. *(Plate 211.)*

Frames are so varied and beautiful it seems sad to find an otherwise fine purse with an inferior, ugly, or inappropriate frame. Above all, a frame must fit the body, being neither too small nor too large. A body may be prettily gathered or smocked into a frame, but when one is stretched into an obviously too wide frame taughtness and ultimate shrinking of the purse from the frame result.

Plate 110 contains some choice frames suitable for beaded or needleworked purses only. American ladies who could afford imported frames must have used them to frame beadwork which occupied so much of their time and labor. Individual companies obtained imported frames, added their own logos, and sought patents for them.

Domestic frames were quite undistinguished. Often of inferior metals, lacking jewels or embossing, they added virtually nothing to the beauty of the purse. This also applies to the narrow steel frames which were widely used on otherwise nicely beaded German and Czechoslovakian purses. They invariably rusted, the silk pulled out of the frame, they were so ugly they greatly detracted from the bead work and a purse thus framed commands a very low price, even though original to the bag.

To counteract the rust, French purses were often made of a substance called *gun metal.* Gun metal, so called because it was once used in the manufacture of cannons and other weapons, was actually more expensive than most brass frames. It was composed of 9 parts of copper and 1 part of tin; a bronze alloy which did not rust, but its dull blue-black color was anything but attractive. It was never wide, embossed, pierced, nor ornamented. Look for the words, "Genuine gun metal-France" inside the purse frame for confirmation of this interesting, albeit ugly, material. (*Figure 238* from Musee de la Mode et du Costume in Paris.)

Frames were, for the most part, made of brass or copper. Brass was highly polished to resemble gold; copper was given a nickel wash or silver plate to imitate sterling silver. Contrary to popular belief, copper is a sturdy metal and is superior to brass which bends out of shape more easily. For some reason, copper was almost always plated though it has a pleasing rosy tone when mellowed. The infamous pot metal was seldom if ever used in frames as it lacks strength, the lead used in its manufacture makes it heavy and it is quite brittle.

Both brass and copper were used to fashion filigreed decorative strips and/or nice

Figure 152

Figure 153

patterns which were machine stamped under tremendous pressure into the frame itself. Applied areas contained such decorations as seed pearls, colored rhinestones, various types of beads, wire drawn into lacy designs, and enameling,

Another frame material was German silver. It is sometimes difficult to distinguish German silver or nickel silver (it will always be stamped under one of these terms) from plated silver or sterling. Beautiful frames of German silver were used, on ring mesh particularly. They are only occasionally seen on the better grade of beaded purses and to avoid repetition are discussed at greater length in other sections of this book.

Silver plated frames were a staple of silver companies and are usually stamped *triple plate* or *quadruple plate*. As the name indicates, such frames were given three or four coatings of silver; they take a good polish and are durable. Both those for home use and those intended for factory installation were drilled. Actually it is difficult to tell the plate from sterling. If there is a doubt, a jeweler can easily test the metal content using an

acid which is not recommended for use by the layman. The frame can be stamped if found to be sterling; both services are very inexpensive.

European manufacturers do not use the term sterling so look for a number instead. Sterling consists of at least 925 parts of pure silver out of 1,000. European silver is not as pure, 800, 825 or more parts out of a 1,000 but is considered fine quality. Neither gold nor silver mines are found (exclusive of Russia) on the European continent and these metals are costly imports used sparingly. The numbers stamped on the frame will not indicate a specific country, but a European origin is certain. Frames such as *Plates 101 and 103* were almost exclusively made in Europe.

A gold wash was often given to sterling then termed *"vermeil"* which causes confusion. Look for the sterling marks or words *sterling silver,* if in doubt. Silver may apply to plate, so look for the word sterling to be certain.

Like most frames intended for use on purses with a distinctive or dominant pattern plated purses tend to be narrow, simply em-

Figure 152–153

Two ornate sterling frames with chatelaine ring/hook. The upper is crowded with cherubs and grape clusters. The lower hook is head of Medusa above fierce dragon-like creatures. Costly and handsome.

167

bossed, in fact rather plain, so when applied to a *busy* pattern the frame will not overpower the body. Some purses are best combined with such simple frames as in *Plate 189.*

Gold has always been considered intrinsically superior to all metals and not in need of embellishment. Aside from engravings, gold frames are most often plain and inclined to be rather narrow. Superb and costly examples such as those used in solid gold ring mesh especially commissioned (as in the previously mentioned Cartier purse) may be set with diamonds, rubies, sapphires, or emeralds, but they are so rare they are seldom ever encountered.

In this connection there are always those who are certain the dealer or other vender is uninformed to the extent they will not recognize a treasure. This *may* have been true at one time, but the collector would be best advised not to underrate anyone, for genuine treasures are few and far between and command as great a price as they warrant.

Even though Chinese and Japanese ladies did not use purses themselves, artisans did make pierced ivory and bone frames for export, in addition to traditionally shaped, beautifully embroidered purses. Some, such as *Plate 549* were huge, shapeless affairs banded with embroidered braids and weighted with silk tassels, or as in this instance, a heavy cinnabar bead.

These carved 6–7 inch frames were made in identical pairs featuring sinuous dragons, chrysanthemums, leaves as shown in *Figure 155.* Extremely brittle, they were easily damaged and were not really satisfactory as frame material. As the patterns were nearly always the same in coloration, width, and decor they are uninteresting and not particularly desirable.

Celluloid made a good but not perfect frame material because it could be impressed with delightful, imaginative designs, could be made in a wide range of colors, closely resembling tortoise shell. It was lightweight, accommodated a matching celluloid chain, the designs could be painted for a nice effect, and best of all, it was inexpensive.

Plate 436 shows how effective even an unadorned celluloid could be, whereas *Plates 169, 192, 411 and 421* are illustrative of molded, painted and applied sections.

Celluloids were not used on French cut steel purses, even though some fine celluloid products were produced there, as they were not rigid enough to support the weight of the beads.

Collectors seem dubious about celluloid frames somehow considering them cheap. They actually are excellent provided they show no evidence of chemical decomposition. Celluloid can turn into a powdery substance if not kept in dry, temperate surroundings. An added disadvantage is the tendency to crack, particularly at the hinges if roughly handled. Purses with celluloid frames are not overly plentiful and add variety to a collection. *(Plates 96, 106 and Figure 150.)*

The least durable frame was a handle beaded to match the body, a metal frame being covered with the same fabric. The beads on the strap took such abuse that the silk frayed and most are found in a poor state of repair. *Plate 97* is a magnificent exception. Note the fine cameo insert on the frame. The fabric covered frame fared no better. Repair is impossible so the whole frame must be replaced; a costly and difficult process. Another exception is the magnificent purse *Plate 203.* Note the mother-of-pearl is divided by an enameled section, and only the strap is beaded. *(Plate 111.)*

French cut steel purses were notorious for the narrow beaded strap threaded through overbound slots left in the body. Superbly beaded in magnificent designs, they simply could not stand the weight of the beads. The strain of being held vertically has left few to admire. *Plates 105 and 238* show the ribbon like strap which was supposed to support these fabulous examples.

Dutch silver, so called because it is embossed with windmills, Dutch maidens in wooden shoes, tulip fields, and similar scenes of Holland was frequently in a wide box shape. It is not silver at all, but nickel or plate.

The width of the frames makes them interesting but of no great value other than curiosity. An open example is shown at *Figure 156.* The body was usually some sort of fabric or textile in coarse needlework.

Frames came in a variety of closures ranging from a circular button which is opened by depressing a metal piece into a slot in the opposite frame. This seems to bewilder

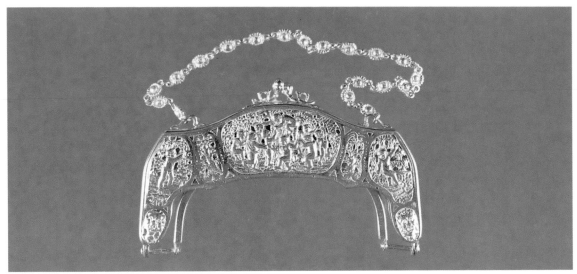

Plate 101

Plate 101

Heavy, wide, embossed, sterling frame with inner bar. Gold plated. Common European classical motif presently selling for several hundred dollars.

Plate 102

Italian mosaic floral. Early 20th century. Drilled area clearly visible.

Plate 103

Twist top. Vermeil with floral and leaf motif. Very heavy sterling.

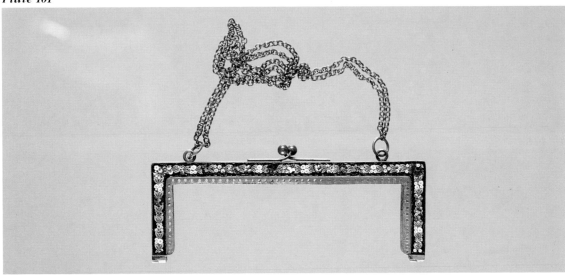

Plate 102

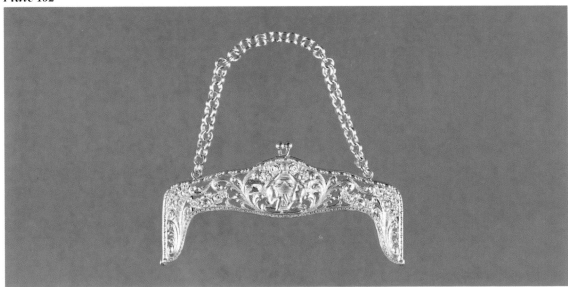

Plate 103

169

failed to enhance the body. Relatively abundant, they are seldom ever found in good condition as the weight of the beads on the delicate net is certain to have caused bead loss in the stress areas immediately below the sides and top of the frame and across the bottom edge. *(Plates 192, 196, 411, 429, 431 and 443.)*

Huge quantities of loomed purses featuring tiny colored cut steel beads were imported from France and Austria in the years immediately following World War I. In point of fact, some women remember this type of purse exclusively, though they will recall only those with the more common four colors; hardly indicative of the artistry which can be found in French cut steels. *(Plates 227 and 249.)*

The loomed purse presents unique problems which are next to impossible to overcome or escape. Responsibility for these shortcomings lies in the construction method. The beads are small rounds of steel exquisitely dyed and of uniform size and shape. They are so heavy that an enormous strain is added to the weak points just noted in the Czechoslovakian purse. A single, thin, silk, vertical thread called the *warp* and another horizontal thread called the *weft* are the sole support of these purses, sometimes reaching lengths in excess of 14 inches and weighing three or more pounds.

They are overbound at the sides but should damage occur at any point, it is next to impossible to repair the rent. The resulting loss of beads is a catastrophe because colored steel cut beads have a tendency to oxidize and the colors are not the same on the unexposed side. It is then difficult to match the shades. French cut steels were also faceted differently and have a markedly dissimilar appearance when mixed. There were many sizes and shapes, and the color range was so extensive repairs cannot be made unless one has a varied stock on hand.

One should not think of these loomed purses as machine made, for most of the operations, if not all, were done by hand. *(Plates 195, 224, 225, 227, 229, 230, 235, 236, 237, 238, 241, 242, 244, 249 and 317.)*

All American cut steel beads were a shiny silver color and even though they were made in numerous sizes and facets they were never dyed. Patterns using American cut steels were inferior, and the American cut steel purse made in the home is in no way comparable to the Austrian and French masterpieces.

Beads could also be applied to materials such as leather, velvet, muslin or flour sacking, various kinds of silks, taffeta, paisley, linen, and many other types of fabric by stamping or tracing a pattern directly on the surface of the material.

Another method used in geometrical patterns was to make a series of dots evenly spaced across the surface of the material covering as many rows as desired, designing a pattern which could be adapted to a section and repeating it over the entire surface. Paisley was easily and effectively adapted to outlining or filling in complete areas especially when steel cut beads were used on the soft colorful Oriental patterns. The pattern was already clearly established and even random paisley beading is marvelous.

A hot sad iron was used to transfer patterns onto the lighter weight fabrics. The graph paper design would then have to be intently followed, row by row, one bead sewn into place at a time to avoid errors in color selection and position.

In the *Encyclopedia of Victorian Needlework,* S.F. Caulfeild devotes no fewer than 13 pages to the ancient art of netting. This is not the delicate lace netting called *tulle,* but the making of net such as is still used in some types of fishing. Every conceivable object capable of being netted is covered from hairnets to hammocks and every net design as well.

Beads were added to netting and some such as the beaded miser purses owned by Boston Museum of Fine Arts, are extraordinarily beautiful. The silk is fine and the colorful netting delicate; the beads usually gold colored. *(Plate 150.)*

American Indian purses form a distinctive category and such was the skill of these artists that it is entirely possible the work was done in a freehand fashion. Depending on the tribe, they were known to have used embossed beading, lazy and spot stitch sewing, weaving and netting techniques. In lazy stitch beading, the rows are short and are fastened to the material only at the ends much like swags. Spot stitch sewing is done by laying threaded beads in a design and sewing them in place with another thread every few beads. This was an excellent method for the innovative and those whose talents extended to envision a finished product at the outset.

The most popular method involved lazy stitching which is emphasized by crowding the beading and raising the designs with padding. The color schemes were brilliant yet pleasing, some have a fresh and crisp quality that no other beaders have ever managed to surpass.

Little will be presented here on Indian work because the North American Indian arts constitute a highly specialized area of study. They should be covered by experts in the field rather than inadequately presented by a novice.

A highly objectionable way to apply beads is by gluing them to any surface. The glue will deteriorate the silk on any material it touches; fabric, leather, or canvas. It forms a hard, impenetrable, messy, yellow glob through which no needle can pass and **renders proper repair impossible.** The area must be cut and the bag is ruined. Inexpert bunglers think they are very clever gluing beads, but it is the most damaging thing which can happen to a purse. Regardless of its condition, if enough time and effort can be allotted, even a hopeless looking bag can be restored. This does not mean that it warrants the required expenditure of time and expense (which incidentally can be enormous) but it **can** be done, whereas gluing is certain to ruin the purse.

The Beads

The size of the beads is of prime importance for the finest purses were knit or crochet of beads so minuscule that a hundred can be held on the fingertip. The smallest size of beads were required in very complicated patterns in order to produce a visually smooth effect similar to an oil painting and to keep the purse size manageable.

Oddly enough, the size of the bead is not as important to the beadworker as the size and alignment of its hole or *pipe*. The best quality beads will thread easily and smoothly regardless of how tiny the hole is. Poor quality beads thread with difficulty and rough holes fray the delicate silk.

Venetian beads were and remain the most desirable and the range of available hues was at one time astounding. Gold and silver lined beads, beads faceted to enhance the light refraction, beads of every shape and hue are still available. Sizes 18–22 are not available to the general public.

Fringes

While it is perfectly true that the vast majority of beaded purses were fringed, not all were. This is not an easy determination to make because the fringe is the most easily damaged purse element and in the course of a hundred years or more, fringes may have been removed, replaced, repaired, or even added. It may well have been a personal choice whether to add or omit a fringe on some purses while on others the fringe is mandatory. A case in point is the intricate arrangement found on French cut steels which may extend for over four inches below the last row on the body itself. The silk on these fringes is usually so deteriorated it is foolish in the extreme to attempt restoration for the inevitable result is further damage and loss of the original pattern.

Care should be taken to determine if the fringe is an extension of the pattern itself for irreparable damage results if the fringe is cut and the body beading is ruined thereby. Fringe repairs in this instance must be incorporated into the body beading, a procedure requiring infinite skill and patience with uncertain results.

Fringes can be repaired, but from frustrating experience I recommend removing the entire fringe and using the following method to recreate the original pattern or originate one of your own design; a most satisfying artistic accomplishment.

First accurately count the number of vertical rows, (usually this will be between one hundred to one hundred fifty rows) and then decide how thick the fringe will be. Starting from either edge, a fringe of fine beads which extends from alternate rows will be pleasing. If the beads are large, allow at least 2–3 rows between loops or swags to prevent crowding. Forty to fifty loops will make an attractive fringe across the average purse. Loops can be intertwined by passing the needle two or three times around each loop to form a visual chain. Be careful to do one crossing at a time to prevent the silk from tangling.

If the original pattern is to be used it is essential to copy it, recording the *exact* number of beads in each loop *in their proper sequence*. It will be immediately apparent two problems must be overcome: there will be an insufficient number of beads to accomplish the pattern in its entirety and the necessary beads will probably not be available anywhere unless an incredible number of salvaged beads are at hand. Beads used in repair must be the same size, cut and color as the neighboring beads or the substitution will be so obvious as to be a distracting and bungling attempt at repair, rather than the unobtrusive effect desired. If perfect matches are unavailable, it is wise to create your own pattern, not diverging too far from the original.

One can modify the pattern by shortening or lengthening the loop either adding from another source, or deleting a sufficient number of beads from each loop to cover missing or sparse loops. If for instance, fifty loops are needed, and there are 152 beads in the pattern, multiply the number of beads required in each color by the number of loops and estimate or count (which will alleviate anxiety) to make certain there will be enough beads of the correct size, cut and color to finish the fringe. Extensive practice will allow you to count one group of beads and approximate other groups to reduce this wearisome but necessary process. It is prudent to err on the side of oversupply, as fringing is time consuming at best.

Some color schemes and patterns which seem garish and inappropriate are often oddly interesting when in place. It is advisable to attach a few loops and determine whether the total effect is harmonious before completing the whole task.

Use pure silk doubled or a thread which will not tangle. Some beadworkers suggest waxing the thread. This is a personal preference which does not appeal to me as it does to others. Pure silk has a slippery surface causing fewer knots and those which will surely result are much easier to untangle than synthetics, cottons, linens or treated threads. An added and great advantage is threading the beading needle! Fine and super fine beads require a number 15 ENGLISH beading needle. If you are unacquainted with this size, it is as thin and flexible as a single strand of human hair. Though the technology is superb, threading it does require practice. Expensive, pure silk now available again from China, is the only twist which will pass through the eye.

In fringing, the lack of a lining is a distinct advantage for the fringe knots can be done from inside the purse, leaving a perfect exterior. The lining can be added once the fringe is completed.

A cursory examination of other purses whose fringes you find pleasing will be most beneficial. Try a simple combination of colors at first and graduate to the interesting patterns offered in full detail by Mary White in *HOW TO DO BEADWORK*, written in 1904; since reissued at a very nominal price by Dover Press in 1974.

Purse Patterns

There were professional European pattern makers as early as the 17th century, but it is doubtful that their designs were intended for beaded purses. Certainly at this early date those below the rank of nobility would not have done beadwork at all for their own use. A queen and her ladies-in-waiting who could afford the costly and rare materials required, occupied themselves with all sorts of needleworks. Some, such as Mary Stuart, Queen of Scots, who spent over half of her life in some form of captivity where needlework was one of the few forms of recreation permitted to her, were experts.

These ancient patterns (17th and 18th century) were expansive and employed more than fifty different shades and colors. They were almost exclusively florals and were adapted for beaded purses from wall hangings or other decorative uses, much like the tapestries covered in Chapter Two. Fortunately there remain two or three publications including Emma Post Barbour's *New Bead Book (1924), Beaded Bags in Crochet and Knitting, Bags of All Kinds to Crochet* by Anna Valerie and the *Hiawatha,* which illustrate the patterns both in enlarged full color artists' renderings and smaller black and white photographs enabling us to see exactly how these antique purses were constructed.

Some patterns simply did not lend themselves to fringes, however simple. One such remains a great favorite and was once made in large quantities because of its relative simplicity and adaptability. There were numerous variations but essentially the dimensions and patterns of the *Steel Spray, Two Wide Panels, Cross Point, The Claridge,* and *The Single Diamond,* were the same. The required beads were large, common, and the silk correspondingly heavy gauge. Once the pattern was established it was repeated for the entire length of the purse and since the color scheme consisted of only one or two shades, practically anyone who could knit or crochet could swiftly and easily make them. *(Figures 173, 174, 175, 176 and 177.)*

Purely for purposes of grouping into various classifications the following alphabetical list seems to cover the various patterns used over the years by both professionals and amateur beaders.

ABSTRACTS
ANIMALS
BEAD AND TAMBOUR
BEAD WITH TAPESTRIES
CHILDREN
DATED AND SIGNED
EARLY SCENIC
EGYPTOLOGY
FABLE OR MYTHOLOGICAL
FIGURALS
FLORALS
FUNEREAL
MULTICOLORED SOLIDS
ORIENTAL THEMES
SCENICS
SOLIDS WITH SWAGS
TURKISH RUG PATTERNS
VENETIAN SCENICS

The lengthy, more choice French and Italian scenics and figurals with lacy and intricate fringes are the most valuable. Children, Egyptian motifs, and Venetian scenes are seldom seen and as a consequence are much higher priced than others.

Purses are found in the following shapes and types of beads and fringing.
Box
Coin compact
Dance purses
Diamond with fret top frame
Gate top
Misers, also called stocking, long, hookers, wallet, all sorts of names
Over the wrist
Pie crust
Reticule
Tam O'Shanter
Tulip

Kinds of beads
bugles
coralene
cut steels
French cut steels
gems as beads
glass
melon seeds as beads
pearls
pony
seed
sequins

Fringes
Dangles
Loops
Netted
Straight dangles

Fi

Plates 133–136

Four bags showing variations in straps, drawstrings, and ambitious pastoral design combined with uniform use of the rounded bottom, beaded gather, three distinct divisions, and preference for florals. Each done in extremely fine beads.

Plate 133

Plate 134

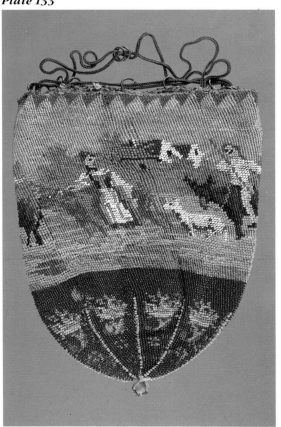

Plate 135

Plate 136

Plate 137

Plate 138

Plates 137–140

Highly imaginative old world scenic featuring moat, castle, walled town, and below an 18th century new world village. Three buildings are common, as in the nicely done one lower right. Probably all were originally fringed with a larger bead than that used on the body. Fringe was often blue or maroon.

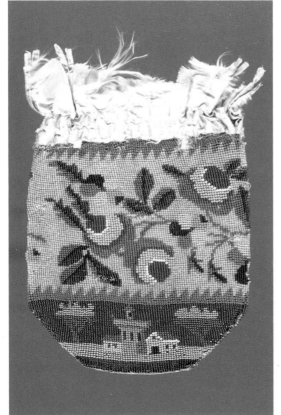

Plate 139

Plate 140

195

198
Plate 145

Misers, Minis, Tam O'Shanters

Misers One of the oldest types of purse still available to the general public originated late in the 1700's. Variously called a miser's, hookers, wallet purse, long purse, stocking purse, and ring purse, they were made by the thousands particularly in England and France. Their popularity was partially due to their speedy construction and continued as late as 1930.

The size of the purse determines whether it was used by a man or woman. A long narrow tubular shape, it was knit, crocheted, or knotted of silk, cotton and even silver thread. A slit was left open for a few inches down the middle and steel rings were slid down to the wider areas to prevent any coins from escaping. The ends were decorated with beads, usually cut steel, and a fringe attached. Those which were beaded through the narrow center portion and were much used, will show raveled silk, for the rings could not slide easily over the beads. The ends were purposely unmatched shapes; pointed, rounded, or squared off, so the user could distinguish by feeling rather than sight whether the coins were gold or silver; or so the story goes. See *Figures 160 and 162* dated 1927 on one side and initials M. D. on the reverse.

Women wore the miser's folded over a belt or folded through the middle and held in the hand. Two very handsome versions are seen at *Figures 147 and 149.* Men thrust them into the pockets of great coats, into the belt, or hand carried them. A man's miser could reach thirty-six inches in length, usually made in navy blue with a red pattern or an bilious pea green which was an extremely popular shade in the 19th century. *(Plate 151.)*

Ladies' versions were colorful, feminine, had pretty floral and other designs and some were terminated by a silver or gold acorn rather than fringes. One interesting variation had a single ring attached to chains in the center of the purse and was worn as a finger purse. It appears to be unique among misers. *(Figure 161.)* When found they are usually inexpensive compared to other more elaborate types of beaded purses.

One of the finest collections of miser's is in the Boston Museum of Fine Arts Costume Department. *(Plate 150.)*

The Tam-O'Shanter (*Figures 167, 169, 170 and 171*) named for its' resemblance to a cap worn by Europeans, particularly the poorer Irish whose homes were sometimes called "shanties". It was a small change purse, knit or crochet in an eight pointed star design incorporating steel cut or other large beads. *Figure 167* shows how the two section top was attached. The caps were made of brass, silver plated or nickel silver embossed with Art Nouveau or classical designs. They were easy to make, inexpensive, useful, popular late into the 1930's and can be bought at a modest price.

The domestic change purses seen at *Figures 163, 164, 165 and 166,* are all variations of the stocking purse on a much smaller scale. They are shown nearly actual size. The dance purses allowed objects to be inseted by separating the cords. They were worn as finger ring purses or chatelaines. One is opened by slanting the bars into the ring. All were commonly decorated with American cut steels.

Figure 160

200 *Figure 162*

Figure 161

Plate 150

also
susp
left
por
orfu
with
to 1

Figures 160–162

Lady's miser's or stocking purse show-ing date and initials. Done in cut steels on black silk.

Miser with chains and finger ring. Chain tassel, cut steel beads. Shows different shaped ends.

Figures 163–166

Four miniature knit coin holders deco-rated with cut steels on black silk. Domestic.

Figure 163

Figure 164

Figure 165

Figure 166

Plate 146–149

Four representa
tiny coin, miser
and dance purs
Green was mos
popular 19th c
tury color choi
Cut steel with l
probably Amer
others are Euro

Plate 150

Seven delicate
ladies' misers
Boston Museu
Fine Arts. No
variety of sha
Decorated in
steels, gold a
brass beads.

Figure 172

Cover of The
Hiawatha Book of
Beaded Bags, 1927
edition. The 10th
edition, it obviously
met with approval.
It included 29 pat-
terns many of which
are in this section. A
partially finished
bag is shown still on
the needles along
with the purse twist
and other items
found with it.

Figure 172

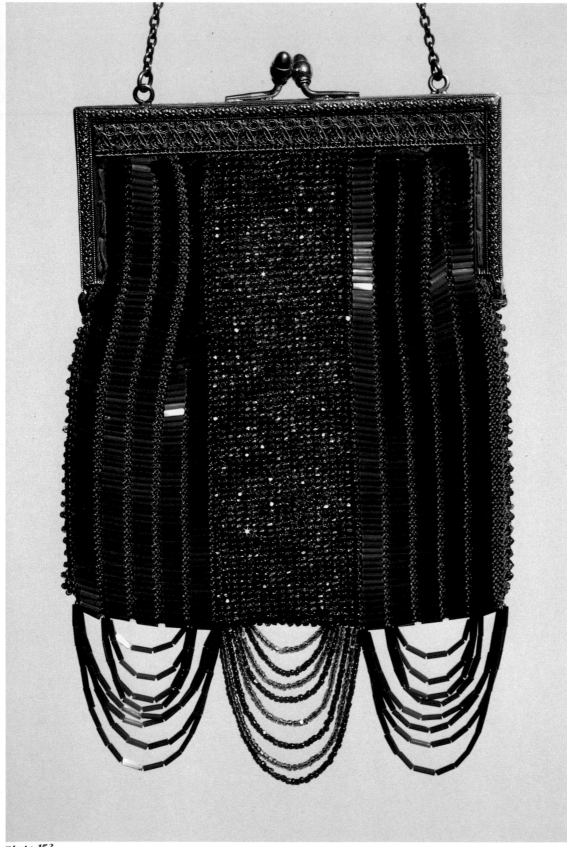

Plate 153

Bugle beads crocket in
rows with bronze
center panel.
Looped fruige. Unusual
treatment of panel
design.

209

Plate 153

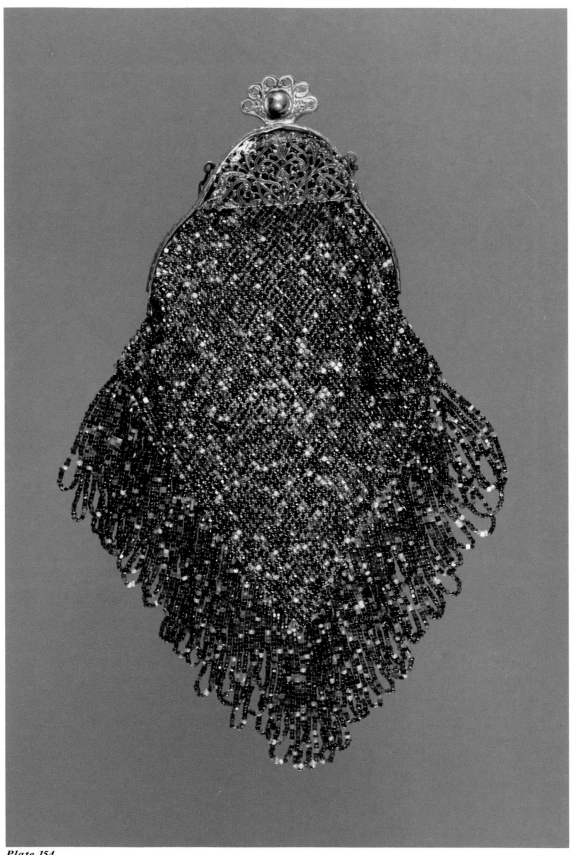

210

Plate 154

Plate 163

Plate 155

Plate 156

Plates 154-158

Diamond shaped bags were nearly always of solid colored, large size beads, depending on thick long, looped fringe for beauty. Used blown out frames. Minimal interior space.

Plate 164

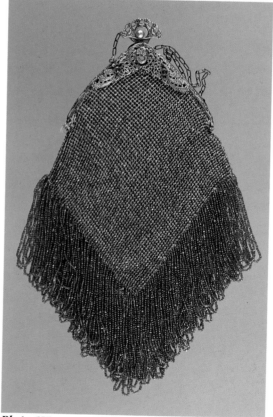

Plate 157

Plate 158

211

Figures 17...

Directions j...
on facing p...
Glitterer is...
popular ch...
casual coll...
(Plate 156,...

Plates 16...

Variations...
panel purs...
ter of the p...
greatly alt...
frame and...
ing use of...
Blown ou...
was comn...

Figures 176-177

Simple patterns such as are found on Page 212.

Page 2

MODEL D10 *Designed by Harriet B. Davis*

Abbreviations Used In This Book

B	Bead or Beads	R	Ridge or Row
K	Knit	P.H.S.	Plain Half Stitch
CR	Crochet	S.C.	Single Crochet
CH	Chain	D.C.	Double Crochet
PL	Plain	H.ST.	Half Stitch
SL	Slide or Slip	B.O.	Bind Off
ST	Stitch		

"THE STEEL SPRAY"—Model No. D10

Materials: 12 Bunches No. 9 "Star Brand" Cut Steel Beads.
1 "Hiawatha" Bag Frame No. 6019/5.
1 Spool Purse Twist.
1 Pair "Hiawatha" Steel Knitting Pins No. 17.
1 Pair "Hiawatha" Knit Pin Protectors No. 93.

The Steel Spray is individual in design and striking in appearance when knitted with steel beads on navy blue purse twist.

Size of Bag: Width at top, 5 inches. Length, 5 inches.

Cast on loosely 54 stitches. Knit back. Knit 2 more ridges to sew into frame. Knit 2, slip a bead knitting it into the next stitch; continue across, knitting a bead into each stitch. Last 3 plain. Back without beads. Continue beading one side, and knitting other plain until you have 7 ridges.

To bring this yoke down into points, on the 8th beaded ridge, knit 4, sl 1 bd, k 1, sl 1 bd, k 1, sl 1 bd, k 1, sl 1 bd, k 1, sl 1 bd, k 2 stitches plain, than knit 5 more beaded sts. and 2 plain, etc. You should have 8 groups of 5 beaded stitches with 2 st. plain between and 4 st. on each edge. Back without beads. Repeat for 9th Ridge.

10th Ridge—Knit 5, sl 1 bd, k 1, sl 1 bd, k 1, sl 1 bd, k 4 plain, then 3 beaded stitches, 4 plain and so on to end. Back plain. Repeat for Ridge 11.

Ridges 12 and 13: Knit 6, sl 1 bd, k 6, sl 1 bd, etc., 6 st. on end. Back plain.

Ridge 14: Knit 3, sl 1 bd, k 3, sl 1 bd, continue across, 3 st. on end. Back the same, slipping bead after every 3rd stitch. From now on you bead the same on each side, except the 1 bead next to the edge stitch remains 1 all through bag and is on the outer side only, not being on the inside of bag. You now have 17 panels beginning with 1 bead.

Ridge 15: Knit 3, sl 2 bds, k 3, sl 1 bd; continue across, increasing the 1 bead to 2 beads on the 1st, 3rd, 5th, etc., panels, making 9 groups of 2 bds and 8 panels of 1 bead.

Ridge 16: The same as 15, only slip 3 bds where there are 2's, leaving the 1's the same.

Ridge 17: Repeat Ridge 16.

Ridge 18: The panels of 3 bds remain as 3's to bottom of bag, while the 1 bead panels divide into two panels of 1 bead each. To do this you knit 2 instead of 3 stitches between all panels, as follows: Knit 1 (or slip the first stitch, if desired) slip 1 bead, k 2, sl 1 bd, k 2, sl 1 bd, k 2, sl 3 bds, k 2, sl 1 bd, k 2, sl 1 bd, k 2, sl 3 bds. You now have 9 panels of 3 beads and 18 panels of 1 bd.

Ridges 19 and 20: Repeat Ridge 18.

(3) Ridge 21 thru 23: Repeat above except increase all 1 bds to 2 bds.
(5) Ridge 24 thru 25: Repeat above except increase all 2 bds to 3 bds.
(8) Ridge 29 thru 36: Repeat above except increase widening panels to 4 bds.
(8) Ridge 37 thru 44: Repeat above except increase widening panels to 5 bds.
(9) Ridge 45 thru 53: Repeat above except increase widening panels to 6 bds.

The above is one-half the bag. Decrease on the other end as you have increased on the first half.

To summarize the bag, the following chart will be found useful:

7 Ridges			Each st. beaded:	2 st. at edge
2 Ridges			5 Sts. Beaded:	2 between 4 edge
2 Ridges			3 Sts. Beaded:	4 between 5 edge
2 Ridges			1 Bead: 6 Sts.	between 6 on edge
1 Ridge			1 Bead: 3 Sts.	between 3 on edge
2 Ridges			2&1 Bead: 3 Sts.	between 3 on edge
2 Ridges			3&1 Bead: 3 Sts.	between 3 on edge
3 Ridges	2 2	2 2	3&1&1 Bead: 2 Sts.	between 1 on edge
3 Ridges	3 3	3 3	3&3&3 Bead: 2 Sts.	between 1 on edge
8 Ridges	4 4	4 4	3&4&4 Bead: 2 Sts.	between 1 on edge
8 Ridges	5 5	5 5	3&5&5 Bead: 2 Sts.	between 1 on edge
9 Ridges	6 6	6 6	3&6&6 Bead: 2 Sts.	between 1 on edge

53 Ridges — ½ Bag.

Page 3

Figure 176

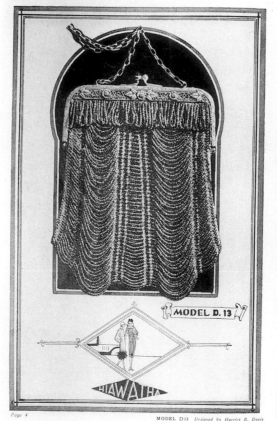

Page 4

MODEL D13 *Designed by Harriet B. Davis*

"THE TWO WIDE PANELS"—Model No. D13

MATERIALS

29 Bunches "Hiawatha" Variegated Beads No. 1105 or Krinkle Lustre Gems No. 35. 1 "Hiawatha" Bag Frame No. 6016/5½. 1 Spool Purse Twist. 1 Pair "Hiawatha" Steel Knitting Pins No. 17. 1 Pair "Hiawatha" Knit Pin Protectors No. 93.

Exquisite combination can be obtained with the brilliant variegated colors of beads and blending colors of silk.

Size of Bag: Width at top, 5½ inches. Length, 4½ inches.

Cast on 50 stitches. Knit back plain. Knit two more rounds or ridges to sew to frame.

Knit 3, drop a loop of fringe two inches long, knitting it into the next stitch. Continue dropping fringe after each stitch until within 3 st of end. Knit these three plain. Knit back plain.

Knit 3, slip 2 beads, k 2, sl 2 bds, k 2, sl 2 bds, k 2, bind off next ten stitches (remembering to knit the second stitch before binding off, or you will take away one of the two you should have on the needle after the two beads are slipped) k 2, sl 2 bds, k 2, sl 2 bds, k 2, sl 2 bds, k 2, sl 2 bds, k 2, bind off next ten stitches, k 2, sl 2 bds, k 2, sl 2 bds, k 2, sl 2 bds, k 3. Knit back the same, only slip 2 inches of beads in the space where you have bound out. This 2 inches of beads suspended from one stitch to the next is best done by cutting a hem measure 2 inches long and measuring same each time, as it remains the same throughout the length of bag.

After passing about the fifteenth ridge, one bead is slipped after the first stitch on either edge and just before the last stitch on each row. (The first 15 being left off in order to have a flat surface to sew to frame sides.)

Remembering there is 1 stitch on each edge and 2 stitches on the needle between all panels or lines of beads, slip beads according to following:

BEADS

3 Ridges	2.2.2	2 Inches 2.2.	2.2.2	2 Inches 2. 2.2
3 Ridges	2. 3.2	2 Inches 2.2.	3.2.2	2 Inches 2. 3.2
4 Ridges	2. 4.2	2 Inches 2.2.	4.2.2	2 Inches 2. 4.2
4 Ridges	2. 5.2	2 Inches 2.2.	5.2.2	2 Inches 2. 5.2
5 Ridges	1.2. 6.2	2 Inches 2.2.	6.2.2	2 Inches 2. 6.2.1
5 Ridges	1.2. 7.2	2 Inches 2.2.	7.2.2	2 Inches 2. 7.2.1
5 Ridges	1.2. 8.2	2 Inches 2.2.	8.2.2	2 Inches 2. 8.2.1
5 Ridges	1.2. 9.2	2 Inches 2.2.	9.2.2	2 Inches 2. 9.2.1
5 Ridges	1.2.10.2	2 Inches 2.2.10.2.2		2 Inches 2.10.2.1
5 Ridges	1.2.11.2	2 Inches 2.2.11.2.2		2 Inches 2.11.2.1
8 Ridges	1.2.12.2	2 Inches 2.2.12.2.2		2 Inches 2.12.2.1

51 Ridges—one-half of bag.

You will observe that only three panels of beads increase in width as the bag progresses, the others remaining in two's throughout the bag. Watch these widening panels to keep the beads smooth on the edges, that is, watch the space and fill it, regardless of the number of beads it takes, if they are running uneven.

THE GLITTERER— MODEL NO. 308—*Continued from Page 25*

10th to 13th R.: Repeat same as 4th R. increasing 2 beads in each R (making 32 B. in each R.) In knitting back on the 13th R. K. 2 Sts. Bind off 1 St., K. 3 Sts., Bind off 1 St. Repeat to end of R., 2 Sts. on end, 28 Sts. on needle. Next ridge begin the panels, K. 2 Sts., Sl. 3 Bds., K. 2 Sts. Sl. 3 Bds. Repeat 3 Sts. and 3 Bds. across, with 2 Sts. on end, making 9 groups of 3 Bds. each with 3 Sts. between. While knitting the panels, slip beads in the back also. Knit 4 more ridges, slipping 3 beads. Knit 23 ridges, slipping 4 beads in each loop. In knitting back on the last ridge, cast on 2 Sts. under each panel.

Knit 4 ridges of single beads and 2 Pl. Sts. on each end of needle. K. 2 ridges plain without beads, K. 4 ridges with beads, K. 2 ridges Pl., K. 4 ridges with beads. This is half the bag.

To make the fringe, K. 1 St. measure 2½ inches of beads, push up close. K. into next stitch, K. 1 St. measure another loop, etc., to end of needle. Knit back plain. Knit up the other side. After knitting the single bead portion, in knitting back on the last ridge, bind off two Sts. for each panel as follows: K. 2 Sts., Bind off 2 Sts. etc., having 28 Sts. on needle for panels. After the panels are finished, cast on 1 St. at top of each panel, to make 37 Sts. for the four single bead ridges, and cast off 1 St. on each end for the last 4 bead ridges. Knit 2 ridges plain and bind off loosely. *Continued on Page 13*

Page 5

Figure 177

Plate 165 A

Brown velvet travel-
ing bag with similar
design to Pictorial
Review Pattern
#12543 on Page 225.

Plate 165 A

217

Plates 167–170

Diversity in baskets, though a decided preference is shown for pedestals. Ribbons and thick fringes were popular.

Plate 167

Plate 168

Plate 169

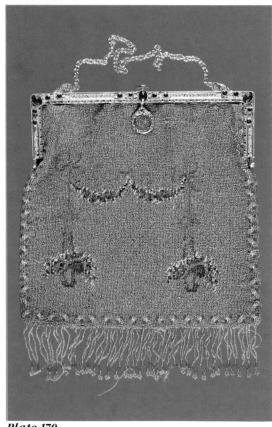

Plate 170

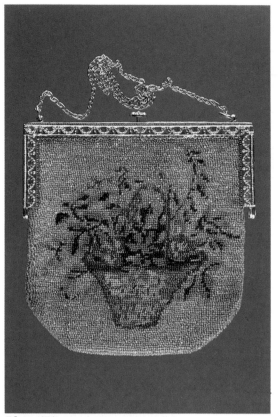

Plate 171

Plate 172

Plates 171–174

Upper left: plain early basket. Upper right: Graceful bow and jeweled frame. Lower left: Cut steel reticule and steel ring on black faille. Lower right: Flat dish-like basket. Velvet lined.

Plate 173

Plate 174

223

Plates 188, 189, 190 and 191. The frames were frequently narrow, fitted with a bar of jade or other precious cabachoned gemstone which slid into an invisible slot. A belting was used to contain the body rather than drilling, which would have been unattractive on such a narrow frame. The beaded bodies must have been contracted from one source as the patterns are so similar. The beads were so small they can barely be seen with the naked eye and the execution of the pattern was flawless. They were popular in the United States during the first quarter of the twentieth century. From every indication they must have been costly.

REPETITIVE GEOMETRICS

Quite stunning is the 7 inch French bag numbered *Plate 202.* Made of silver lined glass beads it was custom designed of midnight blue velvet, lined with striped satin, and framed in sterling. The beading was top stitched to the velvet and was not made in sections as were the pie crust styles.

Simple geometrics may have been designed by their beaders such as *Plates 193, 195 and 206,* but French loomed bags such as *Plate 199,* its marvelous zigzag fringe and scarlet background for the repetitive cut steel cartouches, was no amateurish purse.

Aside from the intricate fringe which is not characteristic of Indian work, *Plate 200* with its bold colors and primitive design is a geometric of generous proportions lined with suede.

A style of purse featuring crystal glass, bright, strong-colored, tubular cut glass beads, and occasionally cut steels (such as were found on fine paisley bags), is perhaps the most popular bag with the general public who are unconcerned with techniques and artistry and may casually purchase one bag in their lifetime. See *Plates 208, 209 and 210.*

It appears to be a combination of shape and blown out frame rather than the patterns which appeal, for great quantities of these bags were made in Germany, Belgium, and to a lesser degree, France. They were small in size, netted, crowded beading, and used large beads which were tamboured into the net. Though effective, they required far less skill in design and/or beading than most other styles. They are extremely fragile and must be lined at all cost to give body to the net.

Czechoslovakia also did distinctive designs on net; usually in large, brilliantly colored beads in similarly shaped bags of a larger size. They seldom used the blown out frame and the straps were often self beaded. *(Plates 192, 196, 204 and 208.)* Note some of these purses had wonderful celluloid or plated frames but others (such as *Plate 194*) had plain almost ugly frames, possibly to avoid competing with the bold pattern.

From every standpoint *Plate 198* is a remarkable purse. The pattern is intense, the header silk perfect, the beading flawless, and the knitting fine. It will not convert to best advantage to a frame and should be left as a reticule. It is a good example of a little used bag, for the circa is early 19th century.

Not all purses with self beaded straps are in a state of disrepair as *Plate 203* attests. The fringe is really outstanding as well, below the balanced but intricate geometrics. This purse also has a unique mother-of-pearl inlaid frame. The beads are large but the knitting is really choice.

TAMBOUR AND BEADS

A narrow but interesting classification of beaded purses combines tambour work with beads. Both the beaded and the unbeaded designs were completely done with a tambour hook. Unless the reverse side of the purse is seen there is no evidence of the beads being so attached, and the design is seen as a series of colorful loops filling in an entire area. The addition of beads was an expensive and tedious process, so purses such as *Plates 212 and 213* were sold under the label of selected department stores and were never inexpensive.

Both the beads and tambour work were pastels favoring such shades as pinks, salmon, blue and lavender. Gold beads were used to outline the beading and emphasize the embroidery. The beaded portions were geometrics or abstracts on a background of small, white, seed pearl or chalk white, opaque beads.

The shapes, sizes, and designs of these purses were amazingly similar. The frames were fitted with a very short chain but were adaptable to being carried as clutches. The saddle style is finished with ropes of gold colored steel beads and the straight model is beaded through perforated sections of the enameled metal. Both the frames and tabs were conspicuously beaded, while raised, bright, enameled sections matched the body design. The fitted lining was slipper satin.

Immediately following World War I those countries producing beads or beaded products, exported evening purses to the United States in tremendous quantities. Belgium and France had suffered great devastation and the world was most sympathetic to their plight.

It is, therefore, not surprising that so many of these small, chalk white and crystal beaded purses are still found bearing labels from those countries. They are so commonplace in fact, that over one hundred were found in one collection. Their abundance relegates them to low prices even though some are quite attractive. The work was nearly always done with a tambour hook following a serpentine single line such as is seen in *Plate 207,* or a more structured pattern such as in the more recent and more elaborate *Plates 212 and 213.* The tambouring on the latter is most assuredly done by machine.

A modified version of the geometric and/or abstract is seen in the honey colored, pan velvet pouch, the sizable pearls are outlined with gold braid. *(Plate 205.)*

Purses such as *Plates 212 and 213.* had the sublime advantage of innocuous color schemes which blended well with any outfit. When tambour work was included it was always pastel florals or merely a filled in area, subdued and often lost among the beads. Still more recently, solid colored, faceted, purses beaded in straight lines, have been done in France with fine enameled frames, satin linings and nice fittings.

Peking glass bracelets used as handles on diamond shaped bags with abstract patterns were popular about 1907. *(Plate 201.)*

The beads were medium to large sized and the side and bottom tassels were anchored by matching large beads. The whole effect was heavy and decorative. The glass bracelets were easily damaged or broken, so they are not too plentiful in a mint condition. Some such as *Plate 197* had no bracelets but were drawn together by a series of silk threads which extended from the crochet top and were then woven or braided together. Though larger than dance purses they were fragile and probably were used for similar occasions.

Plate 175-A

French. Spring fitted enameled top. Beaded tab. Clutch. Circa 1950.

Plate 175-A

Plate 214

Spectacular circular bag with sterling frame. Amethyst stone. Frame is perfectly suited to knit body. Finest beads used in the Moorish pattern. Circular borders. Over nine inches in diameter. Very costly purse.

Pie Crust Shaped Purses

Pie Crust or Circular Bags

Bags made in a circular shape were called pie crust purses in the United States because each of the wedges resembled a piece of pie and the circular shape resembles the bottom pie crust. These old bags date from 1800–1850; assigning a definite date is difficult if not impossible unless some documented proof is established. Proof or no, they constitute a unique and intriguing shape worth a concerted search. It is reassuring to know they may be 140 years old.

Both even and uneven numbers of wedges were used; seven, eight, nine, ten and eleven, being the most common. The number of wedges did not necessarily determine the diameter of the purse, however. *Plate 219* a nine wedge circular purse, is at least 11 inches in diameter, a very sizable purse indeed. Surprisingly more of the larger dimension are seen than the smaller. The wedges or slices when assembled from the center point outward, resemble a kaleidoscope and as can be seen from the examples, none even slightly resembles another.

Unlike purses with other shapes, circular purses were woven together along each section. This required skill both in the knitting and in assembling, for a less than smooth join would be painfully obvious. Once the pattern was established it was repetitious work. Each small section required uniform knitting tension to prevent curled edges.

Fringing added a crucial finishing touch to a circular bag which extended from just below the ends of the frame around the base. An exception is seen in the gusset inset example *Plate 222* which has no fringe, a jewel set frame and drop tab, and plunger closure. The pattern is less distinct than the other four though no less complicated, and fewer shades are used as well.

The frames themselves were perfect or modified rather narrow half circles, though very wide elaborate ones are found. Note that four have twist closures and a link chain handle. Circular bags could not accommodate heavy objects and more than any other purse type, exemplify the paramount idea of beauty in handwork rather than utility. *(Plates 215, 218, 220, 221 and 222.)*

Not all circular bags had designs and those of solid color are not immediately recognized as pie crusts because each segment merges into the next; the purse is seen as a whole. *Plates 216 and 217* are excellent examples. Each features a spectacular fringe. The coral purse contains fourteen spokes and sports a dangerously long fringe.

Eight circular or pie crust shaped bags. Patterned ones resemble a kaleidoscope. Note simple, narrow, twist top frames. Plate 216 has an extreme fringe. Uncommon.

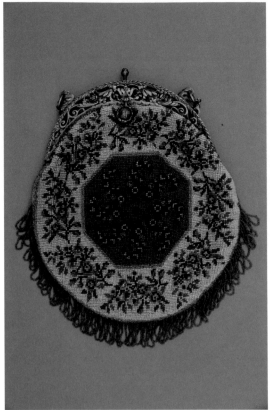

Plate 215

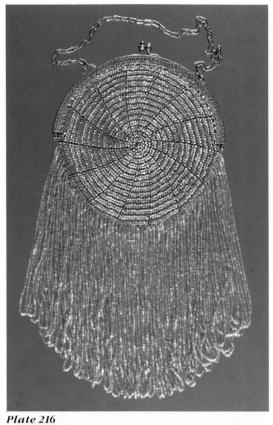

Plate 216

Plate 217

Plate 218

Plate 219

Plate 220

Plate 221

Plate 222

243

Plate 223

Perfectly balanced figural, Silver plated frame. Velvet lined. Simple fringe not typical of French cut steels.

French Cut Steels

Steel Beads

SILVER COLORED STEELS

Two nations can, for all intents and purposes, be considered the chief manufacturers of cut steel beads, France and the United States. Germany did make some cut steels but the major producers were France and the United States.

There are a few essential differences which should be pointed out to enable the collector to quickly differentiate between the more sophisticated French versions and the homespun American.

French cut steels were colored chemically and electrolytically, to produce a magnificent array of hues. They were infinitely smaller and were cut square, faceted, rounded, and tubular shaped. They were nearly always hand woven on a loom but on occasion the plain silver steels were applied to a surface by hand (velvet or paisley were the most effective). *(Plate 318.)* The patterns were very complicated and the fringes were fantastic interwoven webbings extending well below the base.

Possibly my all time favorite purse is *Figure 186.* The French steels are small, silver and the pattern is simple, so is the fringe, but the elegance is understated. The tab is marcasite set, the frame sterling, the lining a heavy satin. It is a large pouched shaped black velvet purse. Only the bottom section of the purse is beaded and that in a simple geometric pattern combined with side fringing.

In the same collection was *Figure 187.* The beading is the same but the pattern is more elegant and quite typically French, reflecting the styles favored during the reign of Emperor Napoleon and Josephine (1804–1815.)

Figures 182, 183, 184 and 185 show some less impressive, small, knitted black silk examples. English script letters A.B. were used on one; round steels were used on the stylized winged horse, small bunches of steels create the effect of blossoms on another, and a very different fringe treatment was used on another.

The fringe extended around the base of *Figure 184* from side to side. The fringe is not free swinging, but does add a finishing

245

touch. The reverse side of this once chatelaine is suede leather and the lining is green tanned leather; quite unusual. The steels in all the foregoing are American and much larger and duller than the French steels. There are many less creative examples which are not worthy of inclusion here.

Another example of French steel cuts in a distinct pattern is at *Figure 180*. It is lined in a dark colored soft suede and framed with the traditional narrow embossed frame and circular tab. It is a very handsome purse made early in the century.

COLORED CUT STEELS

Some of the finest cut steels were at one point made in Austria though they are referred to as French cut steels. Two fine early examples were purchased unmounted and unlined, the labels *Made in Austria*, were still sewn in place. Jeweled Austrian frames are found on some examples but the traditional frames are narrow, simple, unset, and may be of sterling, copper with brass or silver plating, enameled, or fretted.

More contemporary models have a heavy fold over mechanism fitted with a strong spring. Quite characteristic are *Plates 232 and 233*. They are wide, have no fringes, are done in pastels or repeated patterns using three or four basic shades of gold and silver, tend to be rather square shaped, and have ugly, beaded, rolled strap handles which I remove instantly and replace with appropriate chains. Rather than elongated they are always the pouch type of bag. They are nicely loomed and beautifully lined but are a far cry from their earlier counterparts and there is little chance they will be confused with those done half to a quarter of a century earlier.

Page 247 includes some of the geometrics which are a cut above the rather common example *Plate 249*. Why common? The market was at one time flooded with French four color versions. Gold, silver, bronze, and a bright aluminum appeared in monotonous repetition even though the patterns themselves were varied. Sizes ranged from very small 3–4 inches wide by 5 inches or less in length. Medium sizes ranged from 5–6 inches wide to 7 inches long. Large sizes ranged from 7 inches wide to 12–14 inches long, the average being about 9 inches. Extremes in all categories can of course be found, the dimensions given are for those most readily available.

(Although I exhibit thousands of purses at various shows each year, there are always some casual observers who are certain *they* have a purse (one purse of course comprises their collection), which they loudly proclaim has never been seen before. These silly challenges are usually annoying but can be hilarious, as every dealer knows. It is not possible either in written form or through other mediums to cover every conceivable example, but it does not mean that one example is rare or even desirable).

French cut steels are noted for the magnificence of their fringes. Four examples *Plates 224, 225, 226 and 238*, include a scalloped fringe, an asymmetrical step pattern fringe, a random length fish net fringe, and a single strand in various shades of beads. Note the fringes follow the general contours of the pattern and add greatly to the beauty of the purse.

An extremely popular pattern is seen at *Plate 242*. Done in various sizes, it has been seen in bronze and silver, midnight blue and silver, and midnight blue and gold. The two alternate bands reverse directions most effectively.

French cut steel florals were handsome. Strong colors were used, especially reds, and blues. The florals could be centered and boxed or extend vertically, be diagonally placed in a diamond, run horizontally as in *Plate 240*, merge as an all over fabric design, or run in a wide strip such as the grape leaves in *Plates 243 and 244*.

Birds, animals, scenics and figurals may rightfully be considered most unusual. *Plates 223, 253, 282 and 358*.

A curious and highly impractical style is exemplified in *Plates 238 and 245*. Among the finest French cut steels are these marvelous patterns but note the thin strands which are purposely left dangling along the sides. These wee strips were the carry straps for a body so heavy that it sagged woefully through the center. Whether dissatisfaction resulted in their being framed is not known, but far fewer of this delicate, albeit artistic form, are to be found intact today than framed examples.

Plate 224

Plate 225

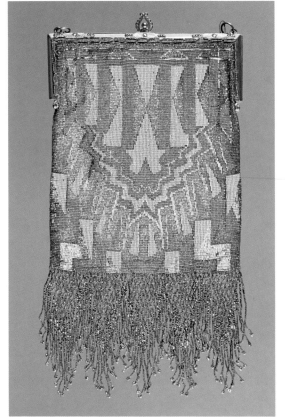

Plate 226

Plate 227

Plates 224–227

Four handsome steels in four color scheme generally associated with French cut steels. These are large, fine quality bags.

Figure 180

In general it can be stated American cut steels were largely confined to outlining paisley patterns, circular solid beading on one side only of the popular leather chatelaine, simple one color patterns on fabrics (usually velvet or silk), solid colored reticules or elongated framed purses, and on rare occasion, as an accent to glass beads.

There were problems aside from excessive weight, chiefly rust. As previously stated, American steels rusted badly when they were left in damp conditions. French steels, for some reason, do not. French steels do oxidize and fade, however. Since American steels were not made in color, this was one problem they escaped.

The French cut steel purse suffers from being loomed on a single thin thread and the sheer weight causes severe damage at the edge of the frame. They are actually too heavy to carry! The insertion of a metal bar reenforcement did not solve the unattractive midsection collapse, which may have led to the demise of this sort of purse. *(Plate 245.)*

Another problem is the deterioration of the silk. Unless the thin thread is backed with material and rewoven it is almost impossible to do skillful restoration of French cut steels. Linings are really mandatory for steels, as puncturing the threads from inside the purse would be more likely than exterior damage. A heavy satin or strong silk should be used and finished with a flower braid.

In view of all the problems, why are steels so appealing? They do have advantages over glass beads for they do not break. They have a gleam which is not possible from glass beads. The range of pigments was nearly as great as with glass beads, though the shapes were relatively limited. Even the simplest of patterns were attractive. Since the patterns were generally professionally styled, they were a commercial product and had to be acceptable to a wide range of people, rather than satisfying a mere individual.

254

Figure 180

Figure 181

Very rare signed
French colored cut
steel. Frame designed
to match body.
Victoria and Albert
Museum, London,
England.

Figure 181

on *Plate 278.* Done in tiny French cut steels the bust is outlined with a similar Moorish architectural treatment. The woman gazes from her window into the starry night beyond. A crescent moon is seen on one side and four slender buildings on the other.

The beads are large and dark, save for those used on the bust. Grape, gold, cobalt, and cranberry glass beads are used on the stylized peacock feathers and other ground details. The fringe is strangely done in rather delicate black and silver steel cuts. The coarse rayon lining is in good condition. It measures ten inches by six including the fringe.

BOUDOIR SCENE

The custom of entertaining in ones' boudoir was not looked on askance prior to the present century; in fact a lady of means habitually spent her day restoring the ravages of the prior evening. Correspondence, business affairs, romantic entanglements, household details, all manner of daily events were properly conducted from the luxury of the bed.

The details of *Plate 270* are a trifle difficult to comprehend as the center of attention is definitely the reclining figure and each of the male visitors appears to be either writing, or serving her in some capacity. The background is odd for it appears to be the exterior of a building or possibly a decorated screen, and the flowers and trees are visible through a French door.

The seated figure dressed in buckle shoes, black satin breeches and black coat resembles Benjamin Franklin who indeed was considered quite a dashing figure at the French court, absurd as it may seem. It is a commanding purse which has both narrative and historical significance. The frame is particularly appropriate to the scene as it adds height and yet is simple. The foreground and fringing are a rich brown, sharply setting off the bed linens.

VENUS

A purse with mythological overtones is *Plate 263.* Aphrodite (Venus) was a major goddess and among her many duties and attributes was dominion over love in both its highest and lowest forms. Here she is shown with her playful son Cupid (Eros). The symbol of love is the bow in her hands and the arrows at her feet. Winged Eros was the youngest of the gods and was a rebellious prankster whom his mother punished by taking his bow and arrows away, as in this instance. Aphrodite is being attended by two of the three graces, Thalia, (She who brought flowers), and Aglaia (The brilliant). There was insufficient room for Euphrosyne (She who rejoices the heart).

The black background is used to best advantage for no color would have allowed the skin tones to project as they do. The crimson skirt is riveting, each of the colors is rich and the fringe and enameled and jeweled frame are outstanding.

NEPTUNE MISERS

Neptune, the god of the oceans (Poseidon), is seen driving his chariot across the waters *(Plate 277,)* his trident (a symbol of the thunderbolt), grasped in one hand. His thick beard, disorderly mane, and distressed features indicate his numerous quarrels with mortals and the gods alike. A passage from *Larousse Mythology* best explains Poseidon: "No one ever disputed Poseidon's rule over the sea. He established his abode in the depths of the Aegean Sea.... When he left the palace he would harness to his chariot swift steeds with golden manes and shod with bronze. Clad in golden armor he would seize a cunningly wrought whip in his hand and hurl his chariot across the watery plain."

Both *Plate 276* and the latter purse are knit of navy blue, heavy gauge silk decorated with uniformly cut American steels. As the subject matter is dignified and classical, the lesser pattern is solid beading or simple lines or arrows. The huge gentleman's miser shows Venus again, as she has always been a favorite mythological subject of artists in many mediums.

SWANS IN THE GARDEN POND

The use of period costumes in designs was really clever for it gave an instant aura of age to a scene which contemporary fashions could not. Clothing was then also more colorful, particularly for the male. Some purses such as *Plate 269* are extremely well rendered, colorful, tender matrimonial scenes, with excellent perspective.

This reticule is small (5 × 8 inches) but it is perhaps the most exquisitely beaded of any figural. Notice the slender legs, the man's extended foot, the slight lean of the female figure, the brilliant red shoes and shaded garments, the minutely detailed background. The sky may be a bit jarring, but it is the perfect rendering of details which sets it apart from other beaded purses.

The late owner of this purse, a prolific collector and purse lover, felt this design was of George and Martha Washington. As to personal likeness it could be any figures appropriately costumed, but those familiar with Mount Vernon will recognize the outlines of the main structure and there is a pond with swans on the estate.

ORIENTALS

In the case of the Oriental motif, the exotic feeling appealed to the domestic beader. As with King Tutankhamen, the opening of trade and culture with the Japanese at the close of the 19th century and the fondness of such master designers as Peter Carl Fabergé and Rene Lalique for things Oriental, stirred American imaginations and appreciation of an obscure culture. *Plate 265* is a classic example of such a design. Most were garden scenes, geishas playfully cavorting with one another, or the traditional satin embroidered blue, white and black designs typical of the Chinese. **(See textiles)** *(Plate 269.)*

COACHING SCENE

Scenics were most often romantic in nature *(Plates 253, 264, 267, 268 and 273)* but *Plate 271* has a decidedly masculine albeit appealing motif. An example of an abundance of detail, the half timbered house and gate-

house serve as a background for a coach drawn by white and brown horses. The driver is sounding his departure or arrival with a golden horn. His coachman's attire is brilliant yellow, blue and red. In the foreground are some colorful barnyard fowl.

Definitely European, Germany is the most likely country of origin for this involved 10 × 8 inch fine beaded purse. As with *Plate 272,* a good fringe would give this purse the finished look it deserves.

HEART SHAPED FACE

There is something vaguely familiar about *Plate 262*. It has to do with snow, skiing, and winter sports. Though not really a figural, it is a unique design which might more properly be called a portrait. It is entirely done in large gold and blue beads. Purchased because, like *Rosebud* it reminded me of something in the dim recesses of memory beyond clear recall.

Plate 254

Plate 254

Intricate scenic with hiker in foreground. Good perspective and fine detail. Jeweled frame/tab.

Plates 276–277

*Navy silk and fine
cut steels were a
frequent choice for
mythical designs
used in this man's
miser and large bag.*

THE BUTTERFLY HUNTERS

This pattern has been done in four different color schemes and at least three different sizes. Was the pattern offered in different dimensions? Did one beader choose to make a more spectacular purse by charting her own? Did each beader alter the color scheme to suit a particular ensemble or just prefer different colors? As each is really richly executed, no one is superior, it is only the differences which are noteworthy. The manufacturers may have adapted this scene to a loomed product *(Plate 282,)* from a very old pattern.

Plate 279 is much larger than the others 9¾ inches wide by 16½ inches long including the fringe. It needs restoration on one side and along the sides beneath the frame. It contains about twenty-five different shades of opaque and translucent beads all nearly the same size. Some are faceted on one side which causes them to sparkle. The skin tones are realistic viewed from a distance and resemble a painting.

More care seems to have been taken in selecting the shading in this example than the others. The lining is sateen and strangely it is in almost perfect condition though it extends awkwardly above the drawstring and considering its immensity it would be best if a rigid frame were substituted for the crochet header.

Plate 282 is done in French cut steels. Unfortunately the colors are poorly rendered. Compared to the color scheme, the body parts and the features are distorted and too intense. The fringe is wonderful. It is done in silver and brass round beads with an open large brass bead terminal. The frame is nicely jewel set with winged cupids and a heavy double chain. Sadly, this is one instance in which the cut steel beads are not beneficial to the pattern, as the gowns merge into the background, the foreground is too bright and the boat and water are indistinct. Size 7¼ inches wide and 11½ inches long. The same pattern was also done in petitpoint *(Plate 281)*. Notice the figures are moving to the right in two examples and to the left in

Plate 276

Plate 277

the other two. As the tab indicates which side is the front, the direction seems to be optional.

The best example from almost any standpoint is *Plate 283*. The fringe is heavy and adds length and a fine finishing touch to the pattern. The frame is handsome, and the color scheme here is the richest.

The very dark background in *Plate 280*

highlights the foliage, and water, and the figures are again rendered in yet another color scheme. The extensive damage is not apparent in the photograph but the absence of a fringe is definitely a drawback.

It is interesting to see how different beaders viewed the same pattern and how much framing and fringing adds or detracts from the total effect.

Plate 278

Exotic design effectively using large glass and steel beads. Moorish motif.

Plate 278

Plate 284

Drawn from the
popular pixie car-
toons, framed twins
(with only a sugges-
tion of features)
were done in Bohe-
mia in the 1920's.

274

Plate 284

Plates 285–288
(On Following Pages)

Children are always engaging whether they are comical (Plate 286) or serene. The plain white background emphases the grape-picker (Plate 287). Plate 288 has very elaborate fringe and framing.

Children in Beads

Children Children were seldom purse subjects except when part of a family grouping or as incidental figures. When they constitute the focal point of a design it is naïve, pastoral, or humorous. One fine collection contained four delightful children, each radically different from the other.

The most humorous one is *Plate 286*. The child's hands are thrust into her apron pockets her long golden braids are tied with large amber colored bows and her feet are encased in Dutch wooden clogs. The face is a comical one; only two coal black eyes, a slash of a mouth, and a dotted nose done without shading in medium coarse beads. The dark blue circles are divided by three rows of random cut jets. Not a sophisticated purse, but a novel one.

Also wearing Dutch shoes is the maiden in *Plate 287* who appears to be a grape harvester. Her face under her wide straw hat is wistfully appealing. The beads are fine, the shading meticulous, the colors vibrant and the pattern probably unique to the beader. The framing leaves something to be desired but this is a matter of mechanics and we are here concerned with designs.

Plates 256, 285 and 288 are more worldly even though the subject matter continues to revolve around shepherdesses, birds and beasts. The distant red roofed summer houses lend a whisper of French court life to the seated figures. *(Plate 285.)* Somehow the girl's profile is quite delicate though that of her companion is indistinct. The animals have bemused expressions. A suggestion of a picture frame is found in the brown scrolling; only a trompe l'oeil, it adds an agreeable third dimension. Only six shades are used in this large scenic giving it a monochromatic look.

The formality of *Plate 288* is not apparent at first glance but look at the structured fringe (which incidentally is fantastic, both as to design and color scheme) the alternating elliptics just below the frame, the symmetry of the figures, combined with a judicious restraint of color, and you have a French pseudo-pastoral in cut steels. Here the girl is a central part, but only a part of the composition.

275

Figure 189

For the Children
*1922 Sears and
Roebuck ad.*

Child's Painted Purse

In 1922, Sears Roebuck featured a little remembered purse which is such a novelty today that it deserves special attention. In a boxed area entitled *For the Children* and priced at twenty-nine cents, a velveteen purse measuring four by four inches is featured. "It looks like a beaded bag, contains a mirror, and has a fancy design," the copy reads. What is unusual about this purse is the fact that the *fancy design* is painted on the velveteen in a series of tiny colored dots which resemble beads without actually being beads. The custom of clothing small girls in the image and likeness of their elders was so ingrained that though it was recognized as eminently impractical to allow them to carry real beaded bags, this charming imitation came close.

It was not the painting on velvet which was novel, for everything imaginable was attacked with the paintbrush from table runners to window drapes, but the desire to mold the child into that detestable phrase, "a perfect little lady" at every opportunity, which is so amusing.

Catalogs (such as Sears Roebuck, Montgomery Ward, Marshall Field, and others) which provided an endless source of entertainment and longing for the marvels contained within their covers, today prove an invaluable resource tool. They are a reliable indicator of prices, materials, sizes, shapes, fads and fashions, and occasionally indicate imported goods as well.

They carefully delineated their terms, pricing structures, ordering procedures, shipment methods, freight rates (even to drop shipment points for every state in the nation). Sample order blanks were included to aid largely unsophisticated customers, and even offered testimonials from their banks in reassurance of their dependability.

In addition to detailed background information, they exhorted the reader through an excess of superlatives and cautioned the urgency of immediate purchase. It is doubtful present day catalogs will be as accurate an indicator of social and economic conditions to future generations.

Marshall Field and Company published a catalog of high quality woodcuts (some items done to scale) rendered in such detail the graphics are works of art. President McKin-

ley's wife actually ordered her inaugural gown from their catalog in 1896.

One purse specifically designated for a child appeared as early as 1902 in a Sears and Roebuck catalog. Ladies' capes, collarettes, and muffs were popular that year and a strange muff-purse for a small child of seven shown with a purse attached to a cord suspended from her neck. The cords were a precautionary measure against loss or damage. The copy read as follows: "White lamb large sailor collar edged all around with Turkish Angora...lined throughout with white satin...a flat muff made of white lamb, trimmed all around with white Angora small purse on top, bow and satin streamers around the neck. $2.25. *Judging from the numbers of orders we get it must be very popular throughout the country. We get orders faster than we can fill them.*"

Goods imported from France were deemed fashionable and usually were proudly declared as such. Imports from other nations were seldom ever announced in advertising so the only means of determining origins were the tiny cloth tags sewn into the linings, or imprinted on the metal frames. These cloth labels (which were only one-quarter of an inch deep and one inch wide made of satin or silk,) were easily detached from the lining and lost, so another means of identification is often needed. The frame may be the only part of the purse made in that country and it cannot be instantly assumed the body was also.

Only constant familiarity with a subject makes for expertise which cannot be gained in any other fashion. Still, it *is* disconcerting to discover a label on a purse which had been thought to have been beaded in one country was in fact made in another! The imported beaded bags found on the same page as the chid's painted purse though not stated as from Czechoslovakia are instantly recognizable as such from their shape, size, type of beads and general appearance. Czechoslovakia (also spelled Checkoslovakia) has been a manufacturer and exporter of these beads for at least a century. Beaded bags were an outgrowth of their bead industry. Unfortunately the colorful and pleasing designs were done on net and the fragile nature of net makes them less desirable than purses done using other beading techniques.

Attractive Values in New Hand Bags

with SAFETY POCKET

Real Pin Seal Something Fine

18K898—Our greatest offer in a full size bag. Tailor made, with very roomy pockets, one on gold colored metal frame. Pocket for powder puff, etc., on flap opposite mirror. Good quality moire lining. Large beveled mirror. Though dainty in appearance, genuine pin seal gives fine service. A high grade gift. Size, 8x5 inches. Black only. Shpg. wt., 1¼ lbs. Each......**$5.45**

$3.75 Large "Pandora" Bag.

18K872 Special value in an extra large size of this popular wide opening bag. Fine quality genuine cowhide with soft suedelike finish. Gold colored metal frame. Serviceable fittings. Coin purse. Good quality moire lining. Size, 7¾x6½ inches. Comes in rich shaded brown color. Shipping weight, 1 pound.

$3.95 **18K812**—Special value in this stunning, entirely new style bag. Fine quality glossy black morocco leather. Beautifully lined throughout with a fancy satin striped material. Attractive narrow silverlike trimming on edge of flap and top of bag. Large roomy pocket. Two small shirred pockets contain fine beveled mirror and coin purse. Size, 9x6 inches. Shipping weight, 1 pound.

$3.19 **18K890**—The better grade Safety Pocket Bag, the kind usually seen at about $4.50. Splendidly built of genuine cowhide leather, seal grain. Three roomy pockets, one on frame. Deep safety pocket for jewelry, etc. Mirror. Good lining. Practical size, 8x4⅞ inches. Highly recommended. **Colors:** Black or dark brown. **State color.** Shipping weight, 1 lb.

$1.69 **18K874** Handsome bag of fine cowhide leather in stylish hand tooled effect. Silverlike edge trimming. Leather lined flap. Deep pockets, one on clasping metal frame. Mirror. A remarkable value. Size, 6½x5¼ inches. **Colors:** Rich dark brown or black. **State color.** Shpg. wt., 1 lb.

$1.98 Distinctive Swagger Vanity Box. **18K841**—Made of good quality leather in beautiful hand tooled effect. Durable all leather double strap handles. Artificial ivory fittings. Finely lined. Coin purse to match. **Colors:** Black or brown. **State color.** Size, 6½x4¾x2 inches. Shipping weight, 14 ounces.

IMPORTED BEADED BAGS

$3.25 **18K804** Our great special value draw string beaded bag. Small beads in fine bright colors, cleverly worked in design. Roomy pocket. Neatly lined. Stylish for dress or shopping. Size, 8¼x6¾ inches. Shpg. wt., 12 oz.

$3.25 **18K807** Bargain in popular framed bead bag. Bright beads in attractive floral design. Rich gunmetal finish frame. Handle of small beads. Nicely lined. A wonder at this price. Size, 6⅛x5⅞ inches. Shipping weight, 12 ounces.

$1.98 Real Cowhide. **18K847**—This is one of our greatest bargains. Stunning tooled effect bag of genuine cowhide with soft suede finish. All leather gussets. Three wide opening pockets, one on clasping metal frame. Long mirror in pocket. Size, 8x5½ inches. Comes in rich shaded brown color. Shipping weight, 14 oz.

$1.38 "Patent" Vanity. **18K836**—Astonishing value in a most favored New York style vanity case. Made of full glossy artificial patent leather, a splendid wearing, non cracking quality. Popular long shape, 7⅛x4½ inches. Purse and comb fittings. Large mirror. Glossy black only. Shpg. wt., 1 lb.

$1.95 **18K794**—Real Pin Seal Bag. An unusual value. Three deep pockets, one on clasping metal frame. Mirror in small inner pocket. Large handkerchief pocket under flap. Neatly lined. Latest style cord handle. 7⅛x4½ inches. Black. Shipping weight, 1 pound.

98c **18K880**—Astounding value, large swagger bag of good quality leather with attractive hand tooled effect. Entire flap leather lined. Attached mirror. Neatly lined. **Colors:** Dark brown or black. Size, 9x6 inches. **State color.** Shipping weight, 1 pound.

For the Children

38c **18K861**—Children's Vanity. Glossy black artificial leather. 5½x1⅝ in. Shpg. wt., 6 oz.

18K826 Soft **45c** brown leather. Opens wide. Nickel plated frame. Mirror. 4¾x4¼ in. Shipping weight, 6 ounces.

29c **18K784** Velveteen. Looks like a beaded bag. Fancy design. Mirror. 4¼x4½ in. Shipping weight, 6 oz.

43c **18K825** Leather Bag. Attached mirror. 5¼x3½ in. Color, dark brown only. Shipping wt., 5 ounces.

$1.55 **18K864**—Bargain value, popular style Pandora Bag. Wide opening roomy pocket on metal frame. Small pocket fitted with mirror. Made of good quality silk poplin with wide satin stripes, a very attractive combination. Has new fashionable double cord handle. Neatly lined. Size, 8x5¼ inches. Shipping wt., 14 ounces.

95c **18K830**—Velveteen bag with fancy metal frame at a sensationally low price. Roomy size. Length, 7½ inches. Wide opening frame. Attached mirror. Good plain lining. Strong chain handle. Tassel trimming. **Color,** black. Shipping weight, 1 pound.

18K892 **98c** Splendid style bag of silk warp moire. Wide opening metal frame. Coin purse on swinging frame. Attached mirror. Edge of flap attractively ornamented with narrow silverlike trimmings. Neatly lined. Stylish braided cord handle. Priced exceptionally low. Size, 7¾x5 in. Shipping weight, 7 ounces.

What About Him?

A fine purse with his name in 22-karat gold letters will delight any man. See page 513.

A—18K818 **$4.75** Extra fine quality bag of rich looking brown calf leather. Wide opening pocket on gold plated frame; also large coin purse on swinging frame. Handkerchief pocket at back. Attractively lined. New style braided cord handle. Beveled mirror. Size, 7⅜x6½ inches. Shipping weight, 1 pound.

B—18K851 **$3.85** New Paris style vanity purse. Combination of genuine brown cowhide with soft suedelike finish and flap and handle of good quality glossy patent leather. Three deep pockets, one on gold plated frame. Handkerchief pocket on inside of flap. Beveled mirror. Size, 6⅛x5⅝ inches. Shipping weight, 1 pound.

C—18K843 **$3.48** Very special value bag in new flat shape style. Good quality leather in tooled effect. Special feature large beveled mirror, 7x5 inches on inner flap. Comes in bronze color (the fashionable greenish brown shade). Size, 7⅛x5¼ inches. Shipping weight, 1¼ pounds.

D—18K859 **$4.38** Splendid value. Very cleverly constructed. When bag is opened it resembles a four-leaf clover, having four separate pockets. When closed, powder puff and mirror can be removed without opening bag. Soft, pliable, fine quality genuine calf leather, in fancy design. Top set with small 14-karat gold clips. Beautiful lining. 9½x7 inches. Rich dark brown color. Shpg. wt., 10 oz.

E—18K846 **$3.59** New York's latest. Soft bag of fine quality dark brown goatskin with filigree lace effect on gold plated frame. Large center pocket opens wide. Coin purse and mirror. Soft, open, side pockets for powder puff or handkerchief. Beautiful lining. Cord handle. 10x5¼ inches. Shipping weight, 10 ounces.

F—18K842 **$4.98** Stunning new style bag in genuine cowhide with soft suede finish. Beautiful moire lining. Large beveled mirror concealed under flap. Most popular high grade bag. 7½x6 inches. Rich shaded brown color. Shipping weight, 1 lb.

G—18K801 **$3.19** Very smart bag. Beautiful combination of brown, soft, suede finished cowhide and genuine black patent leather. Wide opening metal frame. Fine beveled mirror and change purse. Large outside handkerchief pocket. New style braided cord handle. Neat moire lining. Size, 6x4¾ inches. Shipping weight, 8 oz.

H—18K866 **$2.35** Soft style small size bag of good leather, with the latest gold plated fancy frame. Good quality braided cord handle. Beveled mirror. Coin purse. Exquisitely lined. **Colors:** Navy blue or rich dark brown. 6x5½ inches. Shipping weight, 8 ounces.

I—18K829 **$3.48** Entirely different and a big bargain. Large new drop mirror style swagger bag. Good quality leather, in popular fluffed alligator grain. Large roomy pockets. Coin purse. Shirred pocket opposite large mirror inside flap, for powder puff, etc. Neatly lined. 8x5⅞ inches. **Colors:** Gray or dark brown. **State color.** Shipping weight, 1¼ lbs.

J—18K798 **$1.19** Very striking in black and red, as illustrated. Artificial patent leather with genuine glossy leather flap, concealing mirror. Three pockets, one on clasping metal frame. Good cord handle. 6¼x4¼ inches. Can also be had in all black. **State color.** Shipping weight, 12 oz.

126 33K SEARS, ROEBUCK AND CO.

Figure 189

Plate 297

AMETHYST
COLORED BEAD
PURSE

Plate 297

AMETHYST COLORED BEAD PURSE

A successful dealer in antiques must have an appreciation for the merchandise offered for sale, but it is unwise to develop too strong an attachment. No single purse has ever been dearer to me than this one and it was sold with regret. It is a superb example of the artistry and craftsmanship the French lavished upon manufactured goods in general and handmade goods in particular.

A bridge of jewels, pin and bezel set was greatly favored by the Empress Josephine and was a feature of jewelry designed for her. It is a wonderful way of showing off fine stones to best advantage. In this case a bead resembling Royal Azul, one of the least known gems in the world and one of the most beautiful, is used. It is not translucent as the amethyst tab in the center, but densely opaque like malachite.

The body is a plum colored, heavy, velvet decorated with gold colored sequins secured by gold metal beads. Many of the sequins were missing and had to be carefully replaced by removing others from a less valuable purse. It was an incredibly difficult job to sew the sequins to the velvet without damaging or attaching the thread to the lining. The pink stones resemble faceted tourmalines. The perfect Jacquard silk lining is pale pink, finished with matching piping. It is seven inches by seven inches at its widest part.

Plate 298

ADAM AND EVE

Plate 298

ADAM AND EVE

With its fragile drawstring mechanism still in place to illustrate this French cut steel reticule, some unusual aspects should be noted; chiefly its humorous pattern or possibly Biblical truth, depending on one's point of view.

Is it a horned Satan whose stylized trunk stands to the side, or Pan, the Greek god of pipes and flutes? The cherubs appear to have laid aside their quiver of arrows and bow and are busily gathering apples in this Garden of Eden, but Adam and Eve are nowhere to be seen.

Loomed French cut steels infrequently were done in two colors as this one. A highly impractical purse because the weight of the beads on the delicate silk and strap literally tore these purses to pieces. This is a remarkably well preserved example as well as a unique one.

287

Plate 301

GOLD THREAD

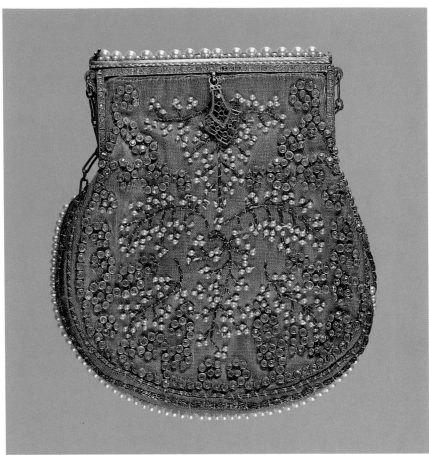

Plate 301

GOLD THREAD

Many antique purses can be used for any afternoon or evening function but this sophisticated example would be best suited to a wedding, opera, ball, reception or a very formal event.

It is a rather small purse, (6 × 6) in a traditional pouch shape. The ground is known as *gold thread* or *gold tissue*. It is a closely machine woven metallic thread upon which a darker gold thread following the confines of a vine, are hand laid and couched. Flat top rhinestones or *diamante* in nice brass, drilled, bezels are arranged in scrolls. Pearls in the shape of leaves are sewn to the body and perfect rows of pearls adorn the gusset base and across the top of the frame. Two thin rows of decorative metal thread are couched and laid on either side.

The tab is set with graduated seed pearls and the frame is further set with faceted rhinestones but they are insignificant to the elegant body. The lining, containing one pocket, is cream colored ribbed silk. The only fitting is a two inch beveled mirror attached to a coin purse done in matching silk. Circa 1920–1940.

290

Plate 302

*ENAMEL BASKET
TOP*

Plate 302

ENAMEL BASKET TOP

Violet satin lining peeks through the latticed or netted areas at the base and top of this French cut beaded purse with its enameled painted top.

This one has an oval sterling frame and cap to which the body is sewn. It consists of a main section of colored iris and leaves on a body of uniformly cut round steels. The flowers are flat cut steels. The netted sections are finished with bead acorns which gives a curious, weighted, sagging appearance much like a hammock, when the purse is not held vertically. The caps and base are closed with a twist and the short carry chain is sterling as well.

Plate 303

AMERICAN CUT
WITH PEARLS

Plate 303

AMERICAN CUT STEEL WITH PEARLS

The majority of the bags in this portfolio are either Italian or French exports, but this lovely knit example is presumably American, knit of a single color cut steels and fitted with a French frame quite similar to *Plate 297*. Pearls are used instead of Royal Azul.

Color variations are created by the use of navy blue and grey silks in a simple elongated pattern. A long collective of cut steel beads is attached on either side as a form of embellishment. Actually the weight of the beads helps this purse retain its shape. Circa 1900.

Plate 304

CHERRIES

Plate 304

CHERRIES

This purse was selected for its unusual pattern, matching frame, the use of American cut steels, effective self beaded strap and its exquisite condition. Now owned by the Los Angeles County Museum, it was part of a most unusual collection. The beads are miniature compared with commonplace American cut steels which tend to be chunky, irregular, lusterless, and generally of poor quality when compared to French or German cut steels.

The cherry and leaf pattern is stunning yet simply done on lime green velvet. The strap is sensibly beaded on the outer side only and the ends are protected by a circlet of beads about two inches up from the eye of the frame.

The frame is covered with a strip of matching velvet, beaded in advance of application. In this instance the material was glued to the frame by professionals, not merely glued as a form of repair.

Plate 305

THE BEADED PAISLEY

No more effective or richer body was ever devised for purses than the Indian paisley. These three examples are beaded with fine uncolored cut steels; actually the patterned wool is so colorful that colored cut steels would have been ineffective. The finer silver-toned cut steels may have been done in France. Paisley was an extremely popular material in the United States and *Lady Godey* books in the mid 1800's were replete with patterns and directions for its embroidery. The high quality frames were never simple, as these examples testify, but amazingly perfect paisley enhancements.

Paisley cloth, so called as it originated in the town of Paisley, Scotland, was made in imitation of fine cashmere. This soft wool came from the Indian Vale of Kashmir and was used for shawls in the 19th century. Paisley is a twill material, made of downy wool and wool and cotton blends.

Antique paisley featured shades of maroon, browns, true red, teal, blue and orange. The patterns originated centuries ago in India and Persia.

Fine paisley is highly prized in Europe and as the antique pieces grow scarcer, specimens in good-to-excellent condition are unbelievably expensive.

The square bottomed example (of superior quality paisley) is a generous eight inches wide and seven inches deep; the circular specimen is five inches in diameter.

Plate 306

Plate 307

Plate 311

TOPIARY TREE

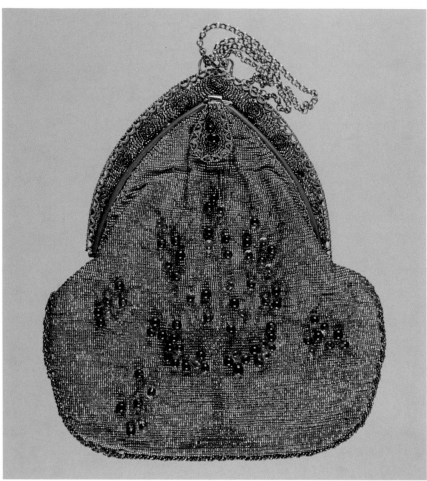

Plate 311

TOPIARY TREE

Large red, blue, and amber colored round beads such as are used in making necklaces and other jewelry, rise above the surface on this French cut steel bag. The use of large, beads which are strung through a special hole at the top of the bead is unique. It allows the beads to resemble various colored fruit hanging from branches.

At first glance it is a trifle difficult to see the container in which this topiary tree is placed because both the container and field are of faded steels. The arched frame is similarly beaded and the reverse side of the frame adds a fretted support. A plaited width finishes the outer edges and beneath the arch of the frame.

Though the steel beads have faded over the years, the silk remains firm and in general the purse is in fine condition. Circa first quarter of this century. The shell pink grosgrain lining is fitted with pockets.

Plate 312

TAMBOUR SEQUINS

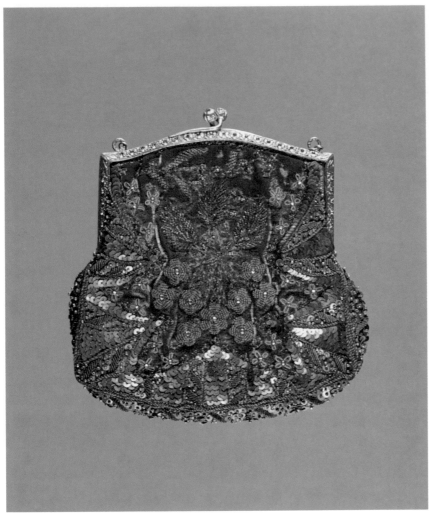

Plate 312

TAMBOURED SEQUINS

An elaborate purse from any standpoint this sequin, bead and chenille combination fails to appeal to many collectors but from sheer complexity of pattern and demanding workmanship, nothing exceeds it. Another French creation, it was done in an age when handwork was still affordable and pride in each finished product was universal. The tiny metal sequins were applied with a tambour hook and the fleurettes were made of countless gold beads finished with a larger bead center. A gold metal braid secures the edges.

The narrow frame is set with small blue rhinestones. The gold is tarnished from age but it is still a refined example of hand tamboured work which is affordable though by no means inexpensive.

Plate 315

GINGER'S VENETIAN

Plate 315

GINGER'S VENETIAN FLORAL

Though by no means as spectacularly large as *Plate 296,* both were once owned by the same lady. Again the white ground; in this case the chalk white beads are accentuated by single colored beads as are used in the florals. The simplicity of the pattern and the bold primary colors make this a truly beautiful purse. The pattern follows tradition in a sense, as it is divided into three distinct fields. The fringe continues the white field, the colors being used sparingly and some distance removed from the body.

The frame is appropriately raised florals and baskets of flowers at the chain rings. A narrow frame allows the body to flare gracefully and presents the pattern to full view, unhindered by folds or shirring.

Only slightly larger than the average purse, it is approximately 7 inches wide at its widest part and 9 inches long.

Figure 190

SILHOUETTE

Figure 190

SILHOUETTE

The human face and form are difficult to capture successfully in beads, so often only a suggestion of the nose, eyes, eyebrows and even the chin are given. A few designs were done in silhouette. One of the finest is shown at *Figure 190*.

When purchased the damage was so extensive and the holes so large, it was put away for several years. It was always a puzzle as to how it should be restored and framed. It is an oversized purse, 16 × 11 inches, and the damage was largely to the top and sides. By adding a wide sterling frame which conformed to the oval cartouche, the damage to the top is camouflaged and the body painstakingly restored. It is done in crystal and black beads exclusively. The crystals were of a peculiar cut and shape and repair had to be done with the beads salvaged from damaged areas. It demonstrates how effective just two colors can be.

Plate 316

WOMAN AND CHILD
WITH SPINNING
WHEEL

Plate 316

WOMAN AND CHILD WITH SPINNING WHEEL

If the human form is difficult to capture in any medium, it is doubly so when rendered as finely as in this purse. Unfortunately it is mounted in a cheap and ugly frame and the fringe adds little or no beautification, as both might.

Why then is it so remarkable as to be in a class by itself? It is the large size, the subject matter, the perfection of the beaded pattern and the composition which are so noteworthy. This is no run-of-the-mill purse, for its' sophisticated and knowledgeable owner has literally hundreds of purses and rightly considers this one her favorite.

Consider the details.... The posts of the chair, the open door which forms a frame for the head of the woman holding the child, the voluminous patterned skirt, the perfect little spinning wheel, the nicely modeled hands, the natural pose of the infant, the distinct facial features, the delicacy of the mob cap and hair ribbons, all given perspective through the use of distant scenery and sky.

The colors are subdued rustic perfection, as is the realistic tableau. The action is centered so the lingering eye catches and appreciates details gradually. The fringe though damaged, is a finishing touch neither detracting nor competing with the body. In some purses the fringe may be more attractive than the body, but this fringe is an extention, not a contention.

Plate 317

ROMAN CHARIOT

Plate 317

ROMAN CHARIOTEER

Even though it has a dreadful fringe, the subject found in *Plate 317* is marvelous. Masculine in feeling, it depicts an ancient Roman driving his leather, two-wheeled chariot complete with faces (an ancient weapon) and shield, behind his over-decorated steed. A small scaled animal can be seen between the horse's hooves. For some strange reason the charioteer sports the double felt crown worn by Egyptian kings a thousand years before the establishment of the Roman Empire. Without doubt the scene is supposedly taking place in the Coliseum and the tiny animal symbolizes the combats staged there be-

tween gladiators and wild animals, not to mention the Christians who met their maker there as well.

It is the imagination, creativity, and the feeling of motion shown in this design which establishes it as the most unique French steel ever. No matter that the artist has confused costumes and centuries; the horse, chariot, lion and man are superb. It is the classic example of the adaptation of ancient works of art to purse designs. Notice the frieze of Roman figures, shown Greek style across the top just under the frame.

The sterling frame has a simple pattern of elongated diamonds across the body and stylized ends. It is well suited to the pattern.

305

Plate 318

BLUE VELVET AND
FRENCH CUT STEEL

Plate 318

BLUE VELVET WITH FRENCH CUT STEEL

A lovely purse is *Plate 318.* The harmonious simplicity of this classic style has a universal appeal to discriminating collectors. The enameled navy blue and gold vermeil frame is engraved *E. Gauthier, rue de petit Champs,* *Paris.* A mirror and coin case are similarly stamped. The body is peacock blue pan velvet with matching velvet strap; the lining a gold taffeta. The gold colored French cut steel beads were skillfully applied in a simple border with a tambour hook.

Plate 319

DON QUIXOTE

Plate 319

DON QUIXOTE

There is something of Don Quixote's Sancho Panza in the mounted figure proudly bearing a royal standard. The horse lifts its slender legs among the hillocks, amusingly set ramrod straight, with stalks of pale blue blossoms. Shadows of gold and green suggest the slopes. The rider appears to be clad in a suit of armor and side arm, while the dappled horse is outlined in gold. Nosegays hover in mid air but no windmill is seen, so perhaps we are wrong and it is another knight en-tirely. Even the fringe is comical, for the colors seem strung at random in long ama-teurish fashion. The basketweave frame is narrow and undistinguished.

The pattern may not be beautiful, but it shows imagination and an attempt to emu-late literature, much like the fable or illumi-nated page taught an ethic by picture and oral repetition. It is the uniqueness of the pattern which makes it choice and shows the range of possibilities available to the skillful beader.

307

Plate 320

BEAD AND TAPESTRY

Another combined type of beadwork is tapestry and beads. It too is far from common. If the category appeals to one's taste, it has a number of characteristics which can be anticipated.

The petitpoint insert will be slightly or vastly different on either side. They tend to be about the same dimensions regardless of shape or pattern. The fringes are heavy, crystal, tipped with a color found in the beading. The frames are narrow and relatively unassuming. I have seen three examples; two were nearly identical and one very different. They were made in Austria where the petit contains thousands of stitches per inch. The pictorial will be scenic, usually a pastoral, though *Plate 320* is a figural.

The beaded portion of the purse is either knit or crocheted. That section of the purse to accommodate the tapestry, is bound off with care and the needlepoint sewn into place with minute stitches. Both sides of *Plate 320 and 321* are illustrated. The enamel and jewel set frame is particularly attractive and increases the value substantially.

Plate 321

The Beaded Scenic

The Two Seasons

The two seasons *Plates 322 and 323* is a fine beaded reticule measuring 8 inches by 10 inches. The crochet header and lining are in excellent condition, but the body has numerous small rents which can be restored successfully. It is the completely unique design which makes this an outstanding bag.

The rectangle enclosing the two seasons is balanced by a lavender motif. The careful choice of colors as well as subject matter demonstrate the effect climate has on both beader and viewer. Yellows are sparingly used or lavishly. Pink, burnt orange, red and touches of pale green convey a spring garden atmosphere. The distant farm house adds to the impression of spaciousness.

The winter scene is chilly, the fields dormant and the trees bare. Even the sun on the horizon lacks warmth.

Whether the same house is depicted depends to some extent on the imagination of the viewer. One thing is certain, the beader was skillful and meticulous in detail. Though purchased in England for a considerable sum, it was most likely made elsewhere.

The Beaded Scenic

Landscapes which do not include figures, or in which the figures are subordinate to the rest of the pattern, may be categorized as scenics.

They are interesting and some are downright beautiful. For the most part they display castles, gardens, woodland scenes, mountains, bodies of water including rivers, peaceful lakes, and an occasional larger water mass such as a bay or inlet. Very ambitious ones incorporate as many details as possible, especially those done in Germany or depicting typical German or Austrian scenes, where the countryside still abounds with views such as *Plates 328, 332, 333, 336 and 339.*

The inclusion of windmills, chalets, formal gardens, pagodas, chateaux, and/or well known buildings such as are found in Venetian scenics or the Crystal Palace (London), make reference to particular countries whether or not the purse is a product of that country.

Plates 326–333

The scenic concentrated on bridges, water, distant mountains, castles, and sky. Exceptions are the inclusion of roses, and windmills in the Spanish and Swiss scenic. How different the same scene appears when a change is made in frame and fringe. (Plate 332–333.)

Plate 326

Plate 327

Plate 328

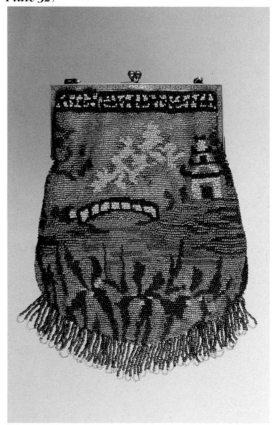

Plate 329

Plate 330

Plate 331

Plate 3

Plate 332

Plate 333

Beasts and Birds in Beads

Birds, animals and children are so hard to find that when a collection contains an example it is cause for joy. The colorful parrot in *Plate 166* was a great disappointment, however, when first seen for it so badly needed attention it was heartbreaking. It is included for it's extraordinary beauty and age even though there has not been time to restore it.

The shape and the sawtooth border at the top frame indicates it was a reticule which was once framed. This example is very large 10½ inches long, (without the gather which will be added to properly complete it), by 6 inches wide, with a narrow sterling silver frame. The opposite side has the usual floral wreath in pastel and white beads. The beads in the design are smaller than those forming the background. An appealing variation is achieved by using assorted sizes and shapes of beads.

This purse does not follow the accustomed divisions for the artist wisely decided a colored tulip bottom would detract from the splendid bird in his floral bower. When the framing was done, probably 75 years after the beading was done, it was lined with a coarse, ribbed, rayon material, a coin container added, and a beveled mirror was attached to the frame. This work was done in a factory situation. There are more than forty different shades used in the design. It is possible a more suitable frame with less rigid square lines can be found to camouflage the needed repairs. It's a wonderful purse in any event!

The mania for peacocks was not confined to the domestic scene for the Indian (Near Eastern) embroiderer working with fine silks, gold and silver thread, gold and silver beads and occasionally sequins, made small, oblong, highly imaginative and delicate clutch bags. Generally they were done on black velvet or a suede like cloth. *(Plates 350 and 351.)*

The metal thread embroidery was so heavily encrusted in one example that the bird is nearly lost in the maze. In the other a wary

Plate 345

Judicious use of white background and brilliant colors makes this an unequaled grouping of birds.

323

Plate 350

Metallic thread embroidery shows the overuse of decoration and the magnificence of simplicity. Both done on suedecloth about forty years ago. Origin: India. Jewelers innovations in bird and animal designs were quickly followed by workers in other mediums in the late 19th century.

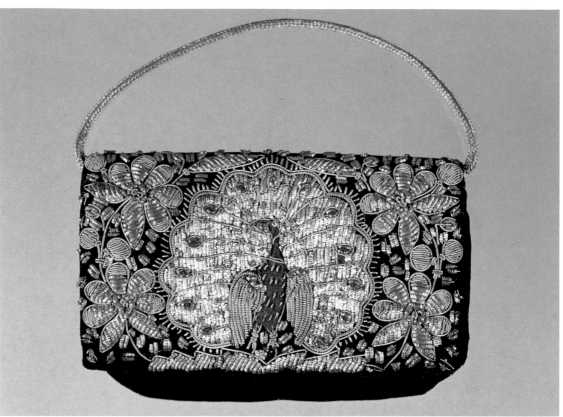

Plate 350

326

Plate 351

Plate 352

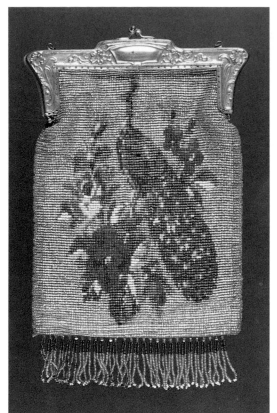

Plate 353

Popular peacock motif may have originated with Cartier jewelers about 1925. Ideally suited to beading it appeared in endless variations. Some birds seem purely imaginary such as those in Plate 355.

Plate 354

Plate 355

327

A particularly fine collection of dolls contains a type of doll which was less designed for play than curiosity. These dolls, nearly 200 years old, display the wares which would have been offered at these fairs and markets. Among the tiny baskets and bottles are containers of beads, needles, and silk threads which highborn ladies used in their fancy work. Careful scrutiny reveals miniature purses prominently displayed among the wares. (See *Plates 382, 383 and 384.*) An ivory case contains the tools which might well have been used in making purses and other accessories of dress.

Is it still possible to manufacture the fine seed beads used hundreds of years ago? The answer is yes. Is it economically justifiable to do so? The answer is an emphatic no.

In order to appreciate this contradiction it is necessary to understand the chemical composition of glass, the fashion in which it was once made and why tiny seed glass beads would be prohibitively expensive if they were currently produced.

VENICE AND THE ISLAND OF MURANO

The Island of Murano lies minutes from Venice, Italy. How many minutes depends on how one arrives. The crowded vaporetti will take about forty-five minutes, stopping at each of the stations along the route to discharge and admit the busy commuter and tourist, but a costly water taxi will deliver one in style, in ten.

As I was suffering from a severe case of flu combined with near exhaustion, we took the water taxi and were met by an English speaking representative of Vetreria Bisanzio glass house. This was a fortunate happenstance for the glass blowers were at work and their seemingly effortless art could be observed first hand. They were busy making the exquisite mirrors, chandeliers, vases, service and decorative pieces for which the island has been famous for centuries. The only change in operations has been in the furances which are now gas powered and produce a uniform 2,000 degrees (centigrade) of heat, where wood and coal furnaces, requiring constant stoking, once produced 1,500 degrees.

Glass is a relatively simple compound consisting of silica, (fine sand) soda or potash, and in some cases, lime or lead and *cullet* or broken glass. These ingredients are heated within the furnaces in a clay pot until they reach a molten state and cooled until the consistency of honey or molasses, called a *batch* or *mass.*

A hollow tube about 4–5 feet long is inserted and a gather is collected. The master blower, called a *gaffer,* assisted by a youthful apprentice, gives the gather a couple of deft twirls and places the tube on a straight metal bar called a *marver* alternately blowing, shaping, crimping, cutting, re-heating, and applying other pipes of molten glass to the sides, lip and standard of the object in rapid, sure movements. The mass must be constantly worked in order that the desired shape is maintained without warping or sagging.

Despite the intense heat of the furnace, the room, (containing about ten master blowers), is not uncomfortably hot for the floor is cement and the light is somewhat muted. So adroit are the workers that none wear gloves despite the fact the glass is red hot. Remarkably few tools are used and these too are basically the same as those used for the last 700 years. (See *Plates 393, 394 and 395.*) Once the object is shaped, and the foot, glass decorations, stem and/or other touches added, the object is left in an annealing oven called a *green oven* for at least 24 hours cooling uniformly and gradually to prevent stress, crazing, or cracking. Engraving, enameling, or other decorative touches are added once the cooling process has been completed.

All the masses appear colorless while being formed. The colors are obtained from the addition of various chemicals such as cobalt, (blue), selenium (red), copper (green), manganese (purple), etc. At one time a staggering 2,300 different shades were produced! The exact formulae are naturally even to this day, a jealously guarded secret of each glass house.

At one time apprentices were drawn only from the immediate families of master blowers and the art was strictly regulated by the city of Venice and The Glassmaker's Guild. A gaffer may take forty years to learn every facet of glassblowing before he is considered a highly paid and equally highly respected master.

By the end of the 13th century all furnaces were required to be located on the Lagoon of Murano as a precaution against the outbreak of fires within the city of Venice. The larger glass houses are still on the island of Murano but smaller furnaces for the enlightenment of the hordes of tourists are scattered about Venice in little shops annexed to the large showrooms which still comprise the major economic base of the city.

Seed beads were made in a slightly different fashion, which is one of the reasons they are no longer made. A gathering was collected on a blow rod or iron and another rod called a *punty* was inserted so the bubble closes around it. The rod was grasped by an assistant who ran with it the length of the glasshouse stretching the bubble into a thin tube to a length of one hundred or more feet. The tube was laid on a wooden framework, cut into smaller lengths, and pushed through a chopping machine.

The beads which were formed were smoothed and cleaned by revolving in water filled barrels. They were then fed into a long machine, gradually heated to six or seven hundred degrees centigrade. This softened the exterior of the beads which were smoothed and polished by a grinding stone as they moved along a conveyer belt. Twenty to fifty kilos (a kilo is approximately 2.2046 pounds) of beads were finished at one time in this concluding process. Finally they were dropped through a sieve and were graded by size and placed in 40 kilo bags for distribution.

Color was achieved by melting colored glass in the pot, dyeing with aniline dyes, or enamels. Enameled beads were the most costly as each color had to be fired at a different temperature. The numerous steps required added greatly to production costs.

Beads are currently made by inserting a hollow tubing inside a mold which is filled with molten glass. Since the beads are no longer of the tiny seed variety, the rods do not require stretching and the process is greatly simplified both as to time consumed and much hand and foot work are eliminated.

Little wonder seed beads, called *perles,* (actually all beads are so called in Europe though they have nothing to do with the natural pearl as we know it) are no longer made. The two essentials for marketing any product are: 1. a demand: 2. the ability to make a profit from its manufacture. Seed beads by their very nature require a great expenditure of time and expertise. There is virtually no demand for seed beads because no one currently wants to work in such a tiny medium.

SEED BEADS AND SOCIETA VENEZIANA CONTERIE

Did I find any of these vanished beads? Curiously, yes. The story is unique enough to deserve retelling.

The courteous salesman, after what he deemed a sufficient length of time spent in the furnace area, *Plate 395* gently ushered us into the elegant showrooms where a dazzling array of items were exhibited for the admiration of the many potential purchasers, who had, incidentally, skipped the furnaces for the plushier ultimate product and knew no more about their acquisitions than when they arrived.

"But there are no beads," we stammered.

"We don't make beads. But there are four firms which may be able to help you, Madam."

Once pointed in the right direction we doggedly set off over bridges and past shops clearly patronized by the Muranese, with their gaudy displays of trinkets and worthless glass items designed for tasteless tourists, and arrived at a large, locked, wooden door. The door opened automatically after the office staff heard English instead of Italian and a pretty girl appeared to assure us that such small beads were no longer made and they had none.

There seemed to be a conspiracy. All Europeans knew the words NO and NONE, I was prepared. Surely the Venetian purse brought from the United States and which by now seemed to weigh a ton, was of *some* use. The pretty girl disappeared up the stairs with it and presently a spirited lady who greatly admired the work, also assured me they had no

337

such beads and she had never seen a purse such as this. I am not one to be easily dissuaded and in the ensuing conversation, it developed that the firm did indeed have old stock which had not been disturbed for generations. Would we like to see the beads? Would we! Does a bee like honey?

The trip to the storage area led past building after building, none of which was visible from the street, for Murano is similar to other Mediterranean countries, a high nondescript wall shields all behind it from intruders and the curious. Barrels of beads lined the pathway to the cave-like storage areas but they were large, brightly colored, modern beads which were of little interest to us. The containers of tiny beads were covered with dust and it was hard to see exactly what colors they were. No matter, if they were for sale we were willing and anxious buyers. In all, fourteen different colors were unearthed and the details of price, quantity, shipping, and various other matters soon resolved.

The charming and helpful lady was studying English at night school and in the course of time she and the Societa Veneziana Conterie would be pleased to assist us with any information which we desired. Before departing Senor Claudio Chiappetta gave us a history of the company which we subsequently had translated. Alas, beads were not considered.

The city of Venice is a static city, buildings may be renovated and conceivably razed, but new construction is almost impossible because of the nature of the canals and the land which surrounds them. This is important in that the landscape features which were present hundreds of years ago are still in use; little changed, and the designs used on beaded purses a hundred years ago are easily recognized today.

Venice is synonymous with her canal system which even today dominates every facet of her existence. Naturally, patterns feature their gondolas, bridges, unique palaces, squares and canals, all of which are incorporated in the examples shown. Saint Mark's famous basilica is featured in *Plates 389 and 391.* A surprising amount of detail is included in all Venetian design purses. Many show

either actual or idealized flowers and trees overhanging the waterways. *Plates 385, 386, 388 and 399* indicate the maze of stairways, archways, and the variety of architecture to be found in this fascinating city. The numerous figures are dressed in period clothing. The gondoliers wear the traditional blue and white middy type of outfit marking their elevated social station, for this occupation was jealously guarded from generation to generation.

Present day actual views of Saint Marks' canals and the Rialto Bridge are shown at *Plates 378, 379 and 380.*

VENETIAN MOTIF

Exactly why the most obvious category escaped me for so long is a mystery. Like most chance discoveries it was suddenly and forcefully evident that the Venetian design in the beaded purses was a natural outgrowth of the location of the ancient bead industry. Where else but Venice? It is no mere happenstance then that the finest purse ever encountered was produced there.

The origin of the word regatta is lost in Venetian history where it originated. The word once referred to the gondola races which were, as the word signifies, competitions; in this case carried out on water. There are a number of Venetian regattas which are causes for much celebration, but this is the most historic. Held since the 12th century on the first Sunday in September, it is called Regata Storca.

The races are preceded by a magnificent procession of historic boats on the Grand Canal, rowed by Venetians in costume. The strolling figures on shore clearly show the designer felt the elaborate costumes would lend authenticity to this purse, little realizing those not familiar with the event could not comprehend their significance.

The costumes, flags, and indeed the ship itself, smack of earlier Mediterranean splendors. The ship is propelled by two tiers of oarsmen, about 38 on the visible side. The furled flag at the mast of the nearest vessel is that of San Marco. From the 11th through the beginning of the 18th century Venice was a world wide commercial power to be reckoned with, augmented by its strategic location in the Adriatic Sea. Though the spice trade constituted the bulk of its early commerce, exploration and the perfection of glass, textiles, and other arts established Venice as one of the world's prime cultural centers. A highly structured, cosmopolitan society evolved as a result of this great wealth.

The beads in this 8½ by 9 inch purse are incredibly tiny, the shading delicately realistic even to the carefully rendered faces. Perspective is achieved by foreshortening. The stunning frame is enameled in black and set with imitation lapiz lazuli. The matching blue faille lining indicates the purse was never used, for it is absolutely mint. *(Front Cover.)*

Because of its condition it is difficult to accurately determine the age but a safe conjecture might be about 1900. Of course the workmanship is professional. Oddly enough it was not purchased in Venice, but in San Francisco. It is as truly an artistic marvel as any painting, statuary, or jeweler's masterpiece and will never be offered for sale during my lifetime, though collectors have offered thousands for it.

Though other purses with Venetian scenes are not as startling, they are all colorful, intriguing, and very significant. Few Venetian design purses are found currently, so few in fact, that their distinction was inadvertently overlooked.

The designer of *Plate 390* may have conjured up the actual setting, but how beautifully the columns frame the campanile and surrounding buildings in the distance. The base of each column, carefully separates the brilliant red wall from the column. In minute detail even the marble deterioration is shown by the shadowy use of deep purple against a light blue sky. This purse lacks a frame, lining, and fringe before restoration. It will be worth the effort.

Signed purses are uncommon and this one *Plate 377* is slightly different than most Venetian scenes. Note the closed gondola and the two gondoliers stretching across the entire width of the body (7 × 5). Gondolas today are open and not nearly so long. This indicates the purse might have been made late in the 19th century. The signature

Richard of Venice is delightfully immodest and one wonders if it was made for/by him, by an admirer, or perhaps it was an early form of advertising.

Note the clear division into three separate areas and the careful attention to keeping the central motif in its position of importance. Actually, the pattern is a simple one, the beads undistinguished as to size and only six colors are used. It is a departure, however, from the expected in Venetian scenes. The opposite side is quite pedestrian; the customary floral wreath done in brilliant colors.

Some liberties may have been taken in respect to the individual canals which crisscross the city, for they are devoid of the lush vegetation shown. The covered gondola is not seen and in its place powered boats churn the water, much to the distress of the slow moving vaporetti and poled boats. In this connection the police run their motorboats at full speed, sirens wailing, and everything scurries for safety. Just what could cause these emergencies several times a day is a puzzle on a island as small and outwardly peaceful as Venice.

Now, refuse is piled along the narrow streets in the ubiquitous black plastic garbage bag collected by a special barge twice daily. How refuse was once disposed of, I shudder to think.

Saint Mark's Square is alive with humanity usually shepherded by a figure wildly waving a huge colorful umbrella in a futile effort to keep its assigned tourist group within shouting distance. Every language known to man is heard here, and no one speaks in tones lower than a roar. Even school children, who seem to be everywhere, scream in an effort to be heard over the din. The square is the hub of all activity and the offerings of the tiny shops range from the crassest of items to glass of breathtaking beauty.

Unless one is aware of their significance the prominence of exotic masks in nearly every shop window must be puzzling. We resisted the temptation to add one to our already bulging baggage with more than a twinge of regret. Having researched their role in Venetian life I felt smug while viewing them. I *knew* their importance, but was nonetheless surprised to see quite so many.

Plates 396–398

Scores of masks displayed in shop windows surrounding San Marco. Popular tourist item but it is doubtful their true purpose is known to travelers.

Plate 396

Plate 397

Plate 398

Plate 399

Early reticule with
accurate detail of
San Marco and the
Doges' Place.

351

Plate 399

collection once obtained contained this same pattern except that the bottom had been cleverly cut away along the points removing the three bottom pansies and tiny looped fringe. It seemed a strange size but no more thought was given it until photographing a collection which contained the full sized version.

In passing it should be noted a sparse fringe is almost always found on this Czechoslovakian black bead background. It is not very attractive, as it is all that usually remains of a much longer fringe. Some bags still have the intricate basketweave fringe intact.

"A rose is a rose, is a rose, is a rose," said Gertrude Stein. She would have found the rose in *Plate 309* irresistible. It is the juxtaposition of roses and what appear to be poppies or a flower with full blown orange, cream, and/or purple petals in sharp contrast which fuses this elegant pattern. The complimenting fringe was commissioned to combine elements of each of the pink and lavender shades with chalk white and crystal. Aside from the fringe, the 9 × 7 inch purse probably was made in Italy and has a fine jeweled frame.

The roses in *Plate 406* are complimented with blue petals, bright red poppies, well placed yellow, green and lavender sprigs and leaves. The wide bands set against the pearl background lend a varied and cheerful tone to this large professionally beaded purse.

In *Plate 447* the roses and rosebuds are the sole flower in a formal pattern also arranged in horizontal strips; the deep blue providing an unusual cartouche for the buds and a foil for the center panel. The blue tips on the twisted fringe unify the design. *Plate 442* is less structured but again it is the blue touches which intensify the rose. Rosebuds are most effective as a border and garlands in the very old purse *Plate 425;* an excellent example of the tulip bottom and divisions cited at the beginning of the chapter.

Pastel roses, and a dahlia like yellow and lavender flowers crowd the next example *(Plate 437)* reaching into the frame and the fringe rather than being framed by them. Very large patterns are best adapted to square frames which do not cut off part of the pattern. The bouquet on the fine bead black ground at *Plate 452* is well adapted to the modified oval shape and is a most impressive purse, measuring more than fifteen inches long and nine inches wide.

Roses are used as a oval frame in *Plate 342* confining the landscape in a unique fashion. Each of the patterns *(Plates 402, 411 and 438)* are quite traditional, the florals are scattered in four and gathered into a grouping in another. The frames are distinctive in each case.

Some florals warrant a brief explanation. *Plate 428* has a frame which opens into a box like shape and the floral wreath is very vivid. *Plate 456* has a similar frame, but note the frame is nicely jewel set, the pattern is very subtly crowded beading. It was done on a delicate net and has a retail price over twice that of the former. *Plate 450* is different! No pastels or bright colors but sophisticated black and crystal fuchsias and daisies with a matching jet set frame. Not your ordinary color scheme, but quite striking nonetheless. Czechoslovakian origin, again with the small black bead ground.

Asymmetrical hydrangeas are massed with nasturtiums in *Plate 309* to create a truly different design united by a checkerboard and single line of blue. The jeweled frame is exceptionally nice.

The bold red, white and navy stripes are a strange background for *Plate 413* with its highly stylized blue flowers and contrasting realistic roses. The frame has variously colored sets and the chain has large glass beads either Bohemian or Chinese.

Bright orange and yellows are used sparingly as a general rule, but in *Plates 426 and 432* these colors are so brilliant they fairly leap off the page. It really doesn't matter that they are just posies of no particular genus, they are sharp, oddly pleasing arrangements.

The passion flower and butterfly are bright but the blue bells catch the eye in *Plate 430*. The ground is black rather than the customary white and the fringe is varigated for emphasis. The butterfly in *Plate 374* (BIRDS AND BEASTS) is very visible against the crystal ground. A plain fringe of crystals is unobtrusive and allows the florals and butterfly center stage.

Plate 441

Plate 443

The flowers in *Plate 444* are so stylized they are difficult to distinguish. Very effective are the white pussywillows against the black ground. This purse has a nice fringe incorporating most of the colors found in the body. *Plate 404* has elongated white flowers with immense dark outer petals which may be asters. Aside from the white portions all the other colors in this reticule are extremely somber. The frame opens into a box shape. This type of frame can be used to reframe a reticule successfully as the sides do not have to be cut down as they would on a traditional straight sided frame.

This bold color scheme was considered smart in the Art Deco period, and was sometimes used on purses of a much earlier vintage. *Plates 412, 415 and 418,* are other examples of dark backgrounds the florals of which are vague esoteric symbols.

Among the thousands of patterns it is most unusual to find actual printed directions for an acquired example. Sixty bunches of dark green glass beads, 1 bunch of amber, 1 of opaque white, 1 of milk white and 1 of glass white, 1 bunch of gold, 1bunch of red, 1 bunch of pink, 2 bunches of yellow green,2 bunches of dark green, 1 bunch of light blue, and 1 bunch of yellow were the surprisingly large number of beads required by The *Priscilla Bead Work Book* (1911) for crocheting *Plate 455.*

The purse is small and rather insignificant, the pattern is not very distinctive even though it is the only decoration as the colors are all so dark. Until the directions were read the background was thought to be black. No fringe is shown in the illustration nor is there on on the purse. It was bound with dark green braid across the top and stiffened with whalebone! The pattern cost ten cents and was printed in black and white.

Ornate is the best word to describe *Plate 433* for every aspect of this example is a zenith. The jewels on the frame are showy; the blue ovals are surrounded by French paste, the fringe is thick and matches the bunches of side fringe which was a very popular touch early in the 20th century. The florals are symmetrical, highlighted by a single blue bead within a gold line.

Italian purses made frequent and beautiful use of white grounds and carefully interspersed colored beads, at times all the same color such as in *Plates 120, 403,* and in *Plate 315,* which features many shades. The clarity of the pattern is so enhanced that individual beads can be counted with the naked eye. The shading which makes this such an superb example would have been lost on a dark ground for the pattern would have submerged into it and been far less striking. The simple frame was not permitted to compete with the body either. The fringe is effective for it continues the white ground and adds length and overall balance. The row of small white beads across the bottom of *Plate 435* do complete the raw edge but leave the field of softly hued flowers looking somehow unfinished. The purse has an old Italian mosaic frame (seen under frames) and it has been seen before in another frame. It was equally pleasing in each instance.

People tend to elaborate on the truth or spin yarns about the provenance of antiques and purses are no exception. Unless there is an undisputable name and/or date, ownership is hard to prove. The following purse *(Plate 424)* is reasonably certain to have been owned by the wife of a prominent San Francisco portrait painter named Mateo Sandona. It was presented early in the century to a lady who was the nurse at her deathbed. A series of borders encloses a floral bouquet and an Oriental motif completes each corner. It is a busy design with teal green, rose, and blue shades predominating.

Plate 438 has a typical floral but an atypical frame of wide sterling silver with sterling jewel set chain. Though the purse is charming, large,and handsome, it is common enough to be of little interest to advanced collectors. It appeals to a novice or person who wishes only one or two beaded purses for special occasions.

Three lone shaded daisies are found at the base of an unusual purse made by an inventive amateur beader. A large wooden, or in some cases Peking glass bracelet served literally as a bracelet or was thrust over the palm of the hand. The shading on this one is subtle and is banded with a beaded circle which could be slid upward or downward to reach

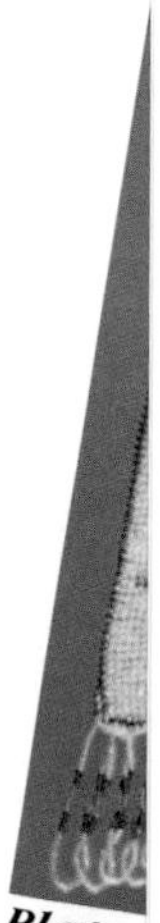

Mandalian If the collector is fortunate, a small shield of china coated paper or an oblong shaped tag may be found in the recesses of Mandalian enameled flat mesh purses. In an age when patents were perhaps even more jealously guarded than today, an innovation of any type was announced to the public along with the patent numbers as proof of claims. The advertising read as follows:

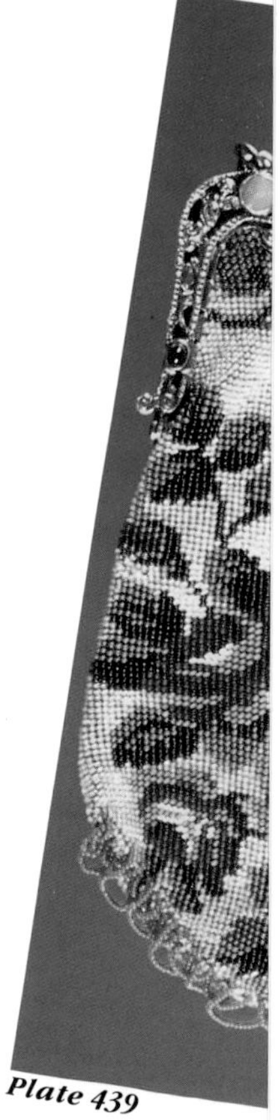

The "Gloria" Bag

Trade   Color Vision Style   *Mark*

Trade   Lustro Pearl Finish   *Mark*

Dampness or Salt Water will not effect

the gloss or smoothness of this Bag.

EVERY LINK GUARANTEED

Please tell your friends about it.

Beware of imitations
None genuine unless stamped
"MANDALIAN"
Originators

Fascinating New Creation

The "Lustro Pearl" Bag

Trade Mark

Process Patents Pending

This bag is finished with essence of pearl,

a very costly solution heretofore confined

to High Grade Pearl Necklaces

can now be had on Mandalian Mesh Bags.

Notice its lustrous and silky finish

originated and made

by Mandalian Mfg. Company. Lustro Pearl

Bags are positively guaranteed to wear well

Pearl Enamel does not chip off

Please tell your friends about the wonderful

wearing qualities of these Lustro Pearl Bags

The Acme of Perfection

Figure 192.

Note that the patents were pending on the second card but had been duly registered on the first card. This indicates that the "pearlized" purse was being sold under the name previously to the 1924 patent grant.

The pearlized finish is so subtle that it can be overlooked unless caught in a particular light and that subtlety is nigh well impossible to capture in a photograph. Glints can be seen in the fringe and teardrop in *Plate 481.*

On April 5 and June 24, 1924, Shatiel G. Mandalia of North Attleboro, Massachusetts, obtained a patent on a process which was variously known as *Lustro Pearl or Color Vision.* He also patented a purse known as the *Gloria.* Over the years these patents were challenged three or four times but verification through a patent search at any United States patent library is readily available. *(Figure 193A–D.)*

Who was Shatiel Mandalia and why is such a point made of his patents? As he left no heirs and very little is known about him today, we were delighted to find some biographical material in three of those publications which are generally regarded as chamber of commerce publicity hype, but which are little jewels of information for researchers nearly three quarters of a century later. The style used in these "who's who's" is typically flowery, but the statistical information should be reliable as it must have been supplied by the individuals themselves.

Shatiel G. Mandalia was born in Constantinople, Turkey, February 10, 1869. He learned English at a missionary school and emigrated to the United States in August, 1890. Upon his arrival in Boston, he was employed in an oriental carpet store. Possibly this is where he developed an interest in art, but it is more likely he had a prior knowledge of rug weaving and the traditional designs which he would employ in his purses at a later date. He began work in a North Attleboro jewelry factory at the age of twenty-three. A short while later he attended an art school in Providence, Rhode Island, for what today would constitute a semester, then returned to North Attleboro as a jewelry tool maker. In this connection it should be noted this city along with Providence, Rhode Island, and Attle-

Plate 439

Plate 4

boro, Massachusetts, had been the center of the manufacturing jewelry industry in North America since 1807, and it was natural for him to locate there. In 1898, he established a cuff link business and eventually specialized in silver plated mesh bags. By the fateful year of 1930 he had 150 employees located in what was known as the Manufacturers Building, selling his products both domestically and in Australia, South Africa and Europe. He wisely protected his enameling innovations from his competitors, (of whom there were many), by the aforementioned patents.

His artistic designs were colorful, balanced and beautiful. In all respects a quality creation, in my opinion, and countless collectors as well. There is an appeal to a Mandalian purse, due to his natural artistic talents and training, which no other manufacturers ever surpassed.

He entered into partnership with a Mr. Caspar in 1898, that relationship continuing until 1908, when Caspar "withdrew." It is not clear whether this means he retired or was engaged in another business. Three years later, he was evidently in partnership with Eugene A. Hawkins at two North Attleboro locations. In 1930, he was one of the sponsors of a centennial publication issued by the city of North Attleboro, as a sole proprietor.

In addition to flat mesh they made dress trimmings called *strip goods* which were sold to the garment industry. These trimmings were pockets, collars, cuffs, belts and decorative pieces made of mesh. Popular until the late 1930's, they were part of every mesh manufacturer's line.

He became active in organizations and clubs in North Attleboro and married Lillian Fuller of Wilton, Maine. Though childless, he is said to have been generous to a nephew named George, who resided with them.

Unfortunately no photograph of Mr. Mandalia could be located for this publication. By 1940 the Mandalian Company was in dire financial difficulties so in 1942–43 he sold out to a well established and financially secure competitor, the prestigious Whiting and Davis Company located in nearby Plainville, Massachusetts. When it became apparent World War II would engulf the world, and the government began to severely restrict essen-

tial metals, Mandalian machines were stored in the Whiting and Davis plant, but the space which they had occupied in the Manufacturers' Building continued to be used for the production of war materials. This prohibition and resulting scarcity necessitated a cessation in the manufacture of metal meshes and thereby mesh purses.

Four outstanding illustrations of Mandalia's versatile skills are seen in *Plates 503, 504, 505 and 506*. As these are large sized purses in absolutely mint condition with unusual patterns, the collector should be prepared to pay much more for them than ordinary metals in small sizes.

Charles A. Whiting

Let us now consider the man whose name is synonymous with mesh purses: **Charles A. Whiting.** *(Figure 191.)*

Charles A. Whiting, the youngest of 11 children, was born July 4th, 1864, in the Abbott Run Section, Cumberland, Rhode Island, just across the river from North Attleboro, Massachusetts; a fortunate circumstance for him indeed. Whiting's parents, Aaron and Adeline, were overseers of one of the many small textile mills in the area. He was 12, when as the story goes, he delivered a cow to a customer in North Attleboro where he must have come in contact with the jewelry industry, for at the age of 16, he took the job of office boy for Wade, Davis Company jewelry manufacturers in the town of Plainville, some four miles distant. Records prior to 1906, will show Wade, Davis Company as located in Wrentham, prior to Plainville's incorporation as a separate entity.

A serious, ambitious and industrious lad, he had been educated through the 8th grade. This was not uncommon at the time, for education was considered a privilege and those who attended school applied themselves with uncommon diligence. The quality of education gained prior to World War I far exceeded that acquired by so many reluctant and belligerent students today.

In 1880, his starting salary was a mere nine cents per hour but he steadily advanced to become a partner in 1890, and the firm's New York representative from 1890–1896. On July

TWO THOUSAND YEARS OF MESH

"There is, perhaps, no one creation of man that has so directly influenced the history of the world as has ring or chain mesh. Dating back to before the year A. D. 1,000, this mesh made into armor, has won or lost wars, and thus affected entire nations. Also, in remembering that arms and armor furnish the best expression of the art and the science of the metal worker of the Middle Ages and of the Renaissance, armor includes in its decorations, gilding, silvering, tinning, damaskeen, niello, even jewel-setting: we can readily appreciate this influence of mesh on history.

"The ornamental designs explain to us stages in the development of religious and civil customs, including pageants and sports. In its mounting, it summarizes the textile art of various periods—appearance, in those Norman days, from the commonest to the most costly of fringes and trimmings further shows the progress of man. The size of armor finally gives us convincing data as to the state of physical development among the men of many nations.

"Chain mail, more or less complete, was used for centuries and was not uncommon even in the Colonial days in America. The Japanese have used triple-linked breast plates as late as 1870, while in the late World War (I) the British used chain mail visors on their steel helmets. This mesh veil, devised by Captain Cruise, R.A.M.C. Oculist to the King, was attached to a metal rod which passed immediately under the brim of the helmet. Few soldiers actually at the front would wear these veils, however, and finding them annoying, would cast them off.

"Since chain mesh played such an important part in armor, let us go back to the beginning of the use of protective armor. Records are scarce indeed for the year A. D. 650, when the Post Roman first made his appearance in a jacket of padded hide. Early Bayeau needlework depicts these pioneers of armor, while a bit later on, needleworks show him in the Frankish period in a suit of scale, (A. D. 850). Still later, in the Norman period (A. D. 1050) soldiers are clearly shown dressed in a hauberk, or coat, of simple interlinked chain mail. This coat, at that time, reached to the knee, and with its long sleeves, and worn over a padded garment, offered good protection against dagger, spear and axe. A padded suit was nearly always worn under armor of all kinds for several obvious reasons. *(Figure 198.)*

"Now let us look at the construction of this hauberk of chain mail or mesh. A shirt in the collection of the Metropolitan Museum of Art contains about a quarter of a million handmade and tempered rings, each carefully formed and each separately riveted. Early chain-mail was made from thin strips of iron rounded with hammers into iron wire and wound about a cylindrical bar. It was then cut with a chisel, the cut ends overlapping, then hammered flat and riveted.

"It is important to mention here that it is the shape of the rivets used in connecting the links, that is supposed to establish the nationality of the craftsmen. The rivets of triangular section are said to appear on European mail, while those that are circular are believed to be of Eastern origin.

"When we stop to think that a skillful armorer might make and weave together two hundred and fifty of these links in a day, it is easy to see that the coat mentioned would have cost its maker, working everyday, nearly three year's work. At modern prices, allowing the maker six dollars a day, the garment would cost over six thousand dollars. As we hold a piece of this chain-mail; or mesh in our hand today, we might well wonder how this material could have protected man against the vicious thrusts of lances, daggers, arrows and even against the early musket ball. That it was effective however, is recorded time and time again, and I will quote a single instance of its virtue.

"When the Crusaders at Tiberas (1187) hemmed in by the Saracens after two days of hard fighting, when most of the foot soldiers were killed or wounded, when hardly a horse in the army could carry its rider, the mail clad knights are known to have suffered no serious casualties. Yet over a thousand of them exposed themselves constantly in battle.

"With the recognition of the importance of chain-mail, its development and improvement naturally followed, and iron mines were sought and guarded much like a gold mine. As early as 1378, iron was mined on a large scale in such places as Sulzbach, Arnberg, and Stahberg, and the fate of people was often decided by this supply or lack of it. Then followed a period of development of the most wonderful metal craftsmen the world has ever known.

"Lighter and finer mesh garments were produced, and soon leg coverings, gauntlets and caps appeared. This was about the year A. D. 1250. Bold and fabulously wealthy knights often rode forth to battle in suits of armor made of gold or silver mesh. But common soldier and noble alike were clothed in chain-mail at any event, and planned and schemed ways of "out armoring" their enemies.

"Chain mesh appeared in the tilting tournaments and duels of the times and even suits of mesh for little children have been found.

"In the year 1350, transitional mail and plate appeared. This follows on with much variation through the seventeenth century.

"Collectors of mail and armor gathered together many of these valuable suits, among these collectors was Charles V whose elaborate collection included his father's armor and many other old pieces brought from Flanders.

"The armor of Joan of Arc with its arm pieces and mittens, and the helmet with a gorget of mail, the border gilt, the inside garnished with crimson satin, is evidence of the skill of the chain-mail craftsmen.

"During the centuries when armor was in use, every town, every prince and almost every castle had an armory or arsenal well stocked with complete suits of armor and weapons.

"With the appearance and effectiveness of firearms, armor gradually disappeared. This, however, was not until late in the seventeenth century, and then only in those more progressive countries where gun powder was first used. Even then, parts of armor were employed in every war up to and including the late World War, (I) as previously mentioned. For close hand to hand conflict, mesh shields and breast plates have been made and used to good advantage in many wars since the advent of firearms.

"With chain mesh being so important from the year A. D. 1050 through the centuries that followed, one might logically expect to find many records of its use. This is not true, largely, I believe, because of the early dates involved. Perhaps, more important is the fact that chain mesh and armor was developed and improved so rapidly that what might have been a long mesh hauberk in one year was often remodeled the next into a short shirt with perhaps chain mesh leg coverings. This changing over of most of this metal mesh, which in those days took so long to make naturally destroyed the evidence of the many types of garments in existence. Because of the early Bayeau needlework before mentioned, we have been able to write our history.

"My great ancestor Nathaniel Whiting settled in Dedham, Massachusetts, about the year 1636. Stories are told and records confirm them, of this sturdy relative of mine, that proves to me that he in turn descended from a long line of *Men in Chain Armor.*

"Possibly the spirit of the knights of old dwells within me, and prompted me to utilize that mesh that many times saved their lives, to make a living for me. At any event, in the year 1898, I found myself manufacturing ladies' bags of mesh. Not unlike the humble beginning of many an enterprise, my first bags were crude and costly. Not only were these efforts costly, but slow as well, for practically all of our work was hand labor.

"Our early methods of assembly were to send the ring mesh out of the factory to private homes where the rings would be linked together in spare time. We made arrangements with needy families in many parts of New England to carry on this work, and it is most gratifying for me to know that we were able in this way not only to get our young business started, but at the same time assist in keeping many homes together.

"Improvements followed rapidly, once we were well underway, and one after another, we have built and perfected machines for many necessary operations, until finally an automatic machine was produced to make the mesh. We now have machines that make mesh at the rate of seven hundred rings a minute, and complete links into mesh at the rate of four hundred thousand a day.

Figures 199 A–B

Steps in the production of modern metal mesh.

Mesh is woven one facet at a time on cylindrical machines. The fabric, called a "stocking," is pulled up and out of the machine and can be cut at any length desired like cloth from a bolt.

The finished mesh is measured and cut by hand to exact specifications. In addition, portions of seams are "knitted" together by hand.

Figure 199A

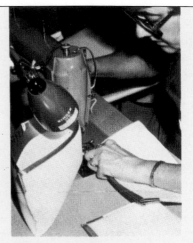

To assure long life and stability, linings are affixed with a special adhesive then machine-stitched for extra durability.

The ancient art of hand spiraling is still used to connect the frame to the mesh with fine coils of wire. In the final step the lining is then sewn in by hand.

At Whiting and Davis skilled craftspeople perform more than 24 hand operations in the finishing of a handbag or accessory.

Figure 199B

"It is interesting at this point to compare our production today with that of the craftsmen in the early Norman period. You will remember that it was estimated that he might complete two hundred and fifty rings a day, and that nearly three years would be necessary for him to complete the one quarter of a million rings necessary for the hauberk. This number we can complete in less than a day, and every ring will be perfect. Today, we operate hundreds of these machines and own, outright, about forty patents pertaining to mesh machinery.

"In the year 1909, our labors started paying dividends in the form of world wide recognition as manufacturers of dainty bags of mesh. Retail stores nearly everywhere clamored for a supply to fill their customers' needs and working night and day, we were able to fill but a small part of these orders. With the demand for bags of mesh came the need of high styling, and I found it necessary to visit the fashion centers both at home and abroad. Hollywood and Paris were visited and today we have close contact with Hollywood and a definite tie-up with Madame Schiaparelli in Paris. You will see in most of the smart shops everywhere, Whiting and Davis bags designed by Schiaparelli, in many shapes and sizes. *(Figure 200 and Plate 460.)* There are new beadlite-mesh pouches with satin lining, with pocket coin purse and French mirror, smart hobnail pouch bags, exquisite armor mesh pouch bags with rhinestone clasps and hundreds of other new Parisian designs in gold, silver and white pearl, all of which are made in the dainty, modern mesh creations by Whiting and Davis with a background that goes back two thousand years."

Mesh Production

Whiting and Davis competitors were hampered by less efficient machines, a limited number of machines, underfunding, and a diversity of production which gave an advantage to the one or two companies specializing in mesh exclusively.

This advantage was apparent in the biographical material appearing in *Massachusetts Industries 1928*, as Charles Whiting related, "Mesh is made on 500 machines installed in the Plainville plant, each provided with automatic stops and individual motor drives, making it possible for a single operator to run a battery of twelve machines. Automatic machines now do practically all of the cutting, splitting and joining of the mesh, operations which formerly were accomplished by hand. . . . today the machines (ring mesh) link the tiny rings at a speed of 400 rings a minute. The new mesh machines are producing effects equal to those of the jacquard loom of the textile industry producing surprisingly novel and beautiful fleur-de-lis, check, mosaic and bird-in-cage patterns in ring mesh."

The artists who created the patterns for metal mesh purses were called *pattern makers* and such famous and influential international fashion molders as Elsa Schiaparelli and Paul Poiret were paid handsome royalties for their endorsements.

Some designs were test marketed in exclusive shops and despite their charming motifs were deemed too expensive or unsuitable in some respect and failed to be incorporated "into the line". As with most manufacturers of fashion goods, those goods which were to appear in the spring and summer were presented to the wholesale market immediately following the Christmas season and the Christmas line, which has always traditionally been the most profitable season, was offered in early summer.

Charles Whiting was known to confer with clients at the dinner table, designing mesh articles to their specifications on the tablecloth. Aside from the design, this would have been a highly technical undertaking for only those thoroughly familiar with every aspect of mesh production would be able to visualize the finished product. In the process a good many tablecloths were ruined.

As a continuing proof of its high standards of business ethics and quality production techniques, purses returned to the Whiting and Davis factory for repair were at first done free of charge. Today high operational costs require the payment of a nominal fee and repairs to flat meshes are made during seasonal lulls as the company continues to service its customers both past and present. Ring Meshes, aside from gold or sterling are not currently repaired and flat mesh repair costs have risen sharply in the past year.

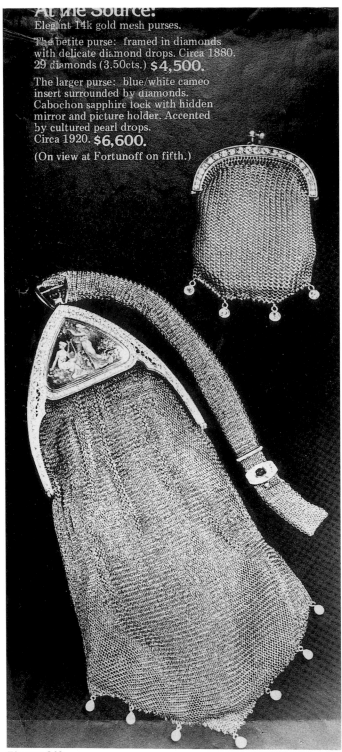

Figure 210

No. 3.
A newspaper reproduction of the famous painting used in our Saturday
Evening Post Two-Page Color "Spread" and our Ladies' Home Journal and
Delineator full page, featuring the DOME SHAPE VANITY BAG and the
PRINCESS MARY MINIATURE BAG,

Figure 211

ket. Their competitors were able to obtain their own mesh making machines by engineering minor modifications to the original patents and obtaining their own patents.

Patent searches are a genuine chore. It is such a confusing and laborious task that there are special librarians who do patent searches only. Moreover, there are only a few such source libraries or patent repositories in the United States.

Patent numbers and dates appeared on the paper inserts used by Mandalian, Evans, Whiting Davis, and other firms to differentiate sources and ward off the competition. Each took inordinate pride in any improvement or technique no matter how slight.

Dates are included on some frames as part of the patent information indicating when the patent was approved, (particularly on frames made by a company named JEMCO, who always included the date). This indicated a new design, locking mechanism, chain, or closure. This lucky circumstance is not the case with mesh purses, as with leathers. The addition of an engraved date is advantageous to a frame or the repousse work. Many women had their name, address, and the year they received a purse added to the frame as a precaution against loss, perhaps with an eye to the future as well, for dated items like signatures on fine art, add immeasurably to the value of an antique.

These patents were important too when the terrible depression ruined so many fine companies and reduced proud men and women to virtual destitution. Scarcity of metals and plant facilities which could not be economically and rapidly converted to the production of war materials, along with lack of funding forced Shatiel Mandalian to liquidate his mesh works. Whiting and Davis who were friendly competition, acquired his holdings in 1942–43 and along with them the rights to his patents.

The pearlized finish Mandalia was so proud of, was a *beautiful* finish obtained from a compound of fish scales such as were used in the manufacture of imitation pearls. Bought in bulk from the fisheries on Cape Cod, Massachusetts, it was used by both Mandalian and Whiting and Davis. Few Whiting and Davis pearlized purses are found today and a Mandalian pearlized purse with teardrops is a prize. Sadly, the end of the enameled mesh era was in sight and World War II was waiting in the wings.

There was a constant change of ownership among the manufacturing jewelers in the Plainville area at the turn of the century. It could almost be compared to warfare for this year's partner was tomorrow's enemy. Add to this, all those with the same family name, (all of whom were engaged in the jewelry business) who incorporated, dissolved associations, changed partnerships again and again in rapid succession, and repeatedly changed the name of the business. There were numerous Sturdys, Evans, Fishers, Franklins, Barrows, and worst of all, Whitings! There was William D.; George A.; F. M.; Frank E.; Clifford C.; and a great many more!

Frank E. Whiting was a nephew of Charles A. Whiting. He and his son, Clifford C. Whiting operated the Chicago office, and were the west coast representatives for the Whiting and Davis firm. Another nephew, Fred M. Cook managed the New York office for nearly half a century.

Charles A. Whiting may have employed his relatives but he himself did no juggling of partners, preferring to be the ultimate authority in the operation of his company.

William D. Whiting and George Whiting were brothers of Charles A. Whiting, who though not in his employ, were local tool and finding suppliers for the jewelry industry at large and undoubtedly did business with the firm, especially when the chain and jewelry division was predominant.

F. M. Whiting was not related but his name is well known among silver circles as a manufacturer of sterling silver flatware. In tracing the art of silversmithing in the United States the Whiting Silver Company of North Attleboro, Massachusetts, ranks among the finest and oldest. Little wonder that serious collectors continually confuse the Whiting and Davis operation with Whiting Silver Company as early Whiting and Davis ring mesh purses were made of sterling silver and gold.

In the interest of historical record and accuracy a list of Whiting and Davis officers is presented here:

Presidents

C. A. Whiting—1907–1940 (Continued on page 405)

Figure 210

This extraordinarily beautiful mesh was recently advertised. The prices reflect the quality which can be obtained in some meshes.

Figure 211

This painting was used in early full color advertisements and later as a line drawing. Child's version is often called a miniature.

Figure 212

*Two versions of the
Princess Mary and a
dome shaped filagree
made of fine wire.
(From 1922
advertisement.)*

Figures 213–214

*A dome shaped
vanity with exterior
compact and a
plainer version. Both
are wrist purses.*

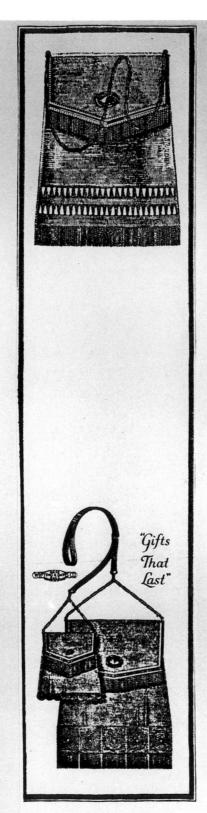

No. 4.
Shows the popular PRINCESS MARY
(top), and the PRINCESS MARY
DANSANT (bottom).

No. 2.
Featuring the DOME SHAPE FILI-
GREE – one of the new Renaissance
design.

Figure 212

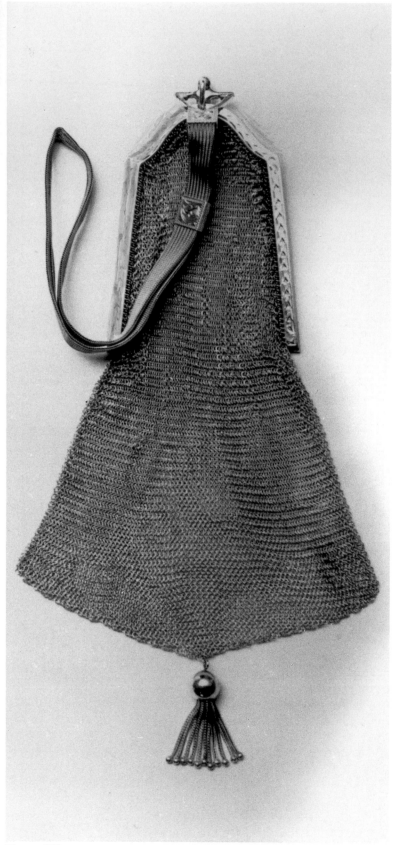

Figure 213

Figure 214   401

Figure 215

The Picadilly with external compact. Heavy gauge wire with a rosette base. Wrist strap of woven metal.

Figure 216

Ad

Figure 215

It's the Mode

For *smart affairs* — the mesh bag!

Contrasting against fur or fabric its lustrous, changeful mesh adds *chic* and charm to even the simplest costume. Its acceptance by women of fashion is a style suggestion to the woman who is mindful of the mode.

In purchasing remember that, altho Whiting & Davis Mesh Bags are both popular priced and costly, the Whiting & Davis name *guarantees* satisfaction, whatever the amount invested.

"Gifts That Last"

WHITING & DAVIS Co.
Plainville, Norfolk County, Mass.

The Whiting & Davis Trademark and Tag guarantee quality. Find them on every bag.

Whiting & Davis MESH BAGS

In the Better Grades, Made of the Famous "Whiting" Soldered Mesh

Figure 216

403

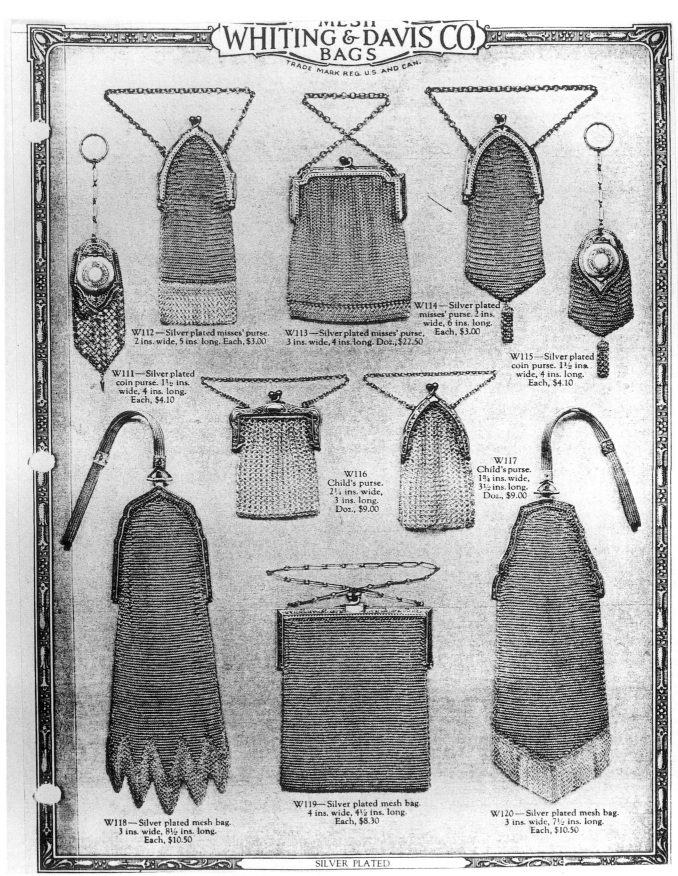

W112—Silver plated misses' purse. 2 ins. wide, 5 ins. long. Each, $3.00

W113—Silver plated misses' purse. 3 ins. wide, 4 ins. long. Doz., $22.50

W114—Silver plated misses' purse. 2 ins. wide, 6 ins. long. Each, $3.00

W111—Silver plated coin purse. 1½ ins. wide, 4 ins. long. Each, $4.10

W115—Silver plated coin purse. 1½ ins. wide, 4 ins. long. Each, $4.10

W116 Child's purse. 2¼ ins. wide, 3 ins. long. Doz., $9.00

W117 Child's purse. 1¾ ins. wide, 3½ ins. long. Doz., $9.00

W118—Silver plated mesh bag. 3 ins. wide, 8½ ins. long. Each, $10.50

W119—Silver plated mesh bag. 4 ins. wide, 4½ ins. long. Each, $8.30

W120—Silver plated mesh bag. 3 ins. wide, 7½ ins. long. Each, $10.50

SILVER PLATED

Figure 218

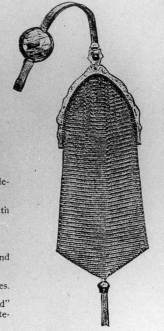
Figure 218

Page from a salesman's sample book showing wholesale prices. Circa 1920.

Figure 219

A page from the Pacific Goldsmith wholesale catalog with Deauville Ad.

Figure 219

407

Figures 230–233

Four miniature meshes none of which measures more than three inches. Upper right has an attached seal; lower left has long chain, large polished spiders and hand fashioned drops, lower right: bracelet attached to draws.

Figure 230

Figure 231

Figure 232

Figure 233

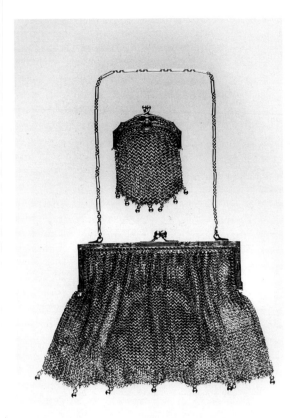

Figures 234–237

*Upper left: Sterling
mesh with ball trim
and double lined
coin purse which
attaches to rings
inside the frame.
Upper right: Sterling
mesh with long
points, balls, and
drawchain. Lower
left: Circular sterling
flat mesh chatelaine,
teardrops, and
repousse frame.
Unusual. Lower
right: Tiny sterling
heavy ring mesh.
Must have been a
coin purse as there
are no attaching
rings. Monogram
center.*

Figure 234

Figure 235

Figure 236

Figure 237

415

and Country, and *Theatre* advising the public to be aware of the metal tags and the trademark stamped on each frame identifying a genuine Whiting and Davis item. *(Figures 24, 218 and 250.)*

In addition to the trademark, name, or other marks of identification some companies used symbols intended for their own benefit. They may indicate when the item was made, which workmen are responsible for inspection of the item, or some particular information which will help in keeping track of their stock. I have noticed the introduction of a series of numbers stamped on current Whiting and Davis bag frames in addition to the banner which is familiar to most collectors. Familiarity with the numbering system should help to more accurately date a particular purse.

Merchandising departments were established in retail outlets while the advertising campaign was intensified. Elaborate traveling displays were contracted with the largest department stores and even mesh making machines were operated in store windows directly appealing to the public. *(Figure 269.)*

These windows must have been dramatic for the draperies were mesh instead of fabric and wax dolls and mannequins dressed in mesh were created especially for them. The store agreed to promote the display, place an order for a stipulated number of bags and the firm name was to be highlighted in advertising and displays. A fairly standard practice today, this was then a novel idea in the marketing of meshes and insured Whiting and Davis something akin to mesh immortality.

Watch Purses

As previously mentioned, watches have always fascinated mankind for the passage of time has a kind of fatal attraction. Aside from the necessity of marking routine appointments and duties, a watch allows us to keep track of time while serving as an ornament as well. A relatively recent jewelry item, slightly more than a century old, the watch had some novel settings in its infancy; to whit, the handbag.

Here it is shown in a "plain Jane" silver plate and in a heavy gauge wire ring mesh with daisy bottom and mock flap. *(Figures 286 and 287.)* The watch was encased in a heavy solid jacket, the winding stem protruding from one side. This allowed the watch to be removed when replating the mesh, repairing or servicing the watch, or removing it for safety sake. Though not visible, the owners initials were often inscribed on the back of the case.

These two examples are not sterling and only the plainer bag has a watch in working order. The watch is seldom perfect and collectors, who are notoriously compulsive accumulators, prefer another purse to restoring the watch.

Those few mesh examples I have seen, (and they are few indeed making the watch purses among the rarest of purses), are large, rectangular, and unstenciled with long carry chains. They are an unfailing source of wonderment to the general public and draw more comment than any other purse regardless of its merits!

Whiting and Davis and the Theatre

For over a half century entertainers and the movie industry have found mesh garments a boon. Metallic mesh is particularly adapted to show business because of its shimmering and sensual qualities. Gold toned mesh resembles spun gold when spot lighting is used to feature a performer. During the early 1920's such theatrical giants as Irving Berlin used mesh costumes in his *Music Box Reviews,* Norman Bel Geddes mesh draped the elephants in Ringling Brothers Circus acts, while Billy Rose obtained special effects from the use of mesh in his *Waterfollies* extravaganzas.

Hollywood used ring mesh extensively in the production of period films such as *The Crusades, Joan of Arc, El Cid,* and numerous others requiring whole armies to be clothed in chain mail. Of course the ring mesh provided was a mere fraction of the original mail weight and was produced at great speed.

In the 1930's mesh scarves and collars were worn variously about the neck, head, shoulders, and the waist. Today they have become elegant halters, blouses, shirts, skirts, and cowls available in a wide variety of colors and hues generally worn in the evening for formal occasions or by theatrical performers.

The flamboyant pianist, Liberace, wore suits entirely made of mesh, whereas other more subdued male entertainers have restricted themselves to jackets of the glittering material. Full length mesh gowns have continued to be a favorite of chanteuses such as Gertrude Neissen, Josephine Baker, Beatrice Lillie, Hildgearde, Diane Carroll, Dolly Parton, The Supremes, and others performing in stage, television and intimate nightclub settings. *(Figures 202, 203, 204 and 205.)*

Lightweight aluminum mesh is now favored over brass or other metals as it allows greater ease of movement and is cooler under the glare of powerful lights. A half century ago such a garment would have cost about $500. In 1988, its custom handcrafted counterpart would cost a hefty $5,000 + or about ten times as much.

In those early days some strange items were also manufactured by Whiting and Davis. One of the most mind boggling was an entire theatre viewing screen made of very porous mesh. How effective it's reflective qualities were is not known. Remember the movies were an infant industry and countless innovations were tried in every aspect of the business. Next came a theatre curtain made of glittering mesh weighing hundreds of pounds, if not tons! It was a durable, fireproof asset to those pleasure palaces which once ringed the nation. They had less appeal for the custodians who from time-to-time had to remove them for cleaning.

Not all the entertainers were professional for in 1926, a proud grandfather had a mesh dress woven for his granddaughter's (Laura Miller Rice) dance recital. Impishly holding an ostrich fan and balancing precariously on one ballet slipper she was photographed for all time in her mesh creation. *(Figure 207.)*

COSTUME COMPACT BAGS

Some charming combinations of purse and exterior compact were attempted with great success in the first quarter of the twentieth century and their popularity with collectors has increased over the years. After World War I, young girls and more liberated older women used cosmetics and even the public application of powder, rouge, and lipstick was not considered a social faux-pas. Purse manufacturers were happy to accommodate.

Among the costume-compact bags, one of the most beautiful was a Dresden mesh displaying either a *swinging* enameled compact set in the center of the exterior frame; or the *corner* compact, which as the name implies, was a rather plainly enameled compact affixed in ornamental metalwork to the upper left hand corner of the frame. Both types of mesh were used in these compact novelties but the flat mesh was not as well suited to the compact as the Dresden. Possibly the color schemes and bolder patterns failed to harmonize with the compact which should have been the center of attention. The floral bouquets shown on *Figure 275* purses 4 and 5 illustrate the point. The enameled barrel slide was well adapted to the simple frame and even the bugle shaped links of the carry chain were enameled in a complimentary shade.

Each of the four models shown is four inches wide but the Dresden mesh appears to be longer. The Ivorytone purse is one third the price of the C4 model selling for $43.50. Those at the bottom of the page have barrel catches and identical compacts but the enameled mesh is $14.50 less than the Dresden. As these are **wholesale** prices from the year 1928, one can reasonably expect the current retail price from an antique dealer to have *greatly increased*. These quality purses were never inexpensive. Collectors should not be unduly alarmed by present day prices if they are found in good condition, especially the choicer Dresden mesh.

A plain gold tone mesh vanity bag is shown at *Figure 214* with a chased monogrammed cover bearing the initials L.M. The beveled mirror was part of the lid and the powder and rouge were in the base.

F&B manufactured a very striking purse measuring four inches long and three inches wide in sterling, *(Plate 457)* which contained an enameled compact, three tassels, three sapphire clasps aligned to the right side. The center portion has a machine turned engraving with the name ISLA bordered by white enameling. The interior has two receptacles probably for rouge and lipstick. It is dated 1923 and has some of the features we associate with Art Deco.

THE PICCADILLY

In 1923 Sears and Roebuck featured a page on mesh bags with well rendered cuts, more than half of which was devoted to ring mesh purses. The bottom half illustrated vanity cases with attached chains or finger rings. Only one purse was of armor mesh. Five years later the reverse was true. Vanity cases had captured milady's fancy and the three mesh bags were relegated to an inferior advertising status. A Whiting and Davis Dresden mesh bag registered as the Piccadilly was referred to as "Piccadilly Style." Relatively abundant, to this day it remains a collector's favorite. *(Figures 224 and 225.)*

A combination of compact and bag was satisfied by placing a diminutive powder container on the exterior of the purse as an integral part of the narrow frame. It was capped by a highly reflective metal surface and tipped with a dangling silver tab which when tugged downward, caused the cover to spring open. In the registered *Piccadilly*, the model name, number, patent date and maker's insignia were to be found on the back of the vanity. *(Figure 215.)*

There were numerous variations on this style. The vanity was to be fitted with a silvered mirror; the shapes ran the gamut from square, to round, to octagonal; the embossing became florid and engraved initials and/or given names were commonplace. A purse called the *Deauville Vanity* incorporated the powder compact into the strap handle itself. *(Figure 219.)*

The narrow, dome-shaped frame remained relatively constant; the bottom finished in ball, curtain, and tassel styles. They were largely heavy silver plated with imitation sapphire fasteners in plated frames, however, both gold and sterling specimens in fine Dresden mesh are obtainable though not plentiful. The precious metals had small genuine sapphire gem set twist closures. The ultimate in this style was reached in a subtly

enameled mesh and generously proportioned vanity such as the elegant example shown at *Plate 486* discussed above. Even the barrel slide fastener and chain links were enameled as well as the frame.

A sterling version seen at *Figure 288* has a wrist strap with affixed coin purse with matching rosette edging on the larger purse as well as the coin. The larger purse contains an octogonal shaped exterior compact though the union of the two purses is presently more unique than the compact.

A coarse mesh capped by a celluloid compact is shown at *Plate 476*. Unfortunately there is considerable fringe damage, but enough of the detail remains so the tab and matching design on the cover can be appreciated for their simplicity.

A much admired tiny purse was made in great quantities in the 1920's and since most of them were of precious metals they are still to be found at antique shows and auctions. The price, which can be dear, is determined by the amount and condition of the enameling, the weight, the fittings, and the overall appeal. Some versions contain coin holders, ivory writing sheets, sterling pencils, an inside mirror, powder and rouge receptacles, and on occasion a money or card clip. It is not uncommon to discover a date, the owner's name, and as on this one, a patent date and manufacturer as well. *Figure 240.* Size 3″ long × 2″ wide as are almost all those of this type.

Hardly larger than an inch-and-a-half in diameter, a diminutive purse with finger ring contains a section for makeup and mirror in one section and a compartment for small articles such as change, key, etc. in the other end. It is made of metal braid and jewel set filagree. Examples are shown in the section on novelties.

Mr. Whiting, The Man Some years ago an acquaintance wished to have an unusual purse photographed and we were puzzled by it. It had one curious feature, a small cross set into the frame and we suspected it had some religious significance. We were delighted when browsing through some advertising material

Illustrations about one half size

1929

W·141   **$21.00 ea.**
Enamel Costume Bag. Pouch Shape. Extra Fine Weave. Silk lined and Mirror. Frame 5 in. wide.

THE POUCH SHAPE
is the newest
WHITING & DAVIS
Costume Bag Creation
Inspired by
PAUL POIRET
celebrated Parisian creator
of costume bag designs
exclusively for this
company

W 142   **$15.00 ea.**
Enamel "Beadlite" Costume Bag. Pouch Shape. Silk lined and Mirror.   Frame 5 in. wide.

W 144   **$27.00 ea.**
"Dresden" Enamel Costume Bag. Pouch Shape. Fine Soldered Mesh. Silk lined and Mirror. Frame 5 in. wide.

W 143   **$6.00 ea.**
Enamel Costume Bag. Pouch Shape. Silk lined and Mirror. Frame 4 in. wide.

W 146   **$21.00 ea.**
"Dresden" Enamel Costume Bag. Pouch Shape. Fine Soldered Mesh.   Silk lined and Mirror. Frame 4 in. wide.

W 145   **$13.50 ea.**
Enamel Costume Bag. Pouch Shape. Extra Fine Weave. Silk lined and Mirror. Frame 4 in. wide.

MESH WHITING & DAVIS CO

Figure 246

425

Four Dresden mesh showing variety of sizes and patterns. It should be pointed out that Dresden mesh was always fringed in ring mesh, never with balls or heavier rings as in flat mesh.

Figure 248

Highly effective black and white ad with a wealth of information.

Plate 468

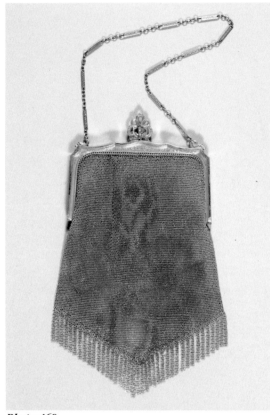

Plate 469

Plate 470

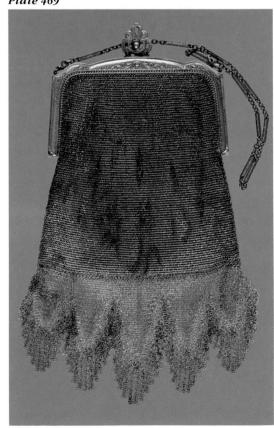

Plate 471

Figure 248

431

Plates 478–481

Four magnificent pearlized Mandalians. Two top examples are baby mesh and almost identical. Bottom left has a base treatment often used by Mandalian. Bottom right has chain and teardrop fringe. Though numerous examples are presented, teardrops are not plentiful. Whiting and Davis examples with teardrops are truly scarce.

Figure 249

Sheet of enameled mesh bags from a jeweler's wholesale book. Circa 1925. Many of the examples are these same designs. Some of these patterns are shown in this chapter. This ad shows original wholesale prices and all pertinent details.

Figure 250

On page 436:

A highly original, beautifully shaped ad. Even more effective without color.

Plate 478

Plate 479

Plate 480

Plate 481

Finest Quality Hard Enameled Mesh Bags
SEASON'S SMARTEST COLORS—FANCY DESIGNS

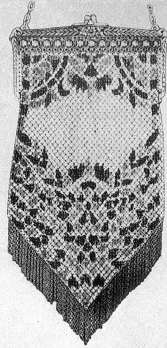
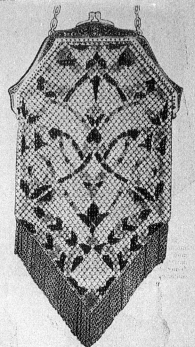

No. B3101—Lustro pearl enameled, white, green, rose, blue and black color combination, very fine baby mesh, silk lined, fancy silver plated frame and handle, 9¼ in. long and 4 in. wide. Price $24.00

No. B3102—Hard enameled, white, green, rose, and black color combination, fancy silver plated frame and chain handle, silk lined, 9 in. long, 4¼ in. wide. Price...........$11.25
No. B3103—Same as above, in white, green, orange and brown color combination. Price $11.25

No. B3104—Hard enameled, yellow, orange, white and black color combination, silver plated frame and chain handle, 7½ inches long, 4½ inches wide. Price $7.50
No. B3105—Same as above, in cream, orange, green and black color combination. Price $7.50

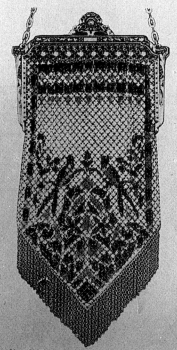

No. B3106—Hard enameled, cream, blue, orange and black color combination, silver plated frame and chain handle, 8 inches long and 3¾ inches wide. Price $6.00
No. B3107—Same as above, in green, black and gold color combination. Price $6.00

No. B3108—Hard enameled, cream, orange, and black color combination, silver plated frame and chain handle, 7 inches long, 3¾ inches wide. Price $4.00
No. B3109—Same as above, in white, green, and black colors, with green gold plated frame and handle. Price $4.00

No. B3110—Hard enameled grey, blue, black, and orange colors, silver plated frame and chain handle, 7 inches long, 3¾ inches wide. Price $4.00
No. B3111—Same as above, in cream, green, purple and black color combination. Price $4.00

Figure 249

435

Hand in Hand with Fashion

Illustrations about one half size

91—"Beadlite" Costume Bag
Silver plated. Silk lined with pocket and mirror. 4 ins. wide.
$13.50 each

92—Enamel Costume Bag
Extra fine weave. Silver plated. Silk lined with pocket and mirror. 4 ins. wide. $18.00 each

93—Enamel Costume Bag
Extra fine weave. 24 karat finish. Antique gold finish frame. Silk lined with pocket and mirror. 4 ins. wide.
$21.00 each

94—"Beadlite" Costume Bag
24 karat gold finish. Antique gold finish frame. Silk lined with pocket and mirror. 4 ins. wide.
$19.50 each

95—"Beadlite" Costume Bag
Silver plated. Silk lined with pocket and mirror. 5 ins. wide. $21.00 each

96—Enamel Costume Bag
Extra fine weave. 24 karat finish. Antique gold finish frame. Silk lined with pocket and mirror. 5 ins. wide. $27.00 each

MESH WHITING & DAVIS CO. BAGS
TRADE MARK REG. U.S. AND CAN.

438

Figure 252

Plate 482

Plate 483

Plate 484

Plate 485

Figure 252

Whiting and Davis 1927 ad showing their use of tear-drops. Full purse was nearly seven inches long.

Plates 482–485

Four Mandalians showing the wide range of patterns offered.

MORE THAN TEN MILLION WOMEN
WILL SEE THESE MAGAZINES
BEFORE
CHRISTMAS

Get aboard the Whiting & Davis "Save a Man" advertising campaign. Thousands of women in *your* community are being told about this opportunity for them to own a genuine Whiting & Davis Mesh Costume Bag this Christmas. Color pages and black and white advertisements appearing repeatedly during the holiday season will bring sales into *your* store.

Don't fail to take advantage of the special offer contained in this folder and send us the enclosed postcard for special display assortment at once. Put them in your windows and on your counters on the beautiful display easel shown (sent free of charge with each bag) and get these extra-profits that we are making possible for you. Your wholesaler has them in stock now. Send us the postcard and we will see that you receive them immediately.

This is the biggest and most intensive advertising campaign ever put behind Whiting & Davis Mesh Costume Bags. We are doing it this year so that you may derive increased business and greater profits by tying up with it. *Only by immediate action on your part can you get this extra profit.*

WHITING & DAVIS COMPANY
World's Largest Manufacturers of Costume Bags
Makers of Costume Jewelry for Everyone
PLAINVILLE (NORFOLK COUNTY), MASS.
In Canada: Sherbrooke, Quebec

New York:
366 Fifth Avenue

Chicago:
F. E. Whiting, 31 N. State Street

*THE BIG
WHITING & DAVIS
"SAVE A MAN"
ADVERTISING CAMPAIGN

We are presenting to more than ten million women of America the opportunity of owning a Whiting & Davis Mesh Costume Bag. All they have to do is send us the name of someone close to them to whom we might make the suggestion of giving a Whiting & Davis Costume Mesh Bag as a Christmas gift.

By returning the enclosed order postcard, *your* name will be registered as a dealer who can supply the wants of prospective customers and we will send you the names on coupons which we receive from your community.

WHITING & DAVIS
COSTUME BAGS

BENEFIT FROM THIS BIG ADVERTISING CAMPAIGN BY MAILING THE POSTCARD RIGHT NOW

450

Figure 263

Figures 264–265

*How can you tell
him what you
really want?*

Every Christmas, to many women, comes disappointment—because the gift most desired is not received.

It is difficult, frequently impossible, to tell "him" your secret wish. Yet, there *is* a way to get the Christmas remembrance you will prize.

The Whiting & Davis Company, creators of the Mesh Costume Bag, devised it. It is very simple, very effective. From an unknown source, Santa Claus perhaps, there comes to "him" the helpful suggestion, "She wants a Whiting & Davis Mesh Costume Bag"—and it is done.

You simply fill in now the coupon below with the name and address of the person from whom you wish to receive a Whiting & Davis Mesh Costume Bag.

Without revealing your identity, a message will go to that person suggesting the desirability of such a gift—always dear to every woman's heart, today doubly so, because of the present vogue of femininity in Fashion.

So, fill in the coupon NOW—for a happier Christmas. The subtle message of gift suggestion will be sent at an appropriate later date to the person whose name you give.

WHITING & DAVIS COMPANY
*World's Largest Manufacturers of Costume Bags
Makers of Costume Jewelry for Everyone*
PLAINVILLE (*Norfolk County*). MASS.
In Canada: SHERBROOKE, QUÉBEC

Always a desired style *accessory*, the return of the ultra-feminine to Fashion makes the Mesh Costume Bag a style *necessity*. As created by Whiting & Davis in a great variety of clever designs and colorful combinations, the Mesh Costume Bag adds the final touch in smart costuming.

Hand in Hand with Fashion

Dresden enamel soldered Mesh Bag, No. W-24. Silk-lined, with mirror. Enamel frame and chain.

Look for this trademark stamped on the frame of every genuine Whiting & Davis Mesh Costume Bag. It stands for over 50 years of creative craftsmanship.

WHITING & DAVIS
Mesh
COSTUME BAGS

WHITING & DAVIS CO.   Dept. J-11
Plainville   (Norfolk County)   Mass.
Gentlemen: Will you send your Gift Suggestion letter to the name and address below—without, of course, in any way revealing my identity. Thank you.

Name...

Street and No..

City........................   State....................

How
can you tell him
what you
really want?

Figure 265

Figure 264

451

STAR SERIES PURSES

When Whiting and Davis decided to issue a series of metal mesh purses featuring Hollywood stars they selected two actors and two actresses, three of whom are still within the memory of at least a segment of the movie going public. The third, Reneé Adoreé, is a puzzle, for she never attained the stature of the others. Though forgotten today, she was once popular in silent films. Clark Gable, Marion Davies, and Charlie Chaplin are properly included. Marion Davies was never an accomplished actress, but her involvement with William Randolph Hearst and his desperate efforts to make her an actress, comprise a fascinating story.

So rare are the portraits that I originally assumed Charlie Chaplin to be much older than it really was. About fifteen years ago a series of portrait purses called **The Stars** was issued much like the more recent **Heritage Collection** series. *(Figure 280.)* Chaplin was done in black and white, and the remaining three in colors. They originally sold for ten dollars and were about five by four inches. For some reason they failed to appeal to the public and were disposed of. Today, if they can be located at all, they are among the costliest of purses! It's the old story of supply and demand. Earlier issues of Shirley Temple and Mickey Mouse were made in childrens' sizes. *(Plate 487.)*

CLARK GABLE

Clark Gable is still remembered as possibly the screen's most durable popular romantic figure, admired by men and adored by women, the mark of a true superstar. *(Plate 488.)*

Clark Gable's real name was the same as his stage name, most unusual in Hollywood. He was born in Cadiz, Ohio, on February 1, 1901. An only child, his mother died shortly after his birth and for a time he was raised by an aunt and uncle. His father, an oil wildcatter, (by all accounts a handsome man who drank to excess), remarried and Clark went to live with him and his step mother, Jennie Dunlop.

Jennie had no children and lavished her whole affection on Clark who was a fairly good student and well behaved. She had high hopes of making a gentleman of him. Bored with farm and small town life, he was 16 when he left school for the theatre though he worked spasmodically in the oil fields and at lumbering.

He was clumsy, awkward, and totally lacking in sophistication, but what he lacked in these qualities he made up for in charm, and a driving desire to became an accomplished actor. In this he was eminently successful. In the process of becoming the king of the film industry he married and moved up the ladder of success through a series of five advantageous marriages. More than a mere gigolo, he became a studio property who worked in over 100 films and was known as a consummate actor, never late; never complaining about working conditions; liked by all in the industry.

His name was magic and if he appeared in a film it was almost always successful. His major achievement was the role of Rhett Butler in *Gone With the Wind,* and he considered it one of his proudest accomplishments.

With all that can be attributed to him as an actor, he was tormented by excessive drinking and smoking, adulation by fans which fostered reckless philandering, and a restless pursuit of the good life which caused his premature death at the age of fifty-nine, on November 16, 1960. He was the last of the great male stars.

CHARLIE CHAPLIN

Charlie Chaplin was a genius of comedy, a talented and farsighted director; a many faceted man who unfortunately ran afoul of so many elements within the government and his own profession that his declining years were spent in self imposed exile in Switzerland. Reams have been written about Chaplin's artistry and his proper place in the development of the film industry.

His purse is sensibly rendered in black and white (the others are in vivid colors) as Chaplin had his greatest successes in that colorless, silent medium. His profile is so famous that even those who have never seen his films recognize the lonely little man with the unflattering mustache, derby and shabby, battered clothing. *(Figure 279.)*

MARION DAVIES (MARION DOURAS)

Marion Davies was born Marion Douras on January 3, 1897, and died of cancer September 22, 1976.

A warm, comical, generous, and beautiful woman, her finer qualities are generally overlooked for the then sensational fact that she was the mistress companion of William Randolph Hearst who loved her dearly for over thirty years. Had they been less visible and Hearst more discreet the affair would have attracted less attention, but this was not to be. *(Plate 487. Figures 277 and 278.)*

Hearst wanted her to pattern her career after that of Mary Pickford, playing demure and innocent girls and to this end he spent seven million dollars promoting her films but her talent was misdirected and squandered. Marion Davies was a comedienne and a good one, but Hearst was adamant. Ironically she did resemble Pickford when her hair was arranged in long curls as *Figure 276* shows and the two were good friends for many years.

She made many films and was a close friend of all the great and near great in the motion picture business. She acted as their hostess at San Simeon, entertaining entire train loads of them as they passed the weekends four hundred miles removed from the Hollywood scene.

Her influence extended to all levels of society and she met every prominent figure of her day from former presidents to scientists. Through Joseph Kennedy (whose name was for years linked with that of Gloria Swanson) she was a good friend of that family and attended their weddings, inaugurals, and other happy events.

The richest woman in Hollywood at Hearst's death, by the early 1970's she had doubled her fortune to twenty million dollars. Her great wealth and subsequent marriage brought her no particular happiness though her charities were legend, especially toward children and hospitals.

The purse is a fair likeness, though the eyes and eyebrows are well delineated, the hair tint is far too dark.

RENEÉ ADOREÉ

Reneé Adoreé whose real name was Reneé La Font, was born September 30, 1898, in Lille, France. She died October 5, 1933, in Tujunga, California, of tuberculosis.

A screen actress and circus performer she danced in the Folies Bergere, and made 38 films in Hollywood between 1921–1930. They ranged from *Made in Heaven* to her last film *Redemption.* The film titles suggest the films were rather risqué. She was in *The Big Parade* which was Marion Davies' all time favorite film.

Following W.W. I things and people French were considered ultra sophisticated and naughty. Many French actresses with names like Fifi O'Dorsay, Anna Held, and Pola Negri enjoyed considerable box office appeal.

She lacks glamour as shown on her star purse, and no photograph could be located to determine what she actually looked like at the height of her career.

Some Rare and/or Unusual Meshes

It is impractical to discuss more than a few of the astounding array of 1,200 different frames used by Whiting and Davis over the years. The modifications were slight in most cases consisting of: a wider or narrower frame, different finishes, different closings, odd piercing or filagree work, embossings, repousse work, enameled designs on sterling, enameled bridge work set into plate, paste stones and invisible hinges.

Among the rare editions was a rigid handled purse *(Figure 298,)* which also failed to excite the buying public. Mr. Rice feels the ratio of sales was about 500 to 1 in favor of the chain link handle. The rigid handle which folded to the side was a nice purse and it is surprising the innovation was not better received. It reflects the resistance to change for the handle was made of polished metal and was quite handsome. So few of these exist today they are as rare as **The Star** purses and offer a challenge for the collector.

Rigid handles were a constant source of experimentation and most of them must have gone down to defeat. *Figure 281* is more material costs, and a demand for larger size purses gave rise to plain mesh more in tune with current casual life styles.

UNUSUAL MESH COMBINATIONS

Some odd combinations appear from time to time which are difficult to place in a proper category. Such an example is *Figure 226* a combination of black velvet and ring mesh overskirt. I strongly suspect this was a marriage formed by removing the top part of the purse (whether frame or compact) and carefully sewing each ring to the velvet reticule leaving the side rings intact for a short distance. Actually it is quite attractive when drawn together. It is possible the mesh was damaged and salvaging a favorite bag was possible by forming this unique union.

Another strange combination was a ring mesh reticule with small glass beads. *(Figure 223.)* Only one such purse has been seen and it is possible it was in the same category with the previous example. If it was a merger of two damaged purses, it was skillfully done even to the addition of the mesh rosettes at the base. This rather poor quality reproduction photograph was used as it was sold many years ago and no more suitable example could be located. It was approximately four inches wide and six inches long.

Armor mesh was lined with satin or silk as a general rule, but a few experimental purses lined with plain mesh are found. One such had a brilliant blue lining contrasting sharply with its silvery spider web exterior design. As the rings faced one another and the flat mesh formed the lining, the danger of catching objects on the sharp edges was reduced. The added weight and additional cost of the metal compared to fabric would have caused this type of lining (shown on the beadlite *Figures 227 and 229*) to be discontinued. It is, therefore a rare example.

MINIATURE RING MESHES

None of the following tiny purses is larger than two or three inches. They were intended to be used as coin purses, although each has more character than bags many times their size. Some collectors prefer these pint size pursettes. The currently revived practice of wearing one about the neck on a long chain is quite fashionable. They are only a fraction of the cost of full sized purses as well.

1. *Figure 232* is made of extremely reflective, brass, wide armor mesh with curved sides and unusually artistic drops; this one looks as if it were beaded. Unlike most meshes, it is of French origin. The frame is nickel plated, embossed brass.

2. *Figure 231.* A letter seal is attached to the rings of this sterling silver coarse mesh. In the days before glues and self sealing envelopes, the seal was applied to correspondence to assure it was read by no one other than the person for whom it was intended. Seals were often made of precious metals, decorated with gems, elaborately scrolled and came in their own little cases. This one may have been added but it is a charming idea.

3. *Figure 230* is also sterling silver and exemplifies the sorority emblems made for special organizations. They may have been awards, college mementoes, or remembrances from one girl to another. They are found from time to time and are sometimes enameled or set with semi-precious stones. They would have been commissioned by individual university clubs and other organizations.

4. *Figure 233.* Another fine mesh with distinctive drops was comprised of a long bar punched at each end; a small solid ball at one end and attached to the ring mesh at the other. A short Dorothy cuff with ball decoration gracefully finished the top. A thin bracelet just large enough to accommodate the fingers is soldered to the chain.

5. *Figure 237.* The sterling coin purse monogrammed GMF looks as if the mesh were heavy wire when actually it is very fine. The rings radiate from the center piece in concentric circles and are joined to the frame through the drillings. I believe this one is hand made and at least a century old.

6. *Figure 242.* The frolicking cherubs on this Italian pewter purse, not much larger than the picture, are deeply engraved. It could be used as an evening purse and undoubtedly was, but it would be equally useful as a card case. The use of antique card cases among business men as well as women is increasing. They add a touch of elegance and if cards are

made to their dimensions, are a useful as well as charming.

7. *Figures 211, 263 and Plate 490.* Because it is difficult to determine size from a one dimensional picture, the childs' size Whiting and Davis is shown next to a full sized Mandalian for comparison. This is the size that is shown in the Christmas illustrations. The small scaled, simple patterns were usually done in pastels.

DRESDEN MESHES WITH ENAMELED FRAMES

Fine Dresden meshes with enameled or jewel set frames are not plentiful and the collector should anticipate paying much more for them than simpler and plainer meshes.

Two of the finest examples are shown here; both are of Whiting and Davis manufacture. *Plate 467* contains a row of seed pearls set in a black enameled surface, edged with a delicate gold colored metal tracery; a matching bow knot set into the corners. The standing shell closure and pearl set drop are elegant touches. The chain is a flat, sturdy braid.

The simple pattern allows the eye to concentrate on the scalloped terminals. Note the attention to detail. As a few rows are made of a larger mesh than the body, they assume a dainty laciness all the more effective when done in a stark white against the subdued pastels.

The same combination of white and pastel enamels is used in *Plate 466.* The modified peacock pastel design is a little more intense, but it is the frame which is so outstanding. Navy blue bandings with white stippling, a prominent tab and standing shell closure are completed with a silver colored snake chain handle. It is such a stunning purse that all who have seen it are not at all surprised at its price tag which is about twice that of less striking meshes.

Relatively large among mesh bags, both of the aforementioned measure five by eight inches, have the original silk linings, and are in superb condition.

Quite a different impression is gained from *Plate 475* with its narrow frame, somber colors, Art Deco design, step cut terminals and matching clasp. The mesh is

Dresden and equally fine, but the frame and overall dimensions relegated this purse to a different price category than the previous two examples.

STENCILING AND ENAMELING

The process used in enameling Dresden mesh was somewhat different than that used in decorating flat mesh. Early in the industry lacquering or enameling was done entirely by hand and frequently done in the home either by a factory employee and members of his family or individuals outside of the factory who worked on a subcontractor basis such as was was noted in an earlier quotation from Mr. Whiting's article dealing with early mesh construction.

Flat enameled metal mesh was accomplished by first applying a background color such as white, a pastel, black, or neutral shade, then positioning a stencil over the mesh and painting in the design by hand. Later this was done by spray-painting. Each color was applied separately and baked before another was added. This was done *before* the mesh was attached to the frame by hand spiraling.

A close examination of enameled mesh will reveal the enamel does not completely fill each spider and even in the days of cheap labor, it would have been prohibitively costly to have filled in the background color skillfully enough to complete the design had the background not been applied first. In addition, designs did not necessarily conform to the shape of the spider. The case is similar to that of an oil painting which is not particularly pleasing when closely viewed; the overall pattern is best seen given some perspective.

Stenciling of the ring mesh actually presented fewer, if different problems. The stenciling could be done directly on the rings and the patterns were indistinct and less structured than those done on flat mesh. It is this shadowy effect which fails to appeal to some people but like the avocado, it grows on one if given a chance. *(Plates 468 and 469.)*

Dresden mesh bags were frequently very ample in size, some of the larger ones measuring eleven inches in length. The delicate patterns tended toward abstractions, muted

Figure 288

Figure 289

Whiting & Davis Mesh Bags

"Gifts That Last"

Paris originated and bestowed the favor of fashion upon the twin mesh bag, which Whiting & Davis now introduce to fashionable America in "The Dansant."

A combination of smart daintiness—the little bag designed for the things one just never can find, and another a bit larger, joined by a silver cord.

Entirely fascinating

WHITING & DAVIS COMPANY
Plainville, Norfolk County, Mass.

Figure 290

The Dansant
Bracelet
Mesh Bag

the latest whim of Paris

Figures 288–289

The twin mesh bag called The Dansant, *made in many variations, often had a compact cover as in Figure 288 or a solid compact case and interior coin purse as in Figure 289. Both Whiting and Davis.*

Gifts That Last

THE real spirit of Christmas is caught in the fine spun gold or shimmering silver of a Whiting & Davis Mesh Bag. Whether handmade, or less costly, this gift is so thoroughly fitting, so entirely captivating to feminine fancy that it contrasts boldly against drab, commonplace remembrances.

Very *new* are bags of SUNSET MESH—a colorful blending of red gold-, green gold-, and platinum-finish—so tarnish and wear proof that they can actually be washed.

For the wee girl there are miniature Whiting & Davis Mesh Bags like mother's. Cunningly made in gold, silver, and less precious metals. Priced to match the tiny wearer.

The Whiting & Davis trade-mark and tag guarantee quality. Look for them on every mesh bag.

WHITING & DAVIS COMPANY
PLAINVILLE, NORFOLK COUNTY, MASS.

The
Princess
Mary

In
Sunset
Mesh

Whiting & Davis MESH BAGS

Figure 291

483

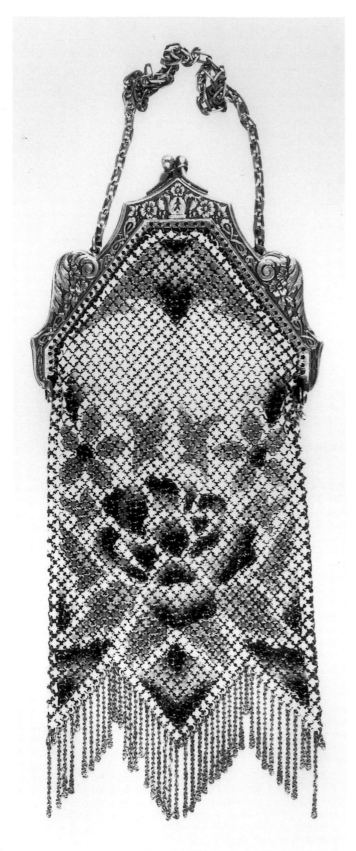

484   *Figure 292*   *Figure 293*

Figure 294

Figure 295

Figures 292–293

Very subtle differences in size, shape, and fringing were overcome by the use of pastels or bold colors on these flat enamel Mandalians.

Figures 294–295

The difference in flat and ring mesh is clearly evident in these two bags which are about the same size, vintage, and use of bold colors.

485

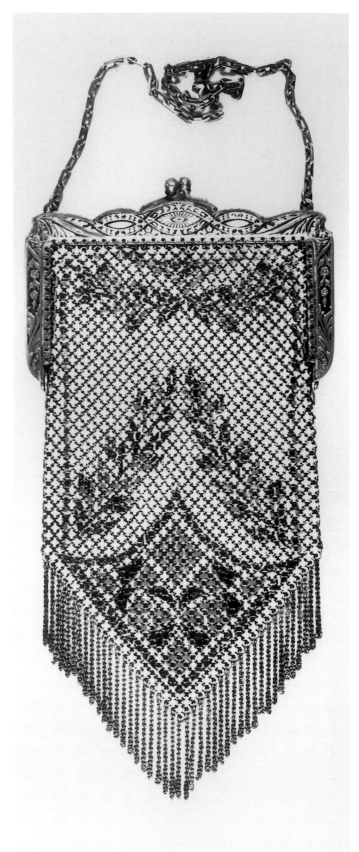

Figure 296

Figure 297

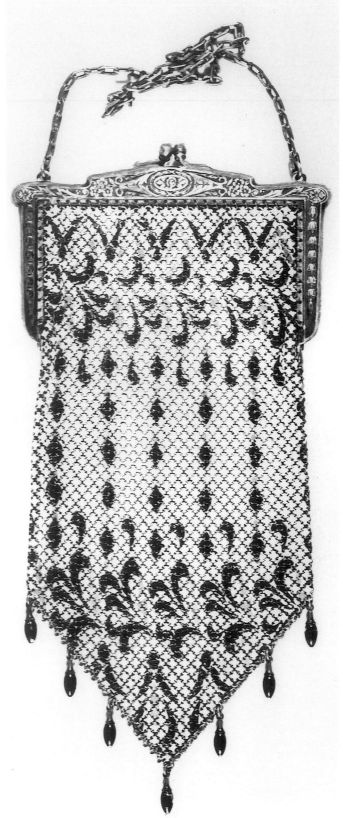

Figure 298   *Figure 299*   487

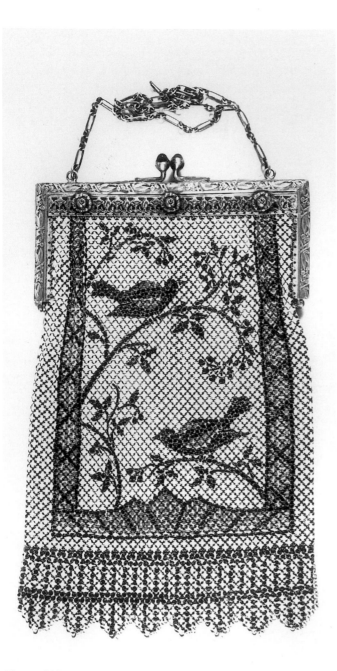

Figure 300

**Figure 300
Plate 489**

*Few naturalistic
designs were used by
either Mandalian or
Whiting and Davis.
Butterflies and birds
were exceptions;
possibly the shapes
adapted well.*

488

Plate 489

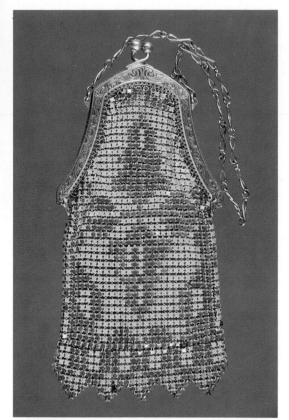

Plate 490

Plate 491

Plate 492

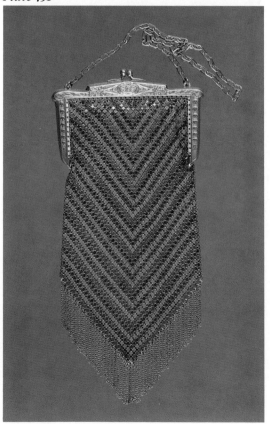

Plate 493

Plates 490–493

Though pink and lavender are favorite shades of all women, few metals use them. Four exceptions are here. Top left is a child's Whiting and Davis. Upper right is a full sized colorful Whiting and Davis. Bottom left is a large, charming, violet pattern atypical of Mandalian. Vandyke skirt was not an earmark of theirs. Bands of pinks, bottom right, are pleasingly simple.

From previous pages 486–487:

Figures 296–297

Bags done for children used the same patterns as for adults often using vivid colors as in Figure 296. The Mandalian at Figure 297 has a classical motif and was done in pastels. Standard size. They may have done miniatures.

Figure 298

Nondescript pattern. Rare rigid handle folded to one side. It should have been very popular but was not.

Figure 299

Teardrop Mandalian done in an unappealing orange and black was also a loser.

489

Plate 494

One of the more esoteric Whiting and Davis offerings was this bezel set topaz bag with topaz chain. The number of topaz varied. The ground was plain, and the effect sumptuous.

Plate 494

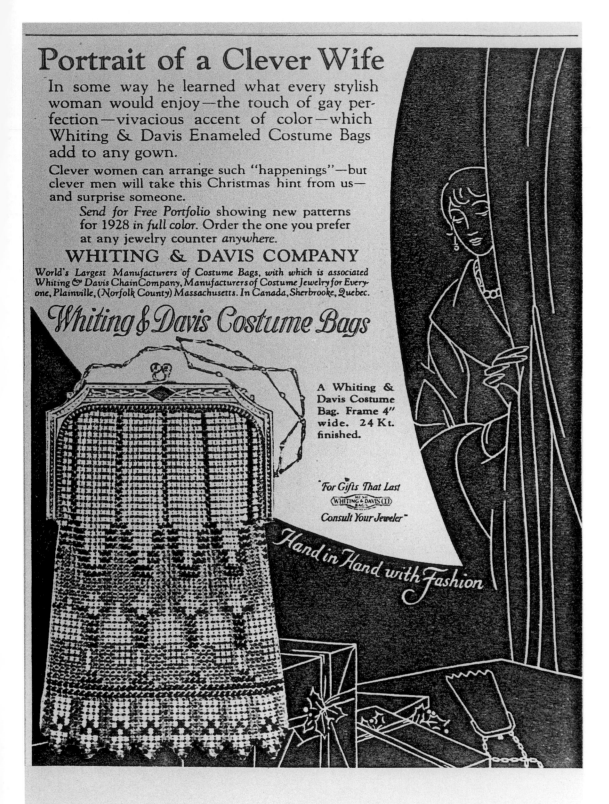

Portrait of a Clever Wife

In some way he learned what every stylish woman would enjoy—the touch of gay perfection—vivacious accent of color—which Whiting & Davis Enameled Costume Bags add to any gown.

Clever women can arrange such "happenings"—but clever men will take this Christmas hint from us—and surprise someone.

Send for Free Portfolio showing new patterns for 1928 *in full color*. Order the one you prefer at any jewelry counter *anywhere*.

WHITING & DAVIS COMPANY

World's Largest Manufacturers of Costume Bags, with which is associated Whiting & Davis Chain Company, Manufacturers of Costume Jewelry for Everyone, Plainville, (Norfolk County) Massachusetts. In Canada, Sherbrooke, Quebec.

Whiting & Davis Costume Bags

A Whiting & Davis Costume Bag. Frame 4" wide. 24 Kt. finished.

For Gifts That Last
WHITING & DAVIS
BAGS
Consult Your Jeweler

Hand in Hand with Fashion

Figure 301

florals, illusions of watered taffeta, and borders. They do not have the crisp, sharp edges found in the flat meshes, but those who prefer subtle graphics on supple mesh should consider the Dresden.

Both Dresden and enameled flat mesh were made for about twenty-five years. No attempt has ever been made to reissue Dresden as has been done with enameled flat mesh, probably because it was usually done on fine ring mesh which is no longer made. Stenciling on coarse ring mesh produced a far less attractive purse and may not even have been called Dresden mesh. *(Figure 283.)*

The bold, warmer, primary colors, of orange, red, yellow, (usually used in combination with the black accents which distinguish the look of the 1930's), were characteristic of both types of these enamels. The patterns are sometimes arranged in straight lines, cubes, dots, and/or symmetrical abstracts. Other examples are jumbled into a veritable crazy quilt lacking harmony both as to color and design.

The more traditional floral, bird, and geometric patterns used muted pastel shades in innovative combinations. Softly feminine, they are enduring favorites.

Machine-made metal mesh does not lend itself to rounded edges so purses are either rectangular or come to a tapered terminal point, although round hand fabricated sterling silver purses are not unknown especially among the early reticules. Machine mesh was produced to lower the cost of production as well as accelerate output and rounded and other novel shapes would require much additional hand labor in fashioning and finishing. It is possible also that the rounded shape would have been limited to a small diameter and been less graceful as well.

The frames used on the Dresden meshes had a tendency to be a trifle wider and plainer than those on other meshes. The pyramid closure was often a ball and socket type and featured a novel serpent chain handle.

During the comparatively few years when enameled ring mesh was made, Germany and France were the only other nations to produce it. There were a number of German mesh makers among them Spidel, best known for their watch bands, who were active just prior to W W I. Anti German sentiment and the Alien Custodial Property Act eliminated them as viable competition to the American mesh manufacturers. Their place in an already diminishing market usurped, they never regained it. This may account for the scarcity of German mesh; it was not ever a serious rival as it was limited in both scope and quality.

German purses of this type are not plentiful, they are, however, instantly recognizable. The Gothic shaped frames are exceedingly narrow, and always have embossed enameling. The patterns are usually a monochromatic, lack luster brown and green combination, and the overall dimensions are small. The frames are plainly marked GERMANY.

EVANS CASE COMPANY

The Evans Case Company began operations in North Attleboro about 1920, incorporating in 1922. Their competitors included Busby and Niles, Payne and Baker, R. Blackington, Mandalian, Whiting and Davis, and numerous others. They manufactured fine ring mesh and armored mesh purses, (the mesh itself was provided by Whiting and Davis) though they ultimately were most famous for their cigarette lighters, vanity items, cosmetics cases, and other silver products.

Evans mesh is not as plentiful as that of other manufacturers and one should watch for the rare mesh bags especially made for organizations and sororities. They have the

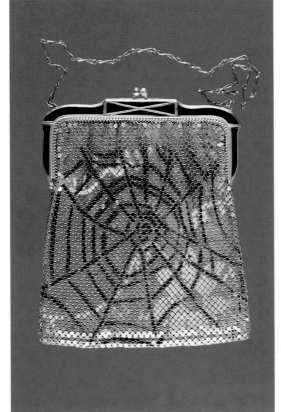

Plate 495

Plate 496

Plates 495–498

Four flat mesh Whiting and Davis purses. Upper left with daisy design is long slender type now ideal for evening wear. Child's purse in pastels. Lower left the popular spiderweb pattern on light-weight wire. Lower right done in similar wire is an abstract peacock feather on gold tones.

Plate 497

Plate 498

493

Plates 499–502

Four predominantly blue toned Whiting and Davis bags.

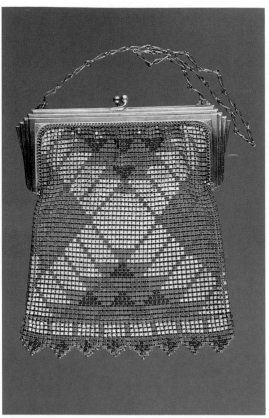

Plate 499

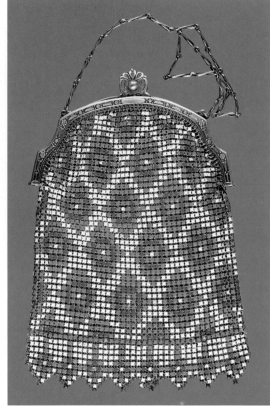

Plate 500

Plate 501

Plate 502

Plate 503

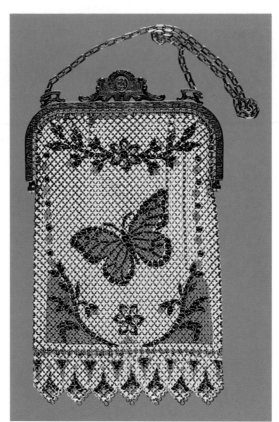

Plate 504

Plates 503–506

Four Mandalian flat mesh bags. Upper left: full blown rose in a jeweled frame. Upper right: another very desirable naturalistic design not typical of Mandalians. Lower left: easily identifiable pattern with enameled and jeweled frame. Lower right: large bag with simple rust design.

Plate 505

Plate 506

495

Plates 507–510

Four Mandalians showing their preference for the pointed end with chain fringe and a wide range of designs. Upper left: a delicate enamel insert in the frame. Upper right: a simple but effective design and chain and teardrops. Lower left: a pair of peacocks. Lower right: a cheerful pattern and embossed frame. Note the wide variety of frames offered by both manufacturers.

Plates 511–513

Three handsome Whiting and Davis bags. Note the preference for squarish shape and vandyke skirts. Upper left: large blue stones in the Greek key motif. Upper right: fret frame complementing the abstract pattern and lacy bottom. Lower left: blue rhinestones and a beaded chain.

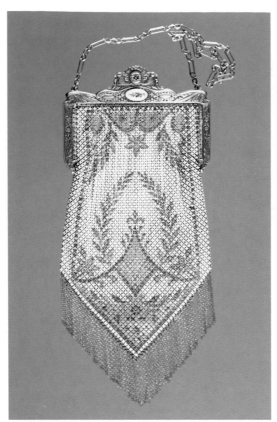

Plate 507

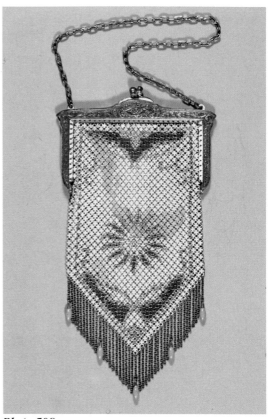

Plate 508

Plate 509

Plate 510

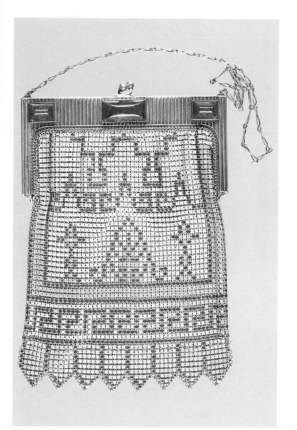

Plate 511

Plate 513

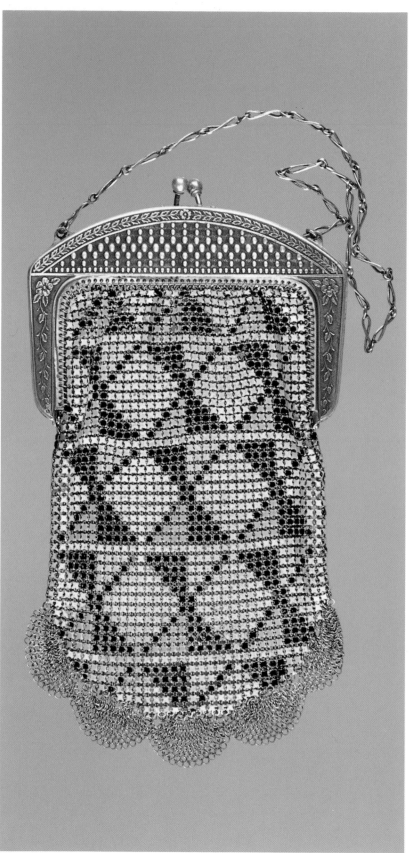

Plate 512

497

Plate 514

Plate 516

Plate 515

Plate 517

Plate 518

Plate 519

Plates 514–519

See previous pages:

(Plate 514) Near Eastern influenced Mandalian with enameled frame; vandyke trim.

(Plate 516) Mandalian with chain and teardrop fringe.

(Plate 515-517) Two versions of the Martha Washington. The green and gold is now restored. The brown bag is lacking the rings but is perfect in all other respects.

(Plate 518) Unique rosebud fold-over with mesh tassel.

(Plate 519) Blown out frame and field of rosebuds befitting its' narrow size.

Plates 520–523

Four Mandalians. Upper left and right: bracelet frames which are flexible and bend to form a box; closed with an over clasp. This version is now extremely choice. Lower left and right are identical except for the color scheme and slight variations in the jewels.

Plate 520

Plate 521

Plate 522

Plate 523

500

finest wire mesh and extremely narrow enameled frame embossed with appropriate insignia. Those I have seen bear some resemblance to German fine mesh purses. The mesh is not decorated, only the frames. Evans ultimately became famous for their vanity purses and compacts which included powder, rouge, and metal lipstick holders. Very often these cases were solid sheets of metal rather than ring or flat mesh, and were exceedingly heavy. *(Plate 459.)*

Whiting and Davis In Our Day

Not often have we the luxury of observing a company in continuous operation for a century plus fourteen years.

What of Whiting and Davis today the reader may well ask? It is a pleasure indeed to relate the company is active, forward looking, has expanded, or perhaps reverted in a sense, to what Charles A. Whiting might view as a modern return to the Whiting Chain Company.

No longer relying exclusively on the purse market they have explored every conceivable accessory potential. The stunning model at *Plate 526* is wearing a bow, blouse, earrings, and purse all made of metal mesh. She might also have selected a 43 inch full length mesh skirt, worn a mesh bow in her dancing slippers, worn a flexible bracelet or necklace, a jewel studded belt, carried a solid or mesh key chain in her purse, along with a mesh covered mini whistle, compact, card case, spray perfume, lipstick holder, lighter, cosmetic case, eyeglass holder, coin purse, and cigarette case!

For the budget minded visitor to the plant, there is a small store where bargains in last seasons' goods are for sale. A single item, to a few of any given kind are to be found here. Mr. Whiting would be amazed to see mesh used in coin purses, wallets, checkbook covers, credit card cases, cosmetic cases, eyeglass cases, key cases, mirror cases, disposable lighter covers, pill boxes, compacts and lipstick holders.

Jewelery items include: Shoe ornaments, head bands, cumberbunds, key rings, snake mesh belts and wide soft mesh belts which tie much like ribbon, leather backed sash belts, combs with mesh strips, metallic bows, mesh rosette barrettes and pony tail holders. Even earrings with dropped mesh strips, inserts and stiff cuffs. The variety of uses for mesh is truly astounding. Necklaces, chains, collars, adjustable cowls, bracelets and clips are here in a wide range of colors and hues.

Some mesh has become supple and soft while other objects incorporate the mesh into rigid metal bodies and cases adding jeweled touches at random. It seems there is hardly a small utilitarian or ornamental object that cannot be adapted to glittering mesh. All this and bags too!

DAY AND EVENING BAG STYLES

How has the appearance of mesh purses changed in a century?

One of the chief ways is size. The emancipated woman may have most, if not all of the items listed above; the antique mesh bag could not begin to accommodate such an array. The softer metals used today, (i.e. aluminum) allow the mesh to drape and fold more softly and weigh less than the alloys once used.

Patterned meshes are less frequently found and not on a regular basis. The patterns themselves are markedly different.

Mesh today tends to have larger spiders; there are combinations of mesh, fabrics and leathers not formerly used; both evening and day purses are fitted with long leather straps for shoulder wear; frames are greatly simplified and enameled frames are no longer offered; jeweled frames are seen in the latest evening bags like those once used on beaded and tapestry bags; most mesh is in gold, silver, white, and black; mesh has become rather a luxury item and is kept under lock and key in the better department stores where sold.

Disco dancing had a profound influence on mesh styles in the 1970's. The bandolier style in glistening fuchsia, red, teal, irridescent colors, as well as the traditional gold and silver were smart and continue in the line. Fluid mesh pursettes in framed and flap styles were attached to thirty inch long chains and worn about the neck. They resembled the coin purses with ball trim formerly found in full sized sterling mesh purses. They were a fashion accent of the decade.

Evening bags of the 1980's tended toward the traditional pouch shapes with an emphasis on black, gold, and silver mesh and wider jewel set frames. Most are fitted with long chain link or snake chain shoulder straps. Clutches with jeweled clasps are also seen.

Aside from the traditional handbag shapes, a season ago, either as innovators or to meet the competition of other purse manufacturers, such shapes as ovals, cylinders, cresents, and barrel shaped evening containers were introduced. These were done in solid metals trimmed with meshes, rhinestones, leathers, velvets, and/or enamels. Both clutches and shoulder straps were available.

Though white, gold, silver, and black remain the most popular colors, there are pastels, paisleys, and colors with such exotic names as vicuna, cognac, holly, berry, and royal purple.

From the Heritage Collection, which the company expects will become the keepsakes of the future, there are bold Aztec and Indian Tai patterns and random prints so colorful they hardly resemble the traditional meshes at all.

EVENING SEPARATES

Soft metal meshes are ideally suited to the glamorous evening clothes now worn by women outside the theatrical community. In fact, evening separates with matching accessories and handbags, are so elegant they are specialized in the most recent wholesale catalogs.

Though mesh in general is not a particularly forgiving material and daring halters are best worn by flat chested ladies, the company offers a modest cowled neck tee shirt in gold, pink, and silver. Many models may be worn reversed with equal effect. Most flattering is a model with a pleated lamé stand-up collar, lamé sleeves to the elbow, and matching lamé belt with rosette. For those with less than perfect bodies and/or advancing years, the cap or mid sleeve worn with either satin or other fabric shirt, or full length mesh skirt is smashing. Matching skirt and blouse appear to be a dress. The younger set can select from floor length, mid calf, to mini skirt styles.

Most dress mesh is plain, but some is woven with a pattern. Primarily it is the draping and shirring which makes the mesh material so handsome.

In 1988, sleek advertising advised the possession of fine mesh removes one from the image of the "girl next door" into a more sophisticated realm. *(Plate 525.)* The company made its reputation on quality goods and though the market has shifted somewhat into the luxury area, it still meets the standards set so long ago.

Today Whiting and Davis has both a domestic and international work force, with regional offices and distributors in such far flung places as Canada, France, Greece, Israel, Singapore, South Africa, and Taiwan.

We wish them another hundred years of excellence.

WHITING & DAVIS
Evening Separates Designs by Anthony Ferrara

Plate 524-A

Plate 524-B

Plate 525

Plate 525

*Definitely not the
girl next door*

505

Chapter 7
Celebrity Purses: Great Purses From Historical Figures

The following twenty-eight purses have been made by, owned by, worn, or been presented to celebrities ranging from the tragic Mary Queen of Scots through cereal heiress Marjorie Merriweather Post Davies and the imperious Mrs. Francis Clark shown arriving at the wedding of Jay Gould.

Not all belonged to women, for Samuel Pepys' wallet was a gift from a Turkish envoy, Wolfgang Amadeus Mozart's was a gift from an admirer, and Loammi Baldwin's needleworked pocket was, according to custom, a present from some female member of his family, probably his mother.

Three were presumably professional models though a far cry from the brassy, ultra worldly models we are now accustomed to find pitching wares from every media. These ladies are so gentle it is difficult to comprehend at first glance exactly what it is they are selling.

Some are lovely, some seemingly commonplace or downright ugly, and some have great historic significance. All are interesting and reveal something about their owners.

The Film Colony

It is very difficult in the fast moving society of the 1980's to comprehend the almost infinite influence which the film industry exerted both nationally and internationally from 1905 through the 1960's.

Richard Schickel in his *Movies, The History of an Art and an Institution,* states that the star system was instituted to insure the early flickers a steady attendance based not on the merits of a given film but on the popularity of a particular personality. The studios carefully established and nurtured the reputation and image of a handful of actors and actresses on both private and public levels.

The *stars* were admired, hated, envied, endlessly discussed by every segment of society and going to the movies became a national passion. The films helped to dispel the horrors of the depression, cheered the lives of the downtrodden (who comprised the bulk of early film devotees), popularized cosmetics, fashions, architecture, furnishings, helped to formulate manners and mores (often giving a false picture of social classes) and disseminated ideas for good or evil. The films unified a nation and helped educate all levels of society; but above all, they entertained to the extent that the stars became venerated, idolized, larger than life paragons to the public, and sadly, often to themselves as well.

Among those most influential in this era were William Randolph Hearst, Marion Davies, Mary Pickford, Douglas Fairbanks Sr., Charlie Chaplin, Louella Parsons, and Clark Gable. Their lives (both personal and artistic) were strangely interwoven as we shall see. Each has a purse included in this section or discussed in the chapter on metal meshes.

Figure 302

Socialite, Mrs. Francis Clark, arriving at charch for the New York wedding of J. Yould.

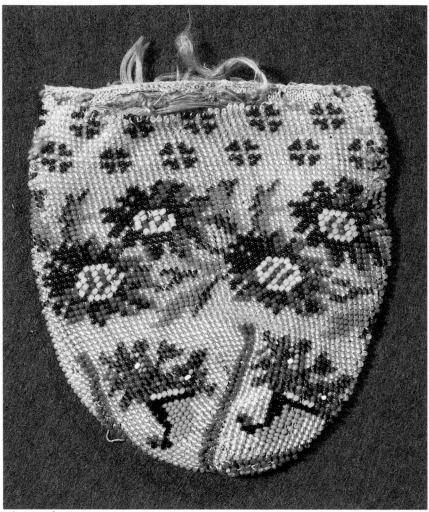

Plate 526

JANE AUSTEN

English novelist, Jane Austen, was born December 16, 1775, into a scholarly family and received a good private education. She had the personal satisfaction of knowing her books were highly regarded during her lifetime.

Her major contribution to society and literature was a refreshingly realistic view of the problems which beset the sexes during the 18th century. She took a less than romantic view of social customs and the absurdity of manners practiced by the British middle and upper classes.

Among her best known books which have a firm place in English literature and remain quite readable even today are: *Pride and Prejudice, Sense and Sensibility, Mansfield Parish, Emma, and Persuasion.*

Exceedingly retiring, little is known about her private life other than that she was a maidenlady. She is thought to have made several beaded purses, in all probability similar to the small knit beaded example shown above. The flower filled cornucopias verify the early use of this motif. As it is only seventy seven rows long, it is a small purse. She died on July 18, 1817.

IMPORTANT AMERICAN NEEDLEWORK

This beautifully wrought petit point purse is documented and dated in the embroidery:

LOAMMI BALDWIN 1764

Loammi Baldwin (circa 1745-1807) was a prominent Revolutionary officer and engineer who built the canal between Concord and the Merrimack. He was also the developer of the Baldwin apple. This piece descended in the Baldwin family until the present time. Condition very good. Bright flowers on a dark green ground. 5" x 8¼" folded.

THE EBENEZER ALDEN HOUSE
Hazel Marcus   Union, Maine 04862   (207) 785-2881

Figure 303

LOAMMI BALDWIN

Not much is known of Loammi Baldwin other than the facts noted in this advertisement. It is one of the early American pocketbooks which is similar to those which can still be found in the costume collections of major American museums.* Like most pocketbooks of this kind it would have been made by his mother, wife, or other female member of his family for the safekeeping of his important papers as well as correspondence, money, and/or legal documents.

Different than most pocketbooks which were done in crewel embroidery, this one is a fine petitpoint, though the designs are strictly primitive, large, and splashy. The pattern was a personal, bright, flowered design on a dark green ground; a cheerful combination and quite fitting for the 18th century when men wore a wide range of colors, laces, and rich materials. It is always advantageous to have the name and date either in beads or embroidery as it firmly establishes the age of an article.

* See museum listings in the Index.

509

Figure 304

CAPTAIN JAMES COOK

This British discoverer of the continents of Australia and New Zealand in 1770, lived from 1728–1779.

Among his achievements, Captain Cook was a cartographer, dietician, a great navigator, and an explorer of both the Atlantic and Pacific Oceans. He charted the continent of Australia and navigated the Great Barrier Reef, itself no mean accomplishment. He understood the importance of diet and provided his crews with citrus fruits and a balanced variety of other foods so they did not suffer from scurvy as did the crews of other ships.

He tried to discover a passage connecting the Atlantic and Pacific Oceans around Canada and Alaska or a North East route around Siberia. He was killed by hostile Hawaiians in 1779, after a lifetime of maritime service to Britain.

Not often is a purse as well documented as this one which belonged to his wife. As the letter which accompanied the purse is difficult to read it is given here: "This bag belonged to the wife of Captain Cook who discovered Australia. She was a ward of Jessie Maton's grandfather and on her death many of Captain Cook's possessions and hers, came into the custody of the Maton family. This bag was given to me by Alice and Jessie Maton when I was at school at St. Johns, Brighton, about 1896. 'Me' was Mrs. Alice Priblett J.P. first lady Mayor of Preston. She died in 1963."

The bag, green with white china and glass beads is thought to have been made about 1750. Note the gold or silver thread side tassels which had been in favor for centuries.

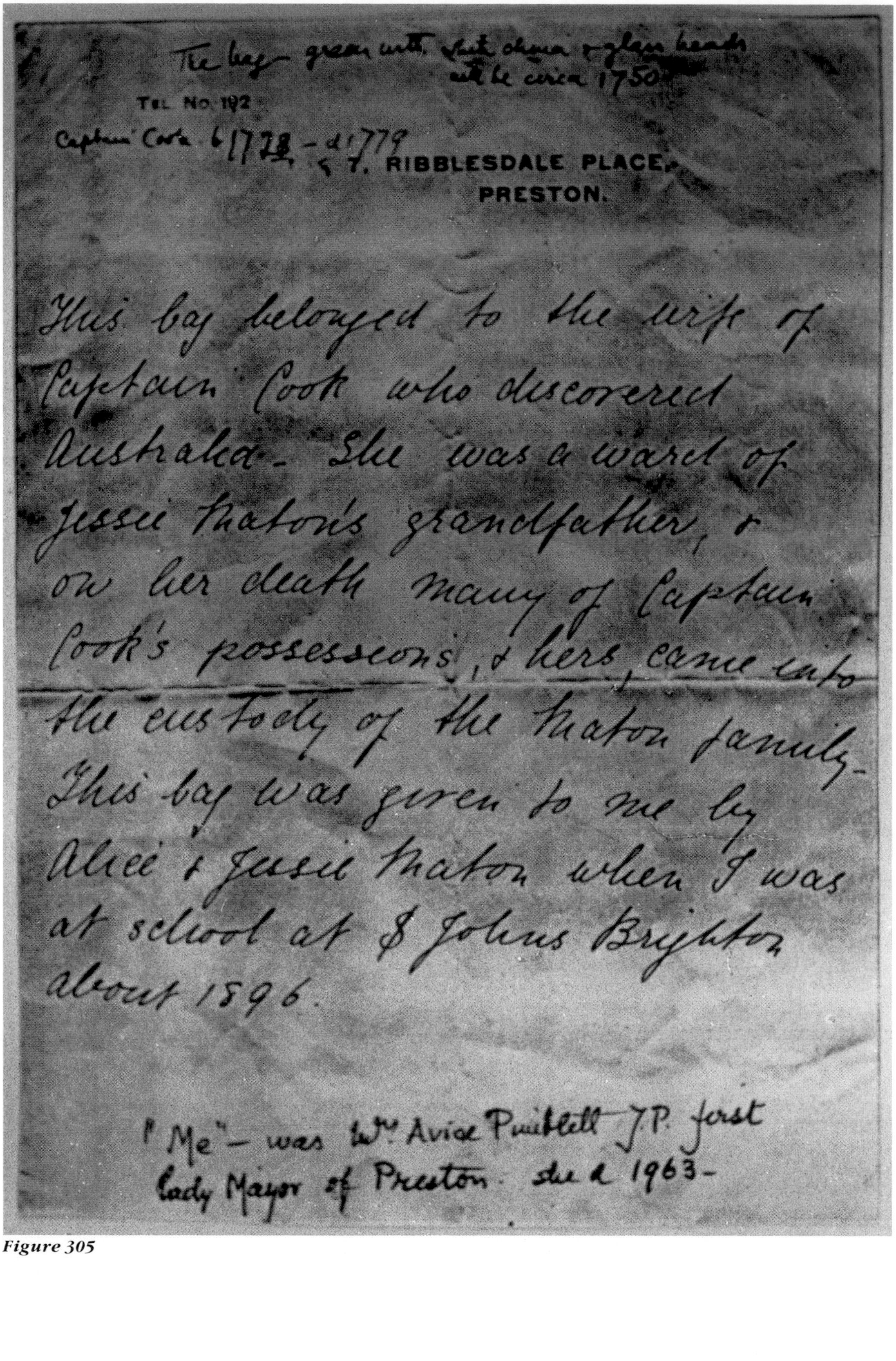

The bag green with white china & glass beads
made circa 1750

TEL NO. 192
Captain Cook b. 1728 – d. 1779

7. RIBBLESDALE PLACE,
PRESTON.

This bag belonged to the wife of
Captain Cook who discovered
Australia – She was a ward of
Jessie Maton's grandfather, &
on her death many of Captain
Cook's possessions, & hers, came into
the custody of the Maton family.
This bag was given to me by
Alice & Jessie Maton when I was
at school at S Johns Brighton
about 1896.

"Me" – was Mrs Avice Pimblett J.P. first
Lady Mayor of Preston. she d 1963 –

Figure 305

511

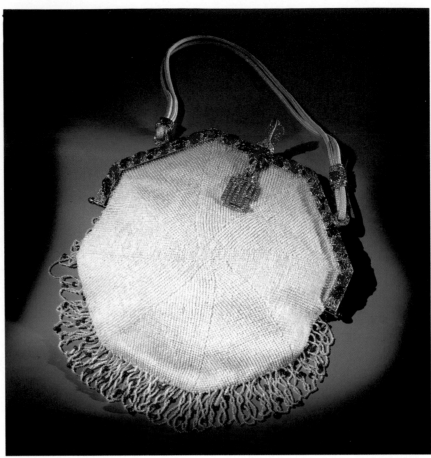

Plate 527

MARJORIE MERRIWEATHER POST DAVIES

Philanthropist Marjorie Merriweather Post Davies was the only child of Charles William Post, founder of the Post Kellogg Cereal fortune. Born March 15, 1888, she lived to see her 85th birthday. Four times wed, she had three children, among them the actress, Diana Merrill. She preferred to be called by her maiden name, though she was wed to two very familiar names in American history; Joseph E. Davies, Ambassador to the Soviet Union and E. F. Hutton of the stock brokerage firm of the same name. Her other two husbands were lesser known.

She received a business education from her father (who also taught her to box, of all things!) in preparation for management of what is now the mighty General Foods Corporation and sat on the Board of Directors, an unheard of practice in her day.

Her fortune was listed at $100,000,000 ranking her in 1957 (*The Rich and The Super-Rich*, Ferdinand Lundberg, Lyle Stuart, New York, 1968) among the richest American women then alive.

Her fabulous purse is six inches in diameter covered solidly with seed pearls. The frame and braided wire handle are of solid platinum set with *genuine* rubies, sapphires, emeralds and diamonds. The standing clasp is a carved ruby and the initials M. P. are done in diamonds and platinum. The fringe is of emeralds, sapphires and rubies entwined with pearls. Many reports of glamorous purses are exaggerated or patently untrue, but this one is just as stated, for its owner could and did live and dress on a grand scale! It is now in the Smithsonian Institute Collection in Washington, D.C.

Figure 306

EMMA EAMES

Though she was famous enough to have been included in the picture files of the Library of Congress, no background information was found concerning this lady. She was probably an actress of some merit. She was appearing in a Shakespearean production, considered properly up-lifting in 1896, when this photograph was taken.

Her handsome reticule is worn old style on a chatelaine belt, much as they had been worn six hundred years before. The shell motif is hung with bits of ornamentation as is the rope twisted flap. It cannot be deter-

mined with certainty whether the material is of soft tanned leather or woven.

Miss Eames' garments are also a curious mixture of rich velvets, slashed sleeves, starched semi-ruff, contrasting with the simple skirt and laced bodice. The costumer was less concerned with historical accuracy than a pleasing ensemble, but it is quite possible the accessory had a significant place in the development of the plot. Both Miss Elliott and Miss Eames were acting in a era when the reticule was firmly entrenched as as an essential part of the wardrobe and the audience would have thought it odd had they not worn one.

513

Figure 307

MAXINE ELLIOTT

In 1890, Maxine Elliott was a rising young star on the American stage. Only an ardent theatre buff would recall anything about her today, so there is little reason to recount too many details of her life. She was a handsome, talented and progressive woman who had the distinction during her lifetime of having a New York theatre named for her in which she gave the opening performance in 1908.

She mastered several Shakespearean roles and was active both at home and abroad. She married Nat Goodwin with whom she shared the stage for many years.

She is shown here in a costume for a Shakespearean production of *Romeo and Juliet.* Her sumptuous dress befits the time period, but again the purse is far too large, the shape entirely wrong; in fact only chatelaines were worn in 15th century Verona, so from an historical sense, it is just plain silly. However that may be, it is very effective and was without doubt made expressly for this costume, as the beadwork and cut work match that of the dress nicely. In the spirit of a virginal fourteen year old girl and appropriate to the plot itself, all parts of the costume are white, even down to the feathered fan and cap.

That cap was very popular at the turn of the 19th century and appeared in beading books along with the purse patterns.

MILI
AND
(186

One
lived
Had
ents
tion
film
ende
have
limit

He
and
disc
made
Geo
your
coul
chilc
him
and
acqu
endu

He
stud
pros
even
ing

He
was
John
Mill
chag

In
was
Hear
lishe
her
duce
and
mut
Hear
her
tain
Mar
in S

LADY FRAI

Hardly any
May Yohe,
daughter of
a pleasing
abroad was
She made h
with Ely B.
discovered
She was n
married Lo
Francis had
most famou
Diamond, f
nately, Lord
having finan
marriage. T
and May re
and final n

Figure 308

MARY GARDEN

The face may not be familiar but the name will be for any opera devotee. Mary Garden, (Born Aberdeen, Scotland, February 20, 1874, Died January 3, 1967) was a lyric soprano who gained instant success and remained a musical celebrity for a quarter of a century. She made her American debut in *Pelleas et Melisande,* February 9, 1908. Two years later she became the leading soprano for the Chicago Grand Opera, retaining her preeminence for over twenty years. Her repertoire ranged from Juliet and Ophelia to Carmen and Salome. She introduced Prokofiev's *The Love for Three Oranges* and *Cherubin* to American audiences.

Tempestuous, extravagant, and theatrical, she embodied those characteristics once associated with the prima donna. Outrageous

behavior was expected, even encouraged, and Mary Garden, like many before and after her, obliged.

She is shown at the height of her career boarding a Chicago train. Her elegant wardrobe exhibits patent leather pumps joined by grosgrain pompoms, topping white silk hose. Her Hudson seal coat has cuffs and hemline of contrasting fur, (possibly stone martin), and a fine chickenwire veiling does not hide the handsome, pear-shaped, pearl dropped earrings.

It is difficult to see the large beaded purse at her side. However, it clearly has a wide sterling frame, heavy chain handle, a bold white beaded pattern on a solid colored body. Such purses were favored in the early 1920's by wealthy and stylish women and are worthy of the prices they command today.

515

Figure 314

MISS A. L. IDE

Absolutely nothing is known of Miss Ide but one thing is certain, she was beautiful. It was not her beauty which attracted my attention (from the Library of Congress Photographic Files) but the rare chatelaine pin she is wearing. It appears to accommodate no fewer than ten hooks though if each space were filled the objects would not fall gracefully.

The four objects she has selected include: a note pad, probably ivory with an enclosed pencil; a scent bottle similar to that worn by Miss Hopper; a long slender etui; and a purse which solves a long standing mystery.

These purses were too large to have been used as coin purses, and their chain arrangement is also incorrect. They were too small to have been used as handbags, and again the chain arrangement would have been incorrect. This photograph and those of Miss Hopper prove these to be what was long suspected. They are undeniably miniature ring mesh chatelaine purses which could be worn as desired either on a long chain about the neck, on a single chatelaine hook, or in concert with several other objects.

Possibly Miss Ide was a model or actress but no background information has been discovered to further identify her. This unusually fine photograph was taken on May 5, 1900, by an unknown photographer.

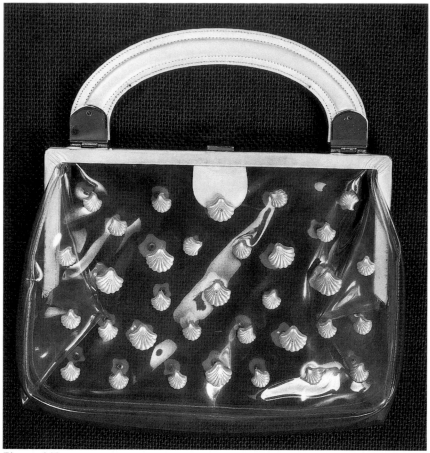

Figure 315

DAME ALICIA MARKOVA

Exactly why this plastic handbag found its way into the archives of The Costume Museum at Bath, England, is a mystery. Since its owner was a premier ballerina and it was purchased from Saks Fifth Avenue in 1955, it may be of significance if not actual monetary value.

Despite her Russian sounding name, Dame Alicia Markova was born in London, England, December 1, 1910. She made her debut at the age of fourteen and her brilliant dancing won her the role of premier ballerina in the Vic-

Wells Ballet by 1933. She was the first dancer to dance the lead in *Giselle* and the full length *Swan Lake*. She became director of the Metropolitan Ballet and a dame of the British Empire before retiring in 1963.

Made of clear plastic and decorated with pink plastic shells, it has a handle and frame of stiffened white kid. Plastic has since become so commonplace and cheap that only very inferior objects are now made from it, but nearly forty years ago it was a novelty with promise. The world of chemistry has moved beyond this plastic and so it may be considered a relic of sorts.

Plate 533

LOUELLA O. PARSONS

Louella Oettinger Parsons, (born August 6, 1893−died December 9, 1972) arrived in Hollywood in 1925. She had a $350.00 weekly contract with William Randolph Hearst to write a daily movie column which would be syndicated world wide in more than 400 newspapers. In a *New York Morning Telegraph* review she had praised a Marion Davies performance and Hearst was rewarding her.

She became a mouthpiece for Hearst and famous for the line, "And Marion never looked lovelier." In accord with his directive that Marion's name was to be mentioned at least once in every Hearst paper printed, Mrs Martin, (Louella had married Dr. Harry Martin, a technical medical film advisor) must have depleted her superlatives many times over. She was, however, an early friend of Marion Davies and a frequent guest at San Simeon.

By 1935, her radio program "Hollywood Hotel" sponsored by Campbells' Soup, (every guest received a case of soup as payment rather than money!) promoted the films Parsons selected. This whetted the appetite of a public already enthralled with movies. Radio itself was a relatively novel medium and both the program and Parsons were wildly successful, so much so, she appeared as herself in a film or two.

Her column was totally devoted to motion pictures and no detail of the stars' private lives, film releases or studio gossip was immune from her relentless pursuit. She got her information from an army of volunteer scouts and spies, including directors and the stars themselves. Stars who failed to keep her informed lived to regret it.

Her arch rival was columnist/actress Hedda Hopper with whom she waged ceaseless warfare in rival publications. Neither refrained from attacking the other in print, along with any film personality unfortunate enough to have tarnished the carefully polished halos placed by the studios in their desperate efforts to achieve sainthood for their properties.

Louella was so feared that lavish gifts were offered as virtual bribes for her silence and/or favorable reporting, among them some elegant gold and precious gem-set purses.

When her estate was auctioned, many of these handbags and jewels were purchased by a Beverly Hills jeweler of our acquaintance who graciously provided a typical 1930−40's example from among a vast wardrobe of purses. Ten inches wide and seven inches deep it is made of large plastic beads divided by gold metal threads. The handle is made of similar oval faceted beads. Despite its commonplace appearance, it like the plastic purse belonging to Dame Markova, was quite costly in its day.

Figure 317

SAMUEL PEPYS, ESQUIRE

Samuel Pepys, (pronounced peeps) was an unusually gifted and fascinating man (1633–1703). He is best remembered for two achievements: the most remarkable diary ever written and the creation, for all intents and purposes, of the British Royal Navy. Under his direction the navy became an established force, not merely a hastily assembled wartime body.

The diary begun on January 1, 1660, records in a form of shorthand such minute details of the everyday life of all who crossed Pepys' path, that it is a *good thing* it was not published until 1825. His biographer, Richard Ollard called it "mutilated and bowdlerised." That it was deciphered at all is amazing! Actually the diary covers only nine years of his life. It constitutes such a complete first per-

son record of momentous events (the Great Fire of London in 1666, the Plague, and court intrigue), that historians and causal readers have been forever grateful.

In his capacity as secretary to his cousin, the Earl of Sandwich, (after whom that staple luncheon goodie was named) he met the famous men of his time. A philanderer of the first water, he carried on a long string of affairs, deceiving his wife with reckless abandon, for after all, women were regarded as either toys or wanton in the 17th century.

The brown morocco leather wallet he received from a Turkish envoy is embroidered in silver wire," Sam: Pepys Esq.(uire)" and was dated 1687, *Constantinople*. At least two other similar wallets, also embroidered *Constantinople*, are still in museums; the one in the Metropolitan Museum is dated 1755. *(See Chapter I)*

529

MARY PICKFORD

Born April 9, 1893, in Toronto, Canada, Gladys Mary Smith was to become the first genuine *movie star* in the star system. At the age of 16 her long blonde curls, innocent manner, and her willingness to cooperate with an infant industry made Mary Pickford "America's Sweetheart"; the most popular actress of all time. She had the good fortune to be at the right place at the right time and it was said she was the only person about whom an entire industry revolved; that industry's most valuable asset.

She was type cast and could not escape the image of pure, innocent determination requiring a childlike quality. This hindered her adult career and did not make for great acting.

Her list of credits, largely silent films under the direction of D. W. Griffith, is extensive. Little wonder for these one reelers were shot at the rate of one a week! Her last film, *Secrets*, was made in 1933. She won the second Best Actress Oscar awarded in 1928–29 for *Coquette*, though she admitted some of her later efforts were poor.

A shrewd business woman, she along with Charlie Chaplin, Douglas Fairbanks, Sr. and D. W. Griffith organized the powerful United Artists Studios in 1919. Previously she had been a partner in Comet and Triangle and Artists' Alliance Studios. She became the first vice president when she and Chaplin were the sole owners before selling out in 1953. An immensely wealthy woman, unlike many other movie stars she kept her fortune intact and in retirement became a philanthropist.

She married Douglas Fairbanks, Sr. one of the most dashing and celebrated actors of all time. She co-starred with Charles Buddy Rogers and married him after her divorce from Fairbanks in 1935. She spent the remaining years of her life with him in seclusion at her palatial estate *Pickfair*, where she died May 29, 1979.

Figure 318

Ultra conservative, in her declining years she considered the film industry had abandoned its leadership position in the entertainment field to sensationalism, sex, and violence.

A diminutive woman, she is seen here alighting from a train at Grand Central Station, March 6, 1926, accompanied by Douglas Fairbanks, Sr. Her purse seems out of proportion to her size and strangely out of color harmony with her dark karakul coat, black shoes, hat and dress. It is not the typical purse and here appears awkward and ill suited. *(Figure 318.)*

Plate 534

DONNA SOMMERS

This blue oblong, metal cased, dyed lizard pursette once belonged to the pop and video artist, Donna Sommers.

Possibly one of a kind, it was designed in Paris by Jacomo. The lining is a deep blue satin with gussets which permit it to open 2¾ inches and it has no fittings. The case is 3¾ × 3 inches and it is interesting that the basket clasp is decorated with the Egyptian motif Lily of the Nile. Heavily embossed on the sides, the back has two sections of lizard divided by an ornate scroll bar. The front is highlighted by a molded cameo, which has been hand detailed, and traditionally mounted on a deep bezel. Here the material is neither rock nor shell, but a stained glass material.

The strap is seven inches long. The purse is very lightweight so it could be worn over the wrist comfortably. An expensive modern purse, it was purchased at auction as a gift for a purse collector.

Entertainers must be noticed, it is an essential part of their career for they are admired for their wardrobe, their general appearance, and their presence, whether on stage or off. This then, is a purse to be seen as part of an ensemble rather than a purse intended to be useful in any sense.

Plate 536

MARTHA CUSTIS WASHINGTON

Martha Custis Washington is shown with her reticule (which she made entirely herself) of brown satin and embroidered with ribbon work. It is the wording which is strange, "Worn by Genl. G. & Mrs. Washington." Why General Washington would have worn it is not clear. It harmonizes with the satin gown she is wearing, but it is not known for certain that she carried it to the first inaugural. All other First Ladies' gowns from the Smithsonian Institution First Ladies Hall, were those worn on this occasion. (In order to give a note of anonymity to each First Lady, mannequins are used bearing no likeness to the actual First Lady.)

A typical reticule, it must have been made about 1789, and indicates how a wealthy Southern lady spent at least a portion of her time when not overseeing a plantation such as Mount Vernon.

Figure 319

Some pu[r]
difficult[...]
specific[...]
case w[...]
twenty-five exampl[e]
lected because of t[h]
value, nor great age, [...]
any of the usual crite[...]

They are merely u[...]
and some, like the 1[...]
so rare I had never [...]
since. This one can [...]
geles County Museu[m]
mine, who wished t[...]
Institute.

Some are indicativ[...]
are not so rare they [...]
purchase. These w[...]
purses, the dance [...]
types. The watch i[...]
rarity as well as the [...]
luloid ring, the six [...]
the sow's ear purse [...]
lutely certain there [...]
world.

This is a fun sec[...]
can find some equa[...]
is what makes purs[...]
hobby.

EDITH BOLLING GALT WILSON

Never known as a shrinking violet, Edith Bolling Galt was the second wife of World War I President Woodrow Wilson, a former President of Princeton University.

Wilson married his first wife in 1855, and was the father of three daughters. When his wife died in 1914, he married the vivacious Edith Bolling Galt on December 18, 1915. He was in his second term of the Presidency when he suffered a series of strokes and Edith was caustically said to have "run the country" for three years until the election of Warren G. Harding in 1920. The country did not fall apart as men were wont to warn, but she was attacked from all quarters. That she did a creditable job, considering the low esteem women were then generally accorded, is to her eternal respect.

The Wilsons had retired to virtual seclusion when this photograph was taken at a reception held in her honor December 8, 1922. She is accompanied by Maryland Governor A. C. Ritchie.

Wearing an ornate beaded gown and hat, this distinguished lady might well have carried another type of purse but she selected this antique (style) as appropriate to the occasion. It is difficult to separate the various articles she is juggling in her gloved left hand; program, corsage holder, and purse ribbons. Apparently the ribbons are over her forefinger.

The dress seems too rich for the simple reticule even though it must have been considered decorative and fitting for the occasion. It contrasts sharply with the heavily beaded gown. It is conceivable Mrs. Wilson made the purse.

535

The final celluloid novelties are the smallest
and certain charmers for any collector. One
is shaped like an elongated egg, the cap held
in place by a simple hook device. A metal
tracery painted black is attached to the bottom ovoid. The finishing touch is a thick
black silk tassel, longer in fact, than the
purse itself.

Because it is tiny and very light weight, it is
attached by cords and rings to a celluloid
ring which was worn over whichever finger
the wearer preferred. Much like the metal
purses or coin purses, these were great favorites for dancing as they are frivolous and yet
contained absolute necessities. *(Plate 542.)*

Though the shapes vary widely, the size
and general appearance of dance purses
does not, as can be seen in *Plates 543–7*.

Set with blue rhinestones and a black grosgrain ribbon strap one dance celluloid purse
has receptacles for rouge, powder, and lipstick. It is 3 × 2½ inches which is standard
for purses of this type, though they may vary
slightly in one or both dimensions.

Another variation had material, usually
silk, in lieu of a solid case (such as the ecru
colored version), complete with gold colored
metal braided tassel. The shirring was done
by hand. This is a particularly nice one as the
casing has jewels and ornamentation.

A very feminine and delicate one has
enameled roses in an inverted horseshoe
shape, with a similar metal braided tassel
and a row of contrasting rhinestones along
the outer edge.

What appears to be a bar is actually a
lipstick holder on the octagonal shaped version. This one is a mere two and a half inches
in diameter set with midnight blue cabachons in a snowflake design. There is a mirror set into each end. The lipstick is still
intact, though a congealed blood red, the
shades favored by *vamps* in the "roaring
twenties".

The two solid cased examples from the
same era have delicate patterns. The size is
relatively the same as the others.

Plate 542

Plate 543

Plate 544

Plate 545

Plate 546

Plate 547

Figure 326

RHINESTONE SET DANCE PURSE

Figures 326 and 327 are somewhat different in that it is cylinder shaped black celluloid, embellished with deeply set clear rhinestones on the cover and along the edges. The interior has a tiny mirror, space for a lipstick and a receptacle for money or some small object.

546

Figure 327

Plate 548

SHELL PURSE

Foster refers to this type of purse (not native to the United States) as a bivalve shell with a metal frame and hinge. She says they were souvenirs of the Crystal Palace Exhibit and seaside amusement parks like Coney Island. Originally they might have had a lining but this example was purchased in the United States and does not have one. They are mother-of-pearl and very small. They are not of any use whatsoever, just decorative, as the shell naturally was exceedingly delicate. They are sometimes sold as pin and needle containers.

The fashion must have spread to the United States between 1860–1914, for numerous shell purses are to be found with enameled designs proudly publicizing a particular city or resort and quite often the date as well. It was another type of souvenir cherished by a society to whom travel was a novelty to be long remembered and discussed.

One reads, "From Atlantic City" and the other "Portland Oregon". It is interesting to note these two locations are on opposite coastlines and would tend to prove how universal the souvenir had become with infrequent seaside visitors.

Figure 328

KOALA BEAR PURSE

This koala bear head is made of some type of cinnamon-colored synthetic fur. The nose is a hard resin or plastic closely resembling the natural species. The amber and black eyes are like the shoe button eyes of old. It is only seven inches wide and six inches long, carried on an eleven inch chain. It is lined with soft, beige-colored suede leather.

Most assuredly it was a child's purse purchased in Australia and brought to the United States as a souvenir. It is not a domestic product.

Despite its initial inexpensive price, few purses have attracted more attention. It is not offered for sale because of its unique resemblance to the actual cuddly animal everyone adores.

Plate 549

CHINESE MOTIF SACK

About the turn of the present century every needlework magazine featured a page or two of useful household items which the home-maker could "whip up in her spare time" (what spare time?) to contain the laundry, hosiery, hankies, dustcloths, lingerie, just about anything that could be stuffed into a soft enclosure. Some, such as this one, were truly works of art.

At least fifteen inches long and half as wide, it is made of heavy persimmon-colored velvet trimmed with five separate strips of exquisitely embroidered braids of varying widths and designs; the major shade closely matching the velvet ground. The bottom is drawn together and counterweighted by a huge Peking glass bead. The carry cords are closed with two painted oval glass beads which are attached to a rectangle of embossed sterling secured by beads.

These oversized rather shapeless sacks were popular for obvious reasons, though this one was not expensive to make for the materials could well have been on hand. Even if purchased specifically for this bag they would have been readily available at a modest cost. They contrasted or combined nicely with particular ensembles and often were made expressly for a particular gown. No beading was required and the woman who was a good seamstress could made one, or have one made, enjoying the same feeling of accomplishment as the woman who did beadwork.

Plate 550

BEADED DIVIDED TOP

Aside from the extraordinarily striking pattern, this floral is the only example of a divided top ever encountered.

The subtle pastels, the unusual combination of flowers including the seldom used lilacs, and the intricate gold lined fringe, are most attractive. The band of beading and the main body are joined by a series of rings; carry chains are run through the open space in opposing directions.

Both the band and body are carefully lined in heavy white grosgrain. The delicate pattern of lilac beads used on the band is quite in keeping with the body and there is no evidence that either has been altered at any time, making this a most unusual purse.

The stiffness of the lining and the heavy beading does not permit the purse to fall gracefully when gathered, however, and its beauty is only seen when it is fully extended. Overall it is one of the most elegant patterns ever seen and is greatly admired. The dimensions are approximately ten inches in length by seven inches wide, with a half inch allowance for the chains.

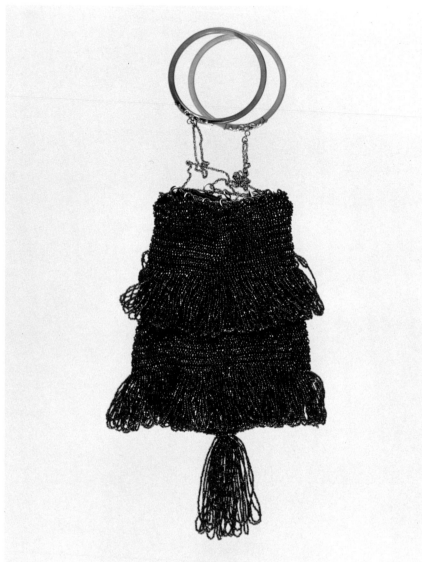

Plate 551

RED BRACELET RETICULE

This knit purse is representative of a group of reticules which close quite traditionally with some type of chain or cording attached to bracelets of one sort or another.

Generally the bracelets are made of sterling or other metal, but in this case, they are a soft celluloid resembling amber, and the chains and embossed fittings are sterling.

The rings are sewn to the edge of the lining and the chains run through them. The lining is a matching red satin material.

The square cut beads are medium fine, knit in rows of three, and the purse measures eight inches by five inches when drawn together.

As previously stated, red is a rarely used color both because of the long standing connotation of wantonness on the part of the owner (whether justified or not) and the difficulty of manufacturing any dye, paint, oxides, or other substance in a true red color. As gold was an essential ingredient, red pigments were the most costly and historically were sparingly used. Additionally, it is a harsh color not suited to large unbroken expanses. Blue, black, dark green, and ecru are the colors commonly used in these modestly priced bracelet variations of the Dorothy bag.

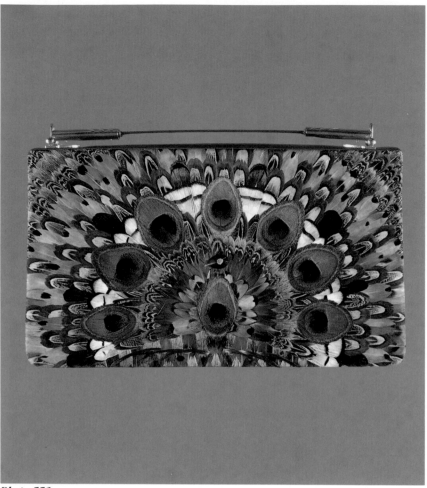

Plate 552

PEACOCK FEATHER BAG

This relatively contemporary smooth leather backed bag is covered with peacock feathers, artistically and harmoniously blended and arranged to simulate a male peacock display. The feathers are painstakingly glued to the leather in a semi-circle on both face and back. It has either been little used, gingerly used, or both, for the condition is remarkably good for such a delicate surface.

Although it could be carried as a clutch, it would be unwise as the resulting friction would cause irreparable damage. The flat, retractable leather strap across the top, slips into decorative metal end pieces in a novel and nice fashion when not being carried.

The black nylon lining has the usual fitted, flat, unweilding compartments with zippered closures. It should be remembered that any purse with zippers is far too recent to be classified as a genuine antique.

It is a purse purposely made to attract attention. Its oblong shape is generously proportioned ($11\frac{1}{2} \times 7$) so it is not utterly useless.

WATCH PURSES

Among the most appealing purses are those which contain a watch set either in the top so as to constitute part of the gate top frame, or as an ornamental part of the rigid frame (See *Antique Combs and Purses,* Page 277). Ring mesh was most often used and ball decoration was almost obligatory.

Always a novelty, there are so few of them today that they have to be ranked as extremely special. This one *(Figure 330)* is sterling mounted and deserves the services of a skilled watch repairman to restore it. Of the three we have seen, two were in running order but neither was sterling mounted. One had an exposed face in a charming celluloid compact pursette, but curiously, the dealer who purchased it did not want the watch, for reasons best known to herself. Only three inches in diameter this pouch shaped mesh was carried on a sturdy metal link chain.

If encountered, the collector can anticipate paying a high price for one, especially if the watch is in working order, for antique watch repair is costly and quality workmen not easily located.

The Art Deco watch (7½ by 6) at *Figure 329* is in working order. Its handsome sterling case is set with marcasites and further embellished by a decorative strip, tabs, and strap holders similarly jeweled. The designer meticulously balanced the entire motif, so a double or false winding stem is found at the left, its tiny shell set with ten marcasites. The body is suede, the strap a heavy double sided satin. Marcasites set on black are truly a rich combination, no other color would give the marcasites such brilliance. Just as carnival glass imitated Tiffany's aurene and other types of choice art glass, so did marcasites double for the diamonds only the very well-to-do could afford.

Unmarked as to origin, the entire purse is an American product for Swiss watches are marked *Made in Switzerland* even though particular makers may not be attributed.

Figure 329

Figure 330

553

BABY PEGGY DELYSIA

The *Baby Peggy* is covered in some detail in the section on metal meshes. This one is shown here in color so the color scheme can be studied and the actual purse observed, rather than an artist's rendering. It is shown approximately actual size.

Plate 553

Plate 554

FRENCH BLUE DIAMANTE

One of the most stunning purses ever seen simply refused to show its beauty photographically.

French designers working about sixty or seventy years ago, were fond of combining rhinestones set in brass bezels and silver/gold embroidery on crepe-de-chine. The bezel was drilled or formed a cup with four sharply pointed ends, much like the spiders used in metal meshes. The ends were forced through the material from the right side and bent over (flattened) to secure them.

Merchandise of a higher quality necessitated the use of drilled bezels sewn onto the material in either a specific or random pattern; often swirls or petal designs. Uncolored rhinestones were usually selected as they blended with almost any costume, but on occasion stones of great beauty and depth of color were used, such as in this purse.

These deep blue stones form the entire outer surface. The four corners of each bezel are joined together to form rows and stoutly overbound at the edges. The midnight blue satin lining is scarcely visible as the beading is so dense. When the light catches the stones at the proper angles, the effect is utterly dazzling.

The frame and chain are sterling. The purse measures approximately eleven by seven inches and because of its elaborateness should be used exclusively for evening wear. Needless to say, it is a valuable purse much beloved by its owner.

Plate 557

TURKISH PRISONERS PURSE

Among the strangest purses must be ranked this purse the band of which reads *Turkish Prisoners*. The three most likely conflicts in which the Turkish military would have participated were The Crimean War, World War I and World War II. The beading seems too old for the latter, and since the Crimean War was waged between 1854–56, this conflict, is in all probability, too early.

Because Turkey is strategically located on the Black and Aegean Seas, Russia has schemed to conquer her for generations. Turkey has had an unfortunate penchant for allying herself with the wrong side as well.

It is quite reasonable that prisoners taken in war would while-away their time with beadwork, especially that done on a loom, for they have been among the world's great-est rug weavers and weaving would not have seemed unnatural to men.

Following the first world war, hospitalized military veterans practiced beading and other types of needlework as therapy for their shattered nerves and as a means of restoring finger dexterity, much as surgeons do today.

Both the black and white beads are very large and unfaceted. The reversed and up-sidedown *R* in the word Turkish is a glaring error which the beader probably was un-aware of until it was too late and he did not bother to correct it.

The purse measures seven and a half inches wide and six inches deep. The size of the beads can be gauged by the depth of the one inch band and the eleven rows of beads covering it. The bands are lined with a strip of flexible metal which can be bent to open and close the purse.

Plate 558

TRIO OF PURSES

These identical black velvet purses joined to a bracelet length chain are something of a mystery. They could have been inserted inside one another and carried as a single purse. Another theory supports the idea they were much like the novelty purses which were carried in groups around 1900. Perhaps the owner purchased one of each size because she liked the style. Who can say? Their present owner purchased them as shown and they are interesting as a trio.

They are pear shaped, and range in size from the largest seven inches by four and a half to the smallest which is three inches shorter but only slightly narrower. They are in excellent condition, are lined with ivory colored silk, and each twist top has a rhinestone insert.

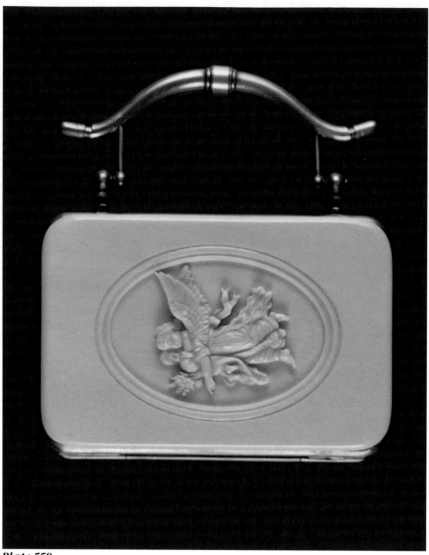

Plate 559

CARVED IVORY

Many years ago, before I had more than a passing interest in purses, this little gem was irresistible and has ever remained so.

It is only two and a half inches wide and three and a half inches long. The front and back are thin sheets of ivory, skillfully fitted into a brass over copper frame. The perfect, brown, cord silk interior is divided into four compartments. They are intended to hold calling cards, a key, a little currency or some very slender and lightweight objects. The curved, solid metal handle is wide enough for a very slender hand or two or three adult fingers.

The deep carving is so poignantly graceful and charming it defies description. A sweet faced winged angel, holding an infant ,seems to float across the face of the carved double oval. The carving is nearly one fourth of a inch deep and each fold of the realistic garments moves.

If this purse was originally owned by a child it was an incredibly careful child, for it shows neither signs or wear nor the slightest damage. It was made between 1850–1870. Though it has no hint as to where it was made, they were popular in England at that time. It is representative of a genre of small purses similar in shape, design, and size, but few are as exquisite as this one.

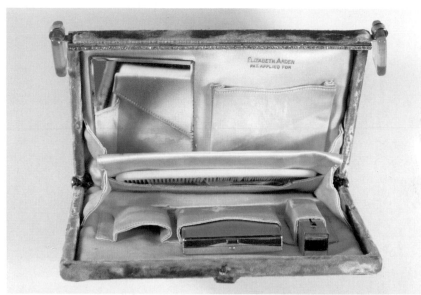

Plate 560

Plate 561

ELIZABETH ARDEN PURSE

Among the rich and super rich, Elizabeth Arden was a name to be reckoned with in the 1920's. Her elegantly understated cosmetic ads, appearing in slick magazines and pitched to society matrons, seldom varied.

This highly specialized lime green velveteen purse (7″ × 5″) would never have been mass produced, say in the sense that a purse for a large department store chain would have been. It has some strange aspects, such as the heavy celluloid oblong rings at either end of the fold over frame which forms a narrow spring flap. The ridge of the frame and drop tab are made of white metal set with insignificant rhinestones.

It is the elegantly fitted interior which makes this an impressive purse. The heavy off-white satin lining is stamped Elizabeth Arden in gold along with the words Patent Applied For. A long center compartment is devoted to non cosmetic areas. The containers for lipstick, powder, rouge, and comb still glow a mellow gold color. Each opening has a narrow, emerald-cut green rhinestone, set in the machine turning. The mirrors have a clarity not seen anywhere today. The cherry red lipstick has a waxy intensity which must have been most startling and unnatural looking.

Though there is no date, the general lines are art deco, as are the square lipstick and end tabs. The satin is shredding along the lines of greatest wear.

561

Plate 562

STEEL WIRE FRENCH—
PAINTING ON IVORY

Dating objects can be a most arduous task but a few guidelines can be both reassuring and timesaving. A case in point is this little iron purse only large enough to fit into the palm of the hand. How old?

The dealer from Maine thought it a favorite of an American Revolutionary general's wife; the name she had forgotten.

I am a natural born skeptic, it sounded interesting but fanciful and it was necessary to use some deductive reasoning to establish a plausible date. It is entirely possible this French purse was made in the opening years of the 19th century and could have belonged to the above mentioned lady.

Vanda Foster relates, "Metalwork also plays an important part in bags of this period, (1800–1900) and some of the most remarkable are made of iron wire, drawn out almost as fine as hair. On a base of fine iron mesh these wires were wound into tight coils and arranged in wheel or flower patterns, the space filled with flower-shaped steel pai-

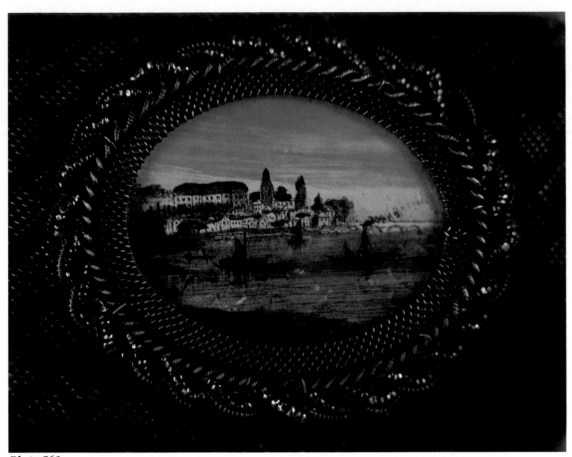

Plate 563

lettes. This type of filagree iron work was first done in Silesia during the eighteenth century, but the War of the Austrian Succession saw the foundries moved to Berlin. During their occupation of Berlin, however, the French copied many of the designs while other countries also experimented with the technique so that, although generally known as "Berlin ironwork, it is difficult to specify the origin of any one piece." This one is marked Deposé a termed used to indicate French origin, so there is no doubt about its manufacture.

The narrow steel frame is attached with seven prominent rivets. What appears to be cut steel beading is a pattern in the wire work itself. The oval reverse painting on ivory depicts a busy harbour, a harbour city and a distant bridge. Cut steel beads and wire rope surrounds the painting and anchors it in place.

The interior, divided into the usual three or four compartments, is covered with thin green silk. The center section has an overclip suitable for the storage of coins. The overall dimensions are a mere three inches wide by two inches deep.

Plate 564

SEED PURSES

Various theories are quite plausible for the substitution of seeds for blown glass beads. Possibly no complicated reasons are necessary, for primitive peoples used whatever materials were at hand with superb results. Mary White in her indispensable little book, *How To Do Beadwork,* refers to this type of beading as open mesh network which forms a sort of curtain.

Every housewife had seeded fruits and vegetables such as pumpkins, various varieties of melons, sunflowers, and fruit seeds. When washed and dried, and possibly polished in some fashion, their interesting shapes and smooth hulls were easily bored or pierced and they were individually strung in mesh-like patterns. The mesh created was attached to a silk, velvet, or satin body and drawn together with wide ribbons in typical reticule fashion. Some beaders combined steel cut and/or glass beads, used as spacers, for variety.

Another seed, such as is shown here, was more exotic; monkey seeds from the Hawaiian Islands. It has a dark, shiny, smooth surface and uniform shape. These seeds were closely arranged vertically in groups of three, interspersed with smaller seeds. The flap and loop fringes include one red glass bead. The handle is cleverly interlooped, quite an achievement for an amateur beader.

An inexpensive purse, this one measures about four inches in each direction. It is in fine condition, whereas most purses of this fragile type are badly damaged. The method of beading is as old as time, but this one was probably made about 1910.

Plate 565

Plate 566

Plate 567

SOW'S EAR PURSE

Since this is truly the rarest purse in all the world, it is fitting to include it here even at the risk of repetition. We beg the indulgence of those who have previous acquaintance with it, for the wisdom contained bears repeating and committing to memory.

"Perhaps the most unusual purse ever made was the result of a dare. Arthur D. Little was the founder of a firm of consulting engineers and experts now 1,300 strong who are capable of solving problems for governments, corporations, individuals, and municipalities. In short, anyone who has a technological, sociological, or agricultural dilemma anywhere in the world may find a solution by consulting this Cambridge, Massachusetts, firm. Dr. Little literally accepted the challenge of "making a silk purse out of a sow's ear" in 1921, by chemically reducing a batch of sow's ears to gelatin and tissues from which a fiber, dyed red was spun and loomed into two miser's purses. The one shown may be seen at their Cambridge headquarters and the other is on display at the Smithsonian Institution in Washington, D. C.

"Quoting from a tongue-in-cheek paper by the firm, 'We admit frankly that it is not very strong or very good silk, and that there is not present industrial value in making it from glue. We have no intention of producing sow's ear silk for the market. We made this silk purse from a sow's ear because we wanted to, because it might serve as an example to clients who come to us with their ambitions or their troubles and also as a contribution to philosophy.

'The most discouraging thing to hear, if you are interested in real progress and in the forward march of events, or more particularly if you have set your heart on doing something that you believe should be done, is some old saw that is repeated merely because the words that tell it have been learned parrot-wise.

'Things that everybody thinks he knows only because he has learned the words that say it, are poisons to progress. The only way to get ahead is to dig in, to study, to find out, to reason out theories and to test them—and then to hold fast to that which is good.'

To which we add, Amen!

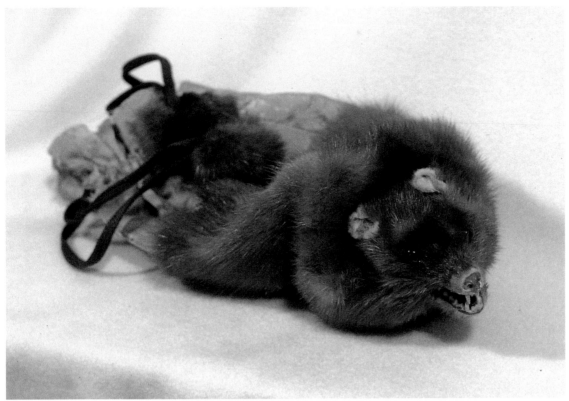

Plate 568

MINK'S HEAD PURSE

A modified version of the muff was introduced, along with the fur scarf, stole, and cape, in the mid twenties, which featured a small animal head, paws, tail, and/or other body parts. Thankfully this grisly practice is out of fashion, as should be the use of all furs.

This little mink, with leather ears and glass eyes, fell victim to the craze. The pelt was attached to a beige, satin damask pouch and completed as a reticule. The actual work may have been done in the home or possibly by a furrier, for there were many more professional furriers seventy years ago than today. The fur is rather coarse now as it has not been properly cared for. It is twelve inches long and six inches wide.

Examples of animal reticules are not plentiful and are relatively expensive. They are mere curiosities and never were practical in any sense.

567

Plate 569

568

Judith Leiber

Handbags/ Accessories

Plate 570

569

Bibliography

Ames, Frances, *The Kashmir Shawl,* Antique Collectors Club, Woodbridge, Suffolk, England, 1986.

Baker, Lillian, *Art Nouveau and Art Deco Jewelery*, Collector's Books, Paducah, Kentucky, 1983.

Braun and Schneider, *Historic Costume In Pictures,* Dover Reprint, 1975, New York.

Buck, Anne, *Victorian Costume,* Herbert Jenkins, London, England, 1961.

Chaney, Lindsay, and Creply, Michael, *The Hearsts, Family and Empire in Later Years,* Simon and Schuster, New York, 1981.

Caulfeild, S.E., *Encyclopedia of Victorian Needlework,* Dover Reprint, New York, 1972.

Clabburn, Pamela, *Beadwork,* Shire Publications, Aylesbury, Bucks, England, 1980.

Dillon, H. A. *Costume in England,* Singing Tree Press, Detroit, Michigan, 1968.

Dubin, Lois, Sherr, *The History of Beads, 30,00 B.C. To The Present,* Harry Abrahams, New York, 1987.

Earle, Alice, Morse, *Two Centuries of Costume in America*, Macmillan Co. New York, 1903 (Dover, 1970).

Edwards, Joan, *Bead Embroidery,* Taplenger, London, England, 1966.

Foster, Vanda, *Bags and Purses,* The Costume Accessories Series, Batsford, London, England, 1982.

Gill, Anne, *Beadwork,* Watson-Guptill, 1977.

Guiles, Lawrence, *Marion Davies,* McGraw Hill, New York, 1972.

Haertig, Evelyn, *Antique Combs and Purses,* Gallery Graphics Press, Carmel, California, 1983.

Hamilton, Charles, F. *Roycroft Collectibles,* A. S. Barnes Inc., San Diego, 1968.

Heath, Mary, Hubbard, *The Elbert Hubbard I Knew,* The Roycrofters, East Aurora, New York, 1924.

Hughes, Therle, *English Domestic Needlework*, Lutterworth Press, London, 1961.

Markrich,Lilo and Kiewe, Heinz, Edgar, *Victorian Fancywork,* Henry Regnery Co, Chicago, Illinois, 1974.

Nadelhoffer, Hans, *Cartier, Jewelers Extraordinary,* Harry Abrahams, Inc., New York, 1984.

Schickel, Richard, *The History of an Art and an Institution*, Basic Books, New York, 1964.

Moore, Doris, Langley, *The Woman In Fashion,* Batsford, New York, 1949.

Ollard, Richard, *The Biography of Sameul Pepys,* Holt, Rhinehart, Winston, London, 1984.

Patch, Susanne, Steinem, *Blue Mystery, The Story of the Hope Diamond,* Smithsonian Institute Press, Washington, D.C., 1976.

Payne, Blanche, *History of Costume,* Harper and Rowe, New York, 1965.

Smith, Patricia, R, *Antique Collector's Dolls,* Collector's Books, Paducah, Kentucky, 1975.

Swan, Susan, *Plain and Fancy,* Holt, Rhinehart, Winston, New York, 1977.

Thornabene, Lyn, *Long Live the King,* G. P. Putnam's Sons, New York, 1976.

Truman, Nevil, *Historic Costuming,* Pitman and Sons, London, England, 1967.

Van Der Sleen, W.G.N., *Handbook of Beads,* Shumway, (1973 Reprint).

Magazines and Catalogues

City Directory of North Attleboro, Massachusetts, 1912.

Emma Barbour's Pattern Book 1921.

Fascination of Exclusivity, Internationaler Reptilleder Verband, West Germany 1983.

TheGreat American Calalog, Oskamp Nolting, Cincinnati, Ohio, 1932.

The Hiawatha Book of Beaded Bags, Bags by Harriet B, Davis, Dritz Traum Company, 258 Fifth Avenue, New York, 1927.

J. Jolles Petit Point Handbook, J. Jolles Studios, Vienna, Austria, 1955.

Lady's Book, 1854-55, Godey's, Philadelphia, Pennsylvaina.

Meeker Leather Manufacturing Comapny Advertisements to Wholesalers 1907–1954 Courtesy William E. Fowks, Jr., Chairman, Meeker Company, Joplin, Missouri.

Montgomery Ward Cataloge, 1907.

Pricilla Needlework Book 1912, Robinson, B., Boston, Massachusetts, 1912.

Sears and Roebuck Catalog, 1922, 1927, 1928.

Various publications from Roycroft Press, East Aurora, New York.

Whiting and Davis Yearly Publications to the Trade.

Manuscripts

Beadmaking in Murano, Venice, Journal of the Royal Society of Arts, London, August, 1919.

Howard, A.L., *Worshipful Company of Glass-Sellers of London,* London, England 1940.

Little, Arthur D., *On The Making of Silk Purses From Sow's Ears,* Cambridge Massachusetts, 1921.

Michelangelo, Pasquato, *Il Vetwo Muranese,* Seduta Plenaria, Venice, Italy, 1953.

Private papers of Charles Rice from his grandfather, Charles A. Whiting.

Index